FLOWERS
at your window

A trailing campanula adorns a cottage window.

Begonias, chrysanthemum and a primula beautifully displayed.

FLOWERS
at your window

Jack Kramer
Consultant: Sue Minter

a Salamander book

Published by Salamander Books Limited
LONDON

A Salamander Book

Published by Salamander Books Ltd,
Salamander House
27 Old Gloucester Street
London WC1N 3AF
England.

ISBN 0 86101 050 7

Distributed in the United Kingdom by
New English Library Ltd.

Distributed in Australia/New Zealand
by Summit Books, a division of
Paul Hamlyn Pty Ltd.
Sydney, Australia.

Credits

Editor: Geoffrey Rogers
Designers: Roger Hyde, Mark Holt

Colour reproductions: Scansets Ltd,
    Middlesex, England.
Bantam Litho Ltd, Essex, England.
Monochrome: Tenreck, London, England

Filmset: Modern Text Typesetting Ltd,
    Essex, England.
    SX Composing Ltd, Essex, England.

Printed in Belgium by
    Henri Proost et Cie, Turnhout.

The springtime blooms of the rat's tail cactus, Aporocactus flagelliformis.

The Author *Jack Kramer writes from personal experience gained during many successful years of growing both indoor and outdoor plants. His beautiful California home is filled with over 300 healthy indoor plants, from stately cacti to delicately fragrant orchids. Known throughout the world for his easy, familiar writing style, Mr. Kramer has contributed articles to a wide range of magazines and is the author of over 50 popular books on gardening subjects.*

The Consultant *Sue Minter is a freelance journalist specializing in gardening subjects who has a keen practical interest in growing plants. Once the buyer of houseplants at Syon Park Garden Center, London, she has since edited a book on the care of indoor plants and a forthcoming book on roses.*

Cut chrysanthemums complement a period window

Contents

Part One

Indoor gardening brings its own rewards: the comforting vitality of living plants to soften and brighten the clinical lines of our homes. In this part of the book we look at the basic techniques you will need to master for assured success with growing and displaying plants; matching plants with your rooms and decor, selecting the best containers, maintaining ideal growing conditions, propagating plants, and dealing with insect pests and disease. Finally, we look briefly at the main groups from which the 200 flowering houseplants featured in part two of the book have been selected

Left: Flowering plants bring color to windows throughout the world. Here a Dutch barge is brightened by potted geraniums, one of the most popular of all indoor plants.

Places for Plants

To enjoy plants in your house or flat, you need to select those that appeal to the eye and complement your decor. It amounts to choosing plants that will grow under the conditions you can offer and then displaying them attractively. In this way flowers and foliage at your windows will always be a pleasing sight.

I am not suggesting you turn your home into a jungle to grow the many indoor orchids, or simulate a desert in your kitchen for the fascinating cacti. It isn't necessary. By judicious selection you can have those orchids that don't require rainforest humidity (there are many) and those cacti that will flourish and flower under average conditions.

So evaluate your conditions, select plants accordingly, and place them strategically for year-long indoor beauty. You can do it, because in the vast world of plants there are hundreds to choose that will grow successfully in your home.

Your choice of plants

Remember the conservatory method of growing plants—warm house, intermediate house, cool house, it was called, and we can take some good advice from this 19th-century concept because there are some plants that thrive in warmth, others in intermediate temperatures, and still others for coolness, and even some obliging plants that thrive in any temperature. Let us look first at what to select in general, and how to make wise choices to create a pleasant indoor garden that is colorful all year long—not only for the first few weeks plants are in your home.

Flowering plants

Only recently have exotic flowering plants entered the home. For decades it was believed that orchids could not produce their beautiful flowers unless they were in a greenhouse, and that gesneriads were impossible to bring into bloom without similar conditions. Today we know that these plants and many more flowering kinds can be successful in indoor gardens. And although it may be true that they will not bear so freely as they do when growing in their natural habitat, they do bloom.

Sun is the prime requisite for blooms,

Above: A small corner needs a small plant; here a Catharanthus roseus.
Right: A large, cool dining room comes alive with a stunning selection of beautifully displayed plants.

but not all flowering plants require intense sunlight. Indeed, many orchids would be harmed by it, and plants such as *Streptocarpus* and *Columnea* would develop leaf scorch. Bright light is adequate for most flowering plants, and at unobstructed windows there is generally enough light for them even when the sun is not shining.

The choice of flowering plants for your windows is vast: handsome geraniums, delightful African violets, stunning orchids, exotic bromeliads. There is also a wide range of bulbous plants—*Achimenes, Allium, Eucharis, Eucomis, Vallota,* and others. All can brighten dreary winter days. It just comes down to the conditions you can offer—warm, intermediate, or cool—and how you care for your plants, and that's what this book is all about.

If your house is hot (a rare condition today)—that is, 75-80°F (24-27°C) during the day and 10°F (5°C) less at night—look to gingers and gesneriads, and some of the bromeliads to provide

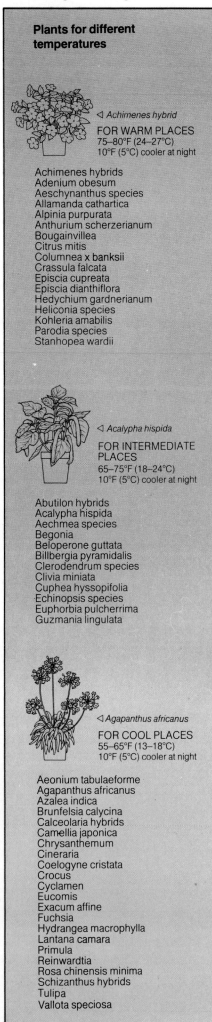

Plants for different temperatures

◁ *Achimenes hybrid*

FOR WARM PLACES
75–80°F (24–27°C)
10°F (5°C) cooler at night

Achimenes hybrids
Adenium obesum
Aeschynanthus species
Allamanda cathartica
Alpinia purpurata
Anthurium scherzerianum
Bougainvillea
Citrus mitis
Columnea x banksii
Crassula falcata
Episcia cupreata
Episcia dianthiflora
Hedychium gardnerianum
Heliconia species
Kohleria amabilis
Parodia species
Stanhopea wardii

◁ *Acalypha hispida*

FOR INTERMEDIATE PLACES
65–75°F (18–24°C)
10°F (5°C) cooler at night

Abutilon hybrids
Acalypha hispida
Aechmea species
Begonia
Beloperone guttata
Billbergia pyramidalis
Clerodendrum species
Clivia miniata
Cuphea hyssopifolia
Echinopsis species
Euphorbia pulcherrima
Guzmania lingulata

◁ *Agapanthus africanus*

FOR COOL PLACES
55–65°F (13–18°C)
10°F (5°C) cooler at night

Aeonium tabulaeforme
Agapanthus africanus
Azalea indica
Brunfelsia calycina
Calceolaria hybrids
Camellia japonica
Chrysanthemum
Cineraria
Coelogyne cristata
Crocus
Cyclamen
Eucomis
Exacum affine
Fuchsia
Hydrangea macrophylla
Lantana camara
Primula
Reinwardtia
Rosa chinensis minima
Schizanthus hybrids
Tulipa
Vallota speciosa

Above: Cacti such as Parodia aureispina make excellent choices for warm, sunny rooms. But remember that they need a cool period in the winter to bloom.

a colorful setting. If your house is cool—65°F (18°C) by day and 10°F (5°C) less at night—then select *Eucomis, Exacum,* geraniums and some orchids. For an intermediate range, consider *Saintpaulia* and *Haemanthus.*

At the same time you are analyzing temperature, think also about light. Some plants, such as gesneriads, do well in bright light, and most of the cacti, such as parodias and lobivias, really need sun.

In a word, make your choices with reference to the temperature and light available in your home. You can then provide the proper soil and water and the right balance of other conditions to create your indoor dream garden.

An added consideration must be size: there are large, medium and small plants, and it is wise to think about this when making selections for a particular area.

Where to display
You can place a specimen plant here or there and leave it at that, but this will hardly add up to an indoor garden. Why not arrange your plants to create a picture? For example, a windowsill can become a garden if you take advantage of such hardware devices as shelves and hangers. Three shelves fastened across a window can accommodate several medium-sized plants to create a display.

A floor installation is another possibility. With this, use galvanized planter bins available from sheet-metal houses, and have these cut to fit your particular area. Fill the bins with gravel to within an inch (2.5cm) of the top and set the plants on the gravel. Keep the gravel slightly moist to provide humidity for the growing plants.

Above: Dipladenia sanderi 'Rosea' is a good choice for a bright room with an intermediate temperature. Double glazing will protect it from the cold.

Suspending plants at windows is another way to make a picture. Use the handsome hanging containers—four to five at a window. Suspend them at different levels—high, low, and in-between, in a staggered design. A straight line of plants is monotonous and also difficult to care for. At varying levels there is more interest and you can easily move among the plants to water them without too much disturbance.

Shelves on poles that attach to ceilings and walls without hardware—'pressure poles' they are called—offer another way to garden indoors. These pressure poles come with trays and make a handsome vertical garden for easy care.

You might also display your plants on a tea table wheeled next to a window. This

Right: Campanula isophylla must have a cool spot to flower well. The light blue looks well with the silver of its companion, Aglaonema 'Silver Queen'.

makes a pretty garden and the table can be moved about as the light changes. Protect the surface with a piece of glass or some tiles and set the plants themselves on saucers to catch excess water.

How to display

For an attractive windows display, don't use too many or too large plants—you don't want a jungle. Select your containers with care. Basically, the standard terracotta pot is a wise choice: it looks good in almost any surroundings, comes in many sizes, and lets moisture evaporate slowly from its walls—a plus for plants.

Decorative containers can also be used, such as a group of china or tole cachepots or some Chinese jardinieres. Many attrac-

Choosing the Best Container

tive glazed containers and handsome porcelain ones are also available. But don't plant directly in these. Instead use standard clay pots and slip these into the decorative ones.

So whether on shelves at windows, on trays, on poles, in planter boxes, or on tables next to the light, your plants can create a cheerful atmosphere in any room. It is all a matter of choosing the right ones for the conditions you have, displaying them properly, and, of course, caring for them diligently so they will thrive.

Containers—new and traditional

In recent years we have been offered not only many new plants but also an array of new containers. Once the clay pot and little else was available, but today florists and nurseries show pots and tubs in various sizes and many materials. Now, selecting a proper container is almost as important as choosing the right plant. Some containers are very ornamental, with outside scrollwork or bas-relief designs. Be sure these do not clash with your furnishings.

The standard clay pot is still with us, but in new designs and sizes. There are also fine glazed pots, ceramic containers, wooden tubs, plastic and metal ones, and majestic jardinieres.

The versatile clay pot

Clay pots are still the most functional because plants grow well in them and the natural clay harmonizes with most furnishings. These containers are available in a number of designs:

1 Venetian pots are barrel-shaped, with a concentric band design pressed into the sides in a scored texture. They are somewhat formal in appearance.
2 The Italian pot modifies the border to a tight-lipped detail. Some have rounded edges, other are beveled or rimless in sizes

Above: Glazed china containers are available in so many sizes and designs that choosing the right one is an enjoyable and rewarding task.

Above: Even clay pots have spruced themselves up and you can now choose (1) Venetian (2) Italian (3) Spanish (4) azalea or (5) cylindrical.
Right: A blaze of flowers from Begonia 'Fireglow' planted in a lead-lined wine cooler provides a stunning accent for a traditional corner.

from 12-14in (30-35cm). These decorative pots are well suited to contemporary rooms and settings.
3 Spanish pots, in many sizes from 8-20in (20-50cm), are graceful, with outward sloping sides and flared lips. They have heavier walls than conventional clay pots, and are suitable for certain period rooms.
4 Azalea, or fern, pots are squat, limited to 14in (35cm), and fine for most settings.
5 The new cylindrical terracotta containers are indeed handsome—a departure from traditional tapered designs. They come in several sizes, the maximum being 16in (40cm) across; good for specimen plants.

Other containers

Glazed containers offer a variety of colors. Choose them with care, because they can be overpowering, especially in large sizes. White goes will with most color schemes, but some of the brighter colors may clash.

As a rule, glazed pots have no drainage holes, so watering plants in them must be done with care; overwatering results in soggy soil that kills plants. Of course, if you purchase undrained, decorative pots, you can take them to a glass store and have holes drilled.

Plastic pots are pleasing, and three or four plants in them look nice on a kitchen

Above: For that special plant why not choose a container made of brass or copper, or perhaps a reed basket to complement delicate blooms?

Below: Plant, pot and decor in perfect harmony. A white porcelain container and a dusty pink wall are superb foils for a specimen begonia.

or bathroom windowsill. The only disadvantage is that, because of their lightness, large plants may tip over in them.

Spun-steel or aluminum containers are sleek and contemporary and come with drainage holes and saucers. Try them for a stylish new look.

Reed, wicker, and bamboo baskets are other possibilities. Use them as cover-ups rather than for direct planting. Put a saucer in the bottom of the basket to catch excess water, and then insert the potted plant. Such natural materials as wicker, reed, and bamboo blend well with plants and harmonize with most decorations.

Baskets come in many shapes—square, rectangular, oval, and round.

Japanese soy tubs and sawed-off wine casks are unique containers, but they do not fit every setting. They suit rustic and informal interiors but are out of place in traditional rooms. Blue-glazed Japanese urns, brass pots and gold-leaf tubs look handsome and lend sophistication to contemporary or period interiors.

Boxes and tubs
These are wooden containers, usually made from redwood or cypress. They are attractive for outdoors, but (except in rare

cases) they are not good indoors. Eventually the wood rots and becomes unsightly because of water stains and acids. However, acrylic-coated redwood containers have recently made their appearance; these handsome pots are fine for some rooms. They are sleek, harmonize with contemporary interiors, and are available in several sizes and shapes.

Concrete and concrete-type tubs are offered in many designs. Given space, they will fit in a modern setting, but generally these do not look well in most rooms, and they are extremely heavy, making them very difficult to move.

Above: Pedestals can be used to raise low-growing plants to a height where they can be better admired; here an Azalea indica with bicolored blooms.

Plant furniture

Although floor plants are fine for many places in the home, invariably there will come a time when, because of space or as an accessory to an interior, you might want only a few medium-sized plants. Plant stands that take little space but still accommodate several plants are the answer; they are available as sleek metal and glass shelving or étagères (wrought-iron stands specifically designed for plants), or perhaps even a small ladder, painted a suitable color, to hold plants. The plant stand is for a grouping of plants; pedestal tables and stands are for a single, larger plant—for example, a hydrangea.

You can also use glass or acrylic shelving to hold a few plants as a room accent. These are generally modern in design, and the green accent of plants is just right for contrast. Use three or four plants spaced accordingly, depending upon how many shelves there are, rather than just one or two plants. Place the plants to either the front or the rear but not in the center, because there they invariably seem out of proportion to the total shelf unit. Wooden shelf units are also available, but these are bulky, and plants—even on saucers—will leave water stains on wood. Glass or acrylic shelves allow light to reach all plants, but wood might block the light.

Wrought-iron stands that look like small spiral staircases are also fine for plants. Shelves are adjustable and generally accommodate one plant. And there is little chance of stain with wrought iron. Place these stands near windows or wherever you need an accent.

Wooden pedestals come in all shapes and sizes, antique or modern, Greek or

Chinese in character. They hold only one plant. These stands are part of the room furnishings and should be chosen to match other furniture in the room. Some are lightweight in appearance, others—the antique type—look heavy and more dominant. For small rooms use a light-weight stand; for larger rooms the old stands make a nice feature.

Plants for stands and pedestals differ in size and character. Generally, a medium-to small-sized plant is what you need, and it should be in proportion to the stand; a

large plant on a small pedestal looks top-heavy. Keep the elements of design in mind: proportion, balance and harmony.

Plant platforms—either small pedestals or homemade wooden stands—can be used to elevate floor plants to the desired height. Some are available commercially, but you may have to make them yourself, or have your local carpenter make them for you. Round plant platforms are better for most plants than square or rectangular ones, although the latter can be used if they fit the decor of the room.

Above: This stand in brass, copper and iron is effective because it holds several plants. The metals complement the foliage, the flower colors of the begonias and the wood and brick behind.
Above right: Plant stands can be used to raise plants into the light. The blue Browallia looks well with white.
Right: Ways to use white; in harmony and in contrast. On the white pedestals white flowering plants are used; in the trough, a contrasting group of chrysanthemums and begonias.

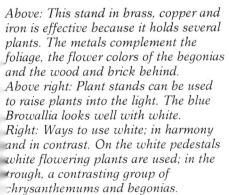

Growing Plants in a Greenhouse

Above: Benches should be at the appropriate height for working with the plants. The recording equipment at top right is available to check the temperature and humidity within the greenhouse.

Greenhouse growing

It is a joy to have a separate place for plants—a greenhouse or even a greenhouse window. There, with full light, adequate humidity, and good air circulation, you can grow almost any plant, and your favorites are probably legion. But avoid crowding, which is indeed a temptation. Some greenhouses I have seen were literally jungles. With such a crowd it is difficult to observe each plant, yet daily inspection goes a long way toward intelligent care.

In greenhouses, too, there is a tendency for conditions to be too good—that is, too high a humidity—and this, coupled with gray days, leads to fungus diseases. It is better to hold to a 50 percent humidity rather than to 90 percent.

Be mindful also of ventilation; the atmosphere should be fresh and buoyant. Also, remember that where there are many plants, there are bound to be many insects, so be prepared for trouble. A few plants at a window do not attract insects as much as, say, 50 or 100 plants in a greenhouse. Above all, keep your greenhouse scrupulously clean, with no debris, and no decayed leaves.

For the most part, plants in a greenhouse are all growing in the same environment. It is hardly possible there to have separate areas of cool, intermediate, and warm conditions; but plants placed at higher elevations will have a warmer atmosphere than those on the benches or on the ground, where it is slightly cooler.

Grow your intermediate type plants at

Above: This greenhouse for cool-loving species has excellent light conditions and automatic ventilation. It's ablaze with calceolarias and cyclamen.

bench level, and under the benches (on slatted platforms), place such cool-preference species as *Exacum* and some of the bulbous plants. Try to elevate the heat lovers to the upper extremes, either on shelves placed above the main bench or suspended from the eaves on plant hangers, or some perhaps in hanging baskets.

Greenhouse conditions and maintenance

Once you have built or purchased your greenhouse, consider such requirements as temperature, humidity, and ventilation. If yours is an all-glass, tightly-enclosed structure, these requirements are vital, because glass is a poor conductor and greenhouses are invariably too hot in summer and too cold in winter. However, if you have avoided the all-glass unit, healthy maintenance will be less exacting. Basically, conditions similar to those in your home—that is, temperatures of 70-80°F (21-27°C) during the day, with some cooling at night—are fine. Humidity of 30-60 percent is acceptable, along with the year-round circulation of air that plants need to thrive and resist disease.

Humidity

For most plants, the average humidity given above is fine. Higher humidity, which is often recommended, can really do more harm than good, because in

winter it is often associated with dark days and so can create a breeding ground for fungus and bacteria.

Keep an inexpensive hygrometer in the greenhouse to measure the moisture in the air. And remember that the more artificial heat you supply in winter, the more moisture will be necessary in the air. On very hot days, keep the humidity somewhat high. At night, humidity, like temperature, should be lower.

As a rule, many plants growing together in a greenhouse will create their own humidity, so special equipment, such as a mister or fogger, is not necessary unless it is very hot. As long as you water routinely, there will be sufficient humidity for plants to create good growth.

Temperature

Many plants prosper at 70-80°F (21-27°C) during the day with a 10-15°F (5-8°C) drop at night. You can maintain this range in your greenhouse without elaborate equipment; only in winter will you need to adjust heat for those very cold nights, and a *few* very cold nights will not harm your plants. What will harm them are sudden changes in temperature, but by careful manipulation of windows and doors, you can gradually reduce the heat of hot summer evenings.

On very warm days, the home greenhouse of wood and glass can get too hot. When doors and windows are shut, the sun can push the inside temperature past 100°F (38°C), and this causes plants to lose moisture too fast. Spray and mist plants with water to keep them cool. Be especially alert in a prolonged heat spell: you can lose plants in a few days if you do

Right: Shade your greenhouse and make use of its full depth. Suspend trailers and warmer species from the roof. Place shade-lovers under the benches.

not cool them by misting or shading.

In winter, don't fret if your greenhouse is somewhat cool. It is better to keep plants too cool than too hot; they can recover from a chill but rarely from dehydration. But on very windy and cold days, when the temperature in a greenhouse can drop faster than you think, make sure you are providing enough heat.

Ventilation
I have always considered the ventilation of my greenhouse more important than either humidity or temperature control, because good air circulation is so important. It provides relief from the sun, helps control such diseases as mildew, and assures good humidity. When I started growing orchids, I was always concerned with humidity and tropical heat, but in a few years I discovered that the plants did not object to coolness; indeed, they grew better as long as there was adequate ventilation.

The atmosphere in a greenhouse should be buoyant and fresh, never stagnant. In nature, you will observe that few plants grow in stagnant places. Even in winter be sure some fresh air enters the greenhouse. Because hot air rises, some windows should be provided at the top of the greenhouse. When these vents are open, warm air flows out to cool the greenhouse and fresh air flows in.

Shading
Direct summer sunshine can heat a greenhouse considerably and wreak havoc on plants. For example, orchids and gesneriads might die overnight if subjected to even one day of temperatures above 100°F (38°C), and leaf temperatures over 120°F (49°C) immediately scorch and kill plant cells. In most areas, unless your greenhouse faces east and so gets only morning sun, you will have to provide some form of efficient shading for the structure.

Above: A greenhouse should contain rising, or 'buoyant', air. You can create it by installing louvred vents in the side and opening roof windows.
Right: This greenhouse needs excellent temperature control because it contains tender plants: hothouse orchids, Medinilla magnifica and caladiums.

Old-fashioned paste or whiting powder can be applied with a spray or paintbrush, but this is a bother and looks ugly. Instead, install movable aluminium- or wood-slatted Venetian blinds or bamboo roll-ups. They cost more than powder or paints, but they look better, are easy to install, and can be opened during periods when there is bright but cool light.

Plastic shading is also a bother and looks terrible. Use some screening that breaks the sunlight yet allows some light through. Even better is special window trellage, which adds charm to a building (this is my preference, after trying other methods of shading). Trellises can be built cheaply and installed with little effort; they will provide almost perfect light for plants, as a pattern of alternating shade and light is created.

Heating
How you heat your greenhouse depends on where you live, the size of the structure, and its design. It used to be that a hot water system was the one means of heating and this depended on a maze of pipes. Today many other types of heating are available. Installing and operating them is not too difficult, but selecting the proper kind of heating fuel—gas, oil, kerosene (paraffin) or electricity—can be difficult.

Before you select your system check local gas and electric rates. Decide which is the most economical for you and then investigate specific systems. For my small greenhouse I use hot air heat by extending one duct directly from the house furnace.

The warm-air, gas-fired heater is popular today; it has a safety pilot and thermostatic controls. You may have to provide masonry or metal chimneys so fumes can be released outside. A nonvented heater does not need an outlet chimney; the inflammable chamber is sealed and outside the greenhouse.

The warm-air, oil-fired heater is small, and can be fitted under a greenhouse bench. It will furnish enough heat for most home greenhouses. It has a gun-type burner, a blower, a two-stage fuel pump and full controls. This type of heater requires a masonry chimney or a metal smokestack above the roof to vent fumes.

Portable kerosene- (paraffin-) burning heaters are available in many parts of the world for heating greenhouses. These are convenient and economical in use, but good ventilation is essential to clear the carbon dioxide fumes away.

Electric heaters are satisfactory for small greenhouses. These units are automatic, built with a circulating fan, but heavy-duty electrical lines are necessary. The heater and thermostats should be installed by a professional electrician in accordance with local electric codes.

How to save heat
There are several ways to 'store' heat in a greenhouse and so save fuel. The methods are relatively simple but they involve the use of proper materials. For example, a concrete floor is a remarkable heat storer: it absorbs enough heat during the day—if the structure faces south—to keep the greenhouse warm for most of the night, even in very cold climates. Masonry walls opposite the glass wall also absorb the sun's heat and store it for night-time radiation; even a wooden wall painted a dark color will save heat.

If you can afford it, use double-layered insulating glass in some areas of the greenhouse, perhaps on the north wall, where the wind is generally strongest. It can save as much as 30 percent of the heat, and even though its initial installation is more expensive than standard glass, in the long run it pays for itself.

Once the greenhouse is built, plant hedges and shrubs along the sides where storms hit the hardest. Such simple landscaping can effectively cut your heating bills. Planting some low-growing trees or shrubs in double rows at the corner of the greenhouse will add to the beauty of the whole area. Such natural barriers also screen out dust, polluted air, and noise.

Heavy plastic sheeting used to 'double-glaze' a greenhouse offers another means of reducing heat costs. Curtains thwart cold drafts and keep the greenhouse fairly warm at night without the necessity of turning up the thermostat. Or better yet, install inexpensive wooden shutters or roll-up blinds.

Weatherstripping, or draft-excluder, sold in packages at hardware stores, can be used to keep cold out and warm air in. These effective products are easy to apply. They can reduce heat loss by about 10 percent, so do not discount them as a gimmick. In Chicago, I always used them on greenhouse windows and they cut my fuel bill quite a bit.

Maintenance
A greenhouse, like other structures, needs periodic maintenance. If you check yours twice a year, you can keep it in good repair with little effort. For example, foundations may develop cracks, but when caught in time they can easily be filled in with a glazing compound. Check the glass for broken panels and the glazing compound that holds the glass in place. If the compound is missing, replace it. Some-

The Versatile Garden Room

times complete reglazing with one of the new materials may be necessary. If you have used putty before, the chances are it has become brittle with time and can be chipped away easily.

Repaint wooden members whenever it is needed. Don't neglect this, because once excess moisture gets into wood, it can travel quickly and cause havoc. If you are painting the inside of your greenhouse, clear out all the plants, rather than trying to do the job with plants in place. This makes it too difficult for you, and paint fumes can harm the plants.

Always check guttered and lipped grooves to be sure water is draining properly. Make any small repairs immediately, rather than waiting until a total replacement is necessary. Use a tar-based paint for gutters because it resists the extra moisture present there.

The garden room
The garden room has become increasingly popular as a place for plants. Primarily, the garden room was the outdoor room or extension of the home; now these areas are virtual greenhouses. The difference between the garden room and a solarium, greenhouse or conservatory is that the latter are generally glazed completely in glass, whereas in the garden room only

Above: The tiled floor of this garden room is both practical and attractive; water marks from pots and soil spillages can be easily cleaned up. The flowering plants here, which include a red Hippeastrum and hanging Columnea, add splashes of color among the ferns and other foliage plants.
Right: The garden room forms a link between the house and the garden. A room of light and greenery, it can house climbers and specimen plants.

partial glass (often just skylights) is used.

Plants for garden rooms vary, but usually large foliage specimens provide the main decoration and smaller flowering plants add color. Large palms are perhaps the favorite for these areas—fishtail palms (*Caryota*) and *Kentia* (*Howeia*). Tree type plants such as *Ficus benjamina* and *Schefflera actinophylla* are popular, as are many of the tall climbing philodendrons and, of lesser importance, dieffenbachias and dracaenas, especially *Dracaena fragrans* 'Massangeana'. All of these plants provide the vertical accent so necessary in large areas such as garden rooms, where ceilings are generally higher than in a standard greenhouse.

Large cacti have also made their appearance in garden areas and many of the tall

Cereus species are often seen. Again the emphasis is on vertical accent to help coordinate the total interior design of such garden rooms.

Garden furniture of various designs is incorporated into the garden room, and it has become a pleasant place for people and for plants—a green retreat where one can forget the outside world.

In a garden room environment plants grow well; many plants growing together create their own humidity and thus the problem of dry air—the nemesis of most plants—is solved. Light is usually excellent. Even one or two skylights (plastic or glass) in an area of, say, 12 × 20ft (3.6 × 6m) is sufficient to allow enough light for most plants to thrive. Temperatures are generally within the house range

namely 65-78°F (18-26°C) during the day and 10°F (5°C) less at night: ideal conditions for most plants.

Plants for garden rooms

Although most of the plants in our descriptive lists can be grown in a garden room, some are better than others, and this includes many of the flowering vines and larger flowering plants. A definitive list of what to grow in such a room is unnecessary—grow what you like. If you do select some of the smaller flowering plants, however, do create a suitable bench or table arrangement. In my garden room I have used plant stands of various kinds for smaller plants and this works well. Larger plants are used as specimen plants on low platforms (4in, 10cm) on the floor.

Many garden rooms have tile or brick floors, so water on the floor does not cause a problem.

If the floor is impervious to water it is a good practice to wet down the paving on very hot days; I do this frequently in the summer to keep the heat down. Whereas greenhouses generally have some shading devices for hot summer sun, garden rooms do not, so wetting down the floor to maintain high humidity during warm weather is advised.

Plants in my garden room are watered with a hose and wand—there is no individual watering. It takes too long when you have over 100 plants. With a watering wand, or lance, I can give moisture to all my plants in about 15 minutes. I do this three times a week in

spring and summer, once a week in autumn and winter. Generally, this schedule works well. Here is what I grow in my garden room:

- Bromeliads (many kinds).
- Orchids (generally shade-tolerant kinds, such as coelogynes, as well as odontoglossums and oncidiums, masdevallias, and lycastes).
- Other flowering plants: an assortment from *Dipladenia* to *Bougainvillea*. I also use hanging containers, and many flowering plants thrive in such a situation.
- Foliage plants: I use palms and *Dracaena marginata* for vertical accent.
- Finally, for that lush green look, large Boston ferns (*Nephrolepis*) occupy the northern corner of the room.

Selecting Your Plants

Let us look now at plants in general – how they grow, what they need, and how to select suitable flowering specimens for the variety of conditions that probably exist in your house or flat – places without sun, centrally-heated rooms and very cool rooms. Let us also look at different methods to encourage your plants to bloom.

The plants we consider first will survive under almost any conditions and in any area — they are the 'easy' ones — but first let us look at plants growing in their native environment.

Consider their habitat

Not very many of our favorite houseplants grow in tropical rain forests. Most flowering plants come from temperate areas where evenings may be somewhat cool (to 60°F, 16°C). So although warmth is essential for some plants, the majority accommodate themselves to average home temperatures of, say, 68°F (20°C) by day and somewhat less at night.

In nature, more plants grow in bright light than in intense sunshine; direct sun in jungles would scorch plants. Such epiphytes as many orchids and bromeliads perch in treetops where light filters through branches and other plants growing there.

In many areas of the world there are distinct dry and wet seasons — it rains for five to six months and is dry the rest of the year — but plants in these areas adjust to the conditions and flourish. Many, like the orchids, have water reservoirs — pseudobulbs — that keep them going through periods of drought. Nature does indeed protect her own.

In nature you rarely find plants growing in a close atmosphere; there is almost always good air circulation, and it is wise to consider this when growing plants at home. Few endure stagnant air conditions. A buoyant atmosphere is what they like. Humidity — moisture in the air — is also vital. Too many indoor plants die because they are exposed to a dry atmosphere. But there are many ways to increase humidity and we discuss this later.

How plants adapt indoors

Plants for commercial sale are grown in

Above: Azalea indica is a temperate plant needing cool, shady conditions. Right: Cinerarias massed at Kew Gardens, London. These plants will grow in a cool, light home environment.

greenhouses where conditions are almost ideal, so it is quite a shock to them to be thrust into a home atmosphere where it is usually cooler, the air less buoyant, and humidity low. But most plants have a will to live and after a few weeks most will adjust to the less favorable environment — some faster than others.

During the vital greenhouse-to-home period, it is essential to give extra attention. For example, don't water copiously until the adjustment period is well under way — too much water can kill. Don't set plants immediately in direct sunlight; in a greenhouse there is shading during the hot summer months. In fact, most greenhouse plants are grown all year round in bright light rather than sunshine. Exposing a newly purchased plant to full sunlight can be very harmful.

When you bring home a plant, place it in an intermediate area of about 68°F (20°C), and water sparingly. If the plant is in a soilless mixture or in a sand-and-

soil mix (which many growers use), it would be wise to repot in fresh nutritious compost after, say, two to three weeks. But do not repot plants in the middle or at the end of their growing season.

Gradually expose the plant to more heat and light; you will have to experiment with placement to determine just where it grows best. Moving a plant a few inches one way or another can make a difference — the air may be more moist in one area, less so in another; there may be a draft in one place; and so on. But once you find the spot that a plant likes, leave it there.

Some plants, such as many orchids, adapt quickly to a new environment; others, such as most cacti and succulents, take longer. If leaves wilt and some fall, don't panic and don't give up. Most plants even-

Some plants need special treatment to encourage them to form flower buds. Above: The Christmas cactus needs darkness 12 to 14 hours a day for six weeks before blooming. But what a stunning reward it gives!
Right: Clivia miniata flowers best in a small pot. If this makes the plant look awkward, stand it in a decorative planter.

tually start to grow and succeed in a new place. It is a matter of patience, observation and proper care. As a rule, if you like plants you will study them, paying attention to leaf color, leaf texture, stem strength and general appearance. Get to know what your plants like or do not like. This makes indoor gardening a pleasurable pastime and not a chore.

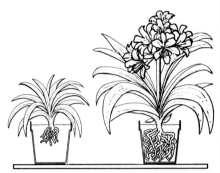

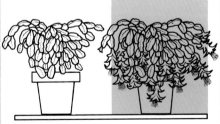

How to coax flowering

Below: Some plants flower when their roots become crowded in a pot. Fearing death, the plant starts the process of reproduction and buds are formed, as in this *Clivia miniata*.

Below: Too much water encourages some species to produce nothing but lush leaves. Reduce watering to obtain fine blooms on this easy to grow orchid *Coelogyne cristata*.

Below: Flowering may be triggered by day length. Short day plants, such as Christmas cactus (*Schlumbergera x buckleyi*) need at least 12 hours dark a day. Long day plants will flower with extra artificial light.

Below: Many cacti, such as the *Mammillaria* shown here, come from countries with hot summers and cool winters. In the house, they will not flower unless they are kept dry for several months at about 40 °F (4 °C).

How to encourage bloom

If someone had told me some years ago that there were ways of making plants bloom indoors I would have been skeptical; but after two decades of success, I can now offer you suggestions on how to achieve beautiful blooms at your windows.

Many plants, such as *Clivia* and *Clorophytum*, will bear only when roots are crowded in the pot; in too large containers, they may take years to bud. Some plants—orchids are a good example—require a drying out period to encourage budding, about four to six weeks with little water. Other plants, such as the Christmas cactus (*Schlumbergera x buckleyi*) require 12 hours of complete darkness per day for four to six weeks before they will bloom.

Another means to induce bloom indoors

Above: A potbound Clivia which has thrived and grown several offsets. This is one of many plants that flower with crowded roots; do not disturb often.

is shock—a period of relative cold. I have had plants bear by setting them outdoors for a few weeks in 50-60°F (10-16°C) —not in winter cold, of course. This method is not suitable for all plants, only for some, and these are marked accordingly in the descriptions given in the second part of the book.

Resting periods

Like people, plants need an occasional period of rest to recoup and prepare for another year of growing. Most rest in winter for, say, six to eight weeks. During

*Above: Oleanders and sun-loving
Mediterranean plants will flower well
in this elegant room. The light from
the large windows is spread by the
white paint, flooring and decor.
Left: Paphiopedilums are orchids that
require rather cool, damp conditions to
thrive and flower. They find a suitable
home in the bathroom.*

this time they need less water than usual
and a somewhat lower temperature (check
for each plant), and no plant food; feeding
during rest can seriously check blooming.
But although the majority of plants rest,
some do not, and require water and food
throughout the year.

The big question then is, when does a
particular plant rest? Although it is difficult to give dates for a particular species,
you can pretty well determine rest time by
checking bloom time and counting six
months forward. Some plants bud in early
spring, others in mid spring, and still

others in late spring. The same sequence of early to late bloom carries into summer and autumn. In winter, bloom time is usually midway in the season, say, February. Check times of bloom in the individual plant descriptions in the second part of the book. Then you can pretty well time the rest period that will encourage budding.

It is not always necessary to move plants for resting; simply water less and do not feed. Plants generally indicate when you should resume watering by some new growth—a shoot here or there.

With bulbous plants (and there are many flowering ones I recommend), the rest period is vital. With bulbs it is a good idea to store them during the dormant period in their pots in a dry shaded place at 55°F (13°C). I store mine in a closed cupboard. When it is time for growth I replant them in fresh compost in the same pots for another year of flowers. For most bulbs it is also important to bring them only gradually into light and warmth.

Where to place

There are really no special places for plants—just different places, such as light, sunny, or dark situations. If you have a window where light is obscured by trees or buildings, or the exposure is northerly, then of course you should select plants that will grow under such conditions.

If you have an expanse of glass with plenty of sunlight, your choice is almost limitless. Consider the exotic tropicals, such as gingers and *Hippeastrum* varieties, and a host of other exciting plants that will bring color to your room.

Of all places, centrally heated rooms pose the geatest problem; the higher the artificial heat, the more the air dries out to make life miserable for most plants. In winter, when artificial heat is at its height, you can increase humidity somewhat by misting plants frequently. The choice for centrally heated rooms is hardly vast, but there are some species that will survive this condition and still grow.

Growing Plants Indoors

If you have selected plants wisely for the conditions you can offer, caring for them will be relatively easy. It is true that some plants require more attention than others, but most, once established, get along pretty well with minimal care. Learn to observe your plants for signs of health or disease.

A long with a suitable location, good soil is essential, also proper watering and feeding. And it is these considerations we discuss now. Of course you will also need some information on how to deal with insects (if they attack) and disease (if it occurs).

Potting mixtures

Plants confined to containers need a rich porous medium in which to grow. Today good potting soils can be purchased in tidy sacks. Some 'houseplant soils' are marked for general use, others are special mixtures for African violets, for cacti, for bulbs, and so on. Basically, good all-purpose houseplant mix is fine; there is no need to buy different mixtures for different plants.

The package of potting soil you buy, however, can be a mystery as to just what it contains. Certainly there is soil but how much? There is no way of knowing. Many mixtures also include fillers, such as sawdust, which will not do your plants any good. How do you know if a packaged soil is good? You don't. It is like purchasing any item; you have to inquire from friends and nurserymen, and then make your own choice. You can also feel the soil in the package—it should be mealy and porous. But beyond that you have no way of knowing what you are buying.

So for those who are not satisfied and want to prepare their own potting soil (which is fine), here is the mixture (by volume) that I have found satisfactory for most houseplants:

$\frac{1}{3}$ sterilized garden loam
$\frac{1}{3}$ humus
$\frac{1}{3}$ sand

For cacti and succulents I use:

$\frac{1}{2}$ sterilized loam
$\frac{1}{2}$ sand

You can make a big quantity of potting mixture ahead of time and store it in a dry, cool place, rather than prepare a small

Above: These saintpaulias will grow more rapidly and use up more food under artificial light than the begonia, right, in natural light. The begonia should need repotting less often.

batch for immediate use, which can be a bother. When you do make a mix, combine all materials thoroughly so that they are evenly distributed.

For bromeliads and orchids, you will need a potting medium other than soil; most of these are epiphytes (or air plants) and don't grow well in soil. The mixture I use for bromeliads is $\frac{1}{2}$ soil and $\frac{1}{2}$ fine-grade fir bark; and for orchids I use medium- or large-grade fir bark (no soil).

Bulbous plants are favorites of mine and through the years I have found that they thrive in a relatively rich mixture, although some garden writers claim they do well in a sandy soil. I use this mixture for bulbs:

$\frac{1}{3}$ sterilized loam
$\frac{1}{3}$ humus
$\frac{1}{6}$ sand
$\frac{1}{6}$ charcoal chips

Those are my preferred mixtures, but just as each of us has a favorite apple pie recipe, so gardeners have their soil prefer-

ences. Stick to whatever has been success-ful for you, but if you are a beginner, you may find my recommended mixtures helpful to start with.

Potting and repotting
The first time you move a plant or a seedling from a nursery container into a new pot it is called potting. Repotting is moving a plant from its pot to another one, usually of a larger size. Select a pefectly clean container. If you are using a new clay pot, soak it overnight so it will not absorb a lot of water from the soil. If you are reusing a pot, scrub it with hot water and soap and rinse it thoroughly.

To prepare a pot for planting, spread a 1in (2.5cm) layer of pot shards (broken pieces of pots) over the bottom. Sprinkle this with charcoal chips, about a handful for a 6in (15cm) pot. Arrange a mound of potting mixture and center the plant on it.

Steady it with one hand and with your other hand fill in and around it with fresh potting mixture. If the plant rests too low in the pot, add more mixture; if it is too high, remove some. The final soil level should be 1in (2.5cm) below the rim of the pot, thus allowing space for water, and a proper stem height for the plant—not too deep nor too shallow. If you pot a plant too deep you risk crown rot; if it is too high, it will look awkward.

Finally tamp down the soil and knock the base of the pot gently against a step or table; after the soil settles, the need for more may be indicated.

Press down with your thumbs to pack the soil around the collar of the plant. You want it secure and this is important; air pockets cause roots to reach for moisture and so produce straggly growth.

Finally, water thoroughly, and as the water drains out, water again.

In repotting, the main consideration is safe removal from the old container. A

Above: Potting a cactus can be a painful experience, so use gloves. Very hairy or spiny plants such as this Echinocactus grusonii, may trap particles of the soil mix. A suitable shallow pot or pan is ready to receive the plant, and tweezers and brush are on hand to tidy up the cactus once potted.

plant that pushes roots out of the drainage hole or a plant that appears crowded usually needs repotting. But there are exceptions. You may want to keep a plant potbound to force it to bloom, as with clivias for example.

To repot, loosen the old potting mixture by drawing a blunt stick in a circle just inside the pot. Now grasp the plant by the collar and try to tease it from the pot—don't pull hard or you will injure or even break the roots.

If the plant does not come out easily, spread aluminum foil over the soil, invert

Above: How to pot a large cactus. (1) Put in plenty of pot shards. (2) Pour in sufficient gravel and soil mix to support the plant. (3) Position the cactus on the soil mound, using gloves or newspaper to protect your hands. (4) Water thoroughly, using spout. Right: Patience rewarded; a stunning array of cactus plants in full bloom.

Left: Seedlings of many types of orchid can be easily repotted as they develop. They are grown in fir bark chips, which cling to the rootball as the plant is transferred from one pot to another. Polystyrene pieces ensure good drainage.

Right: The diagram sequence shows the essential stages in potting a plant. (1) Put in a few pot shards (broken pieces of pot) to ensure good drainage and to prevent loose soil falling through the single, large hole in most clay pots. (2) Pour in some potting soil, allowing space for the plant. (3) Center the plant on the soil and care-fully fill in around it, shaking the pot to settle the soil. (4) Firm the soil with your fingertips to prevent air pockets forming around the roots.

the pot, and knock the edge hard against a desk or potting bench. If the plant still won't budge, you will have to break the pot with a hammer and gently remove the rootball. (It may seem foolish to break a pot to remove a plant, but it is better than pulling out the plant and so retarding growth for several months. Besides, you can always used the broken pot pieces for drainage.) Try to keep the rootball intact. Finally crumble away some of the old potting mixture and trim any rangy brown roots judiciously. Then follow the recom-mended procedure for potting.

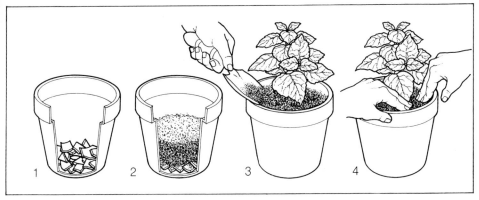

When to pot a plant

Plants confined to a container use up the nutrients in the potting mixture in a given time—generally in one year or less. However, if you give plants supplemental feeding (add nutrients to the soil with plant food), you can keep a plant in the same potting soil for perhaps two years. But additional feeding—too much plant food—can harm a plant by burning roots, so I suggest only moderate feedings at specific times as outlined in the plant descriptions. Even so, repotting is eventually necessary to promote plant health.

There are several old-fashioned ways to determine whether a plant needs new soil—if you see roots coming out of the drainage hole of the pot, or if the soil seems caked and dry. A better and more efficient way of knowing when to repot a specific plant is to repot plants in 4-6in (10-15cm) containers every year, those in 7-9in (18-23cm) containers every 18 months, and those in pots over 10in (25cm) in diameter every second or third year. The best time of the year to repot a plant is at the beginning of the growing season, which for most is in the spring.

The process of repotting a plant may seem troublesome and time consuming but if you want healthy plants (and who doesn't) you will have to provide the fresh potting mixture for plants to live. Soil that has been depleted of nutrients simply will not keep a plant alive, and too much feeding can harm a plant as poisonous residues may build up in the soil.

When you are giving plants new soil you also provide a larger pot—certainly the plant has grown and more room is necessary for its roots. I use a pot 2in (5cm) in diameter larger than the old pot. This has worked well for my plants.

Generally, the above when-to-pot rules apply, but—as always—there are exceptions to the rule. Many plants—clivias, for example—like to grow potbound: that is, they like their roots crowded in a container, and repotting can set them back considerably, and even thwart blooming. In the plant descriptions I have noted these; usually it is the bulbous plants that resent repotting, but nature always provides. Most bulbous plants do not require repotting every year or so, because they have their own food reservoir, the bulb.

Above: The water level in a humidity tray must be below the pot to avoid waterlogging. The plant will benefit from the damp air, rising around it.

Above: A container with wet clay granules will provide the humidity that the cyclamen and saintpaulias need. Misting is impractical here; it would mark both table and blooms.

Below: The fleshy leaves of this Paphiopedilum have developed crown rot through overwatering. This common cultural fault drives air out of the fir bark medium, causing it to stagnate.

Several other plants from various families also resent repotting, and for these subjects it is best to topdress the soil rather than do a complete repotting. Topdressing is digging out the top 2-3in (5-7.5cm) of soil and replacing it with fresh potting mixture. You will find notes on these plants in the descriptions.

Humidity

Lack of humidity is the major cause of plant demise in the home. Dry air desiccates, resulting first in leaf drop and eventually in death. Humidity (the amount of moisture in the air) should be between 30 and 40 percent for plant health and, incidentally, for good human health as well. If your house is equipped with a humidifier system both you and your plants will greatly benefit.

A less sophisticated way of increasing humidity is to set pots on a gravel layer in a bin. Keep the gravel moist but never soggy. You can also spray plants frequently with water, and I opt for this method. It is simple and inexpensive, and takes only a few minutes each time. Use any misting bottle, such as the laundry type, or buy one at the nursery made especially for this purpose. You can mist all plants except hairy-leaved ones such as the hirsute begonias, and succulents.

Of course, a group of plants will furnish its own humidity because plants give off moisture through their leaves. The more plants, the more humidity—but avoid the dangers of overcrowding.

Light

Many flowering plants prefer as much sunlight as possible, say, three to four

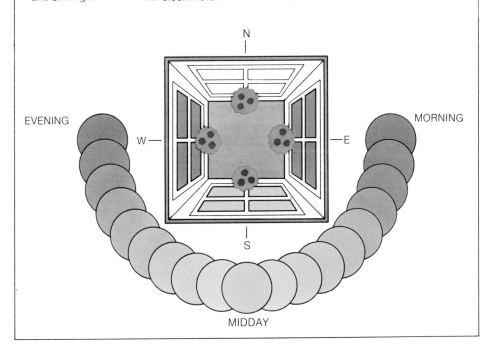

N

EVENING

W — — E

MORNING

S

MIDDAY

Above: These gardenias need the bright light close to the window. But remember that autumn and winter cold can strike through glass. Move them in at night; never leave them behind drawn curtains.

at a western exposure; and for such plants as *Exacum* and some orchids, a north light will suffice. There are indeed plants for every window.

For maximum exposure, plants must be close to windows; the farther away you place a plant, the weaker the light. If you want plants for temporary decoration on tables or desks that are not next to windows, return the plants to windows after a few days.

Light, lamps, and plant life

A plant in a dim corner may live for a few months, but it won't prosper *and mature* there, because without sufficient light it is unable to complete its life cycle. Light is necessary for the plant to be able to produce plant foods from the carbon dioxide and water that it absorbs. The duration of the exposure to light determines the amount of food produced and thus whether the plant will grow well and bloom successfully.

If the window light is dim, you can depend on artificial light to help your plants grow. You can use artificial light as a supplement for plants receiving natural light, or treat the growing area as a separate entity away from windows.

Plants under artificial light grow all the time, as opposed to plants at windows, where the light may sometimes be clouded. So under lights you will have to water plants more than at windows, feed them

hours a day, but if you cannot provide this, do not despair, because many plants do well with only bright light (no sun). Some even adjust after a time to a rather dim north window. In summer, protect plants against strong light that can cause leaf scorch. A curtain or even a screen at the window is helpful. Through the rest of the year no protection is necessary.

For most plants light from an east, west, or south window is fine. In order of preference, east light is best—it is the morning light, neither too strong nor too weak. West light, like east, is of moderate strength. Light at a southern exposure is brightest during midday. North light is obviously weaker than light from the other directions.

Set plants that need sun at a south or east window; those that want bright light

more, and be even more careful about supplying enough humidity.

How plants use light

In the rainbow we can see the prismatic colors, violet, indigo, blue, green, yellow, orange, and red. Plants require blue, red, and far red light to produce normal growth. Blue enables them to manufacture food substances; red controls the assimilation of these, and also affects the plant's response to the relative length of light and darkness. Far red works in conjunction with red light in several ways: it controls seed germination, stem length, and leaf size by nullifying or reversing the action of the red rays.

Plants grow best when they receive adequate levels of blue and red light—both of which are produced by standard fluorescent lamps—and also of far red light, which comes from incandescent bulbs (reading lamps). (Some studies indicate that the rest of the spectrum is also necessary for plants to thrive, but experiments continue, and incontrovertible evidence has yet to be produced.)

Above: Do not assume that a pale-leaved plant is underfed. Too much light can also bleach leaves (left). A normal Aglaonema is shown at right. Below: For healthy growth, plants need blue, red, and far red light. Fluorescent lamps can be used to supply the first two quotients and incandescent lamps provide far red light.

Duration of light

The dark period is a crucial time for plants, and darkness means exactly that—absolute darkness, no ray of light. Some plants require a short day and some a long day, and others are neutral or flexible in their needs. We cannot determine an exact pattern for every plant. Fortunately for indoor gardeners, most houseplants are in the neutral category and will flower and set seed without precise timing of the dark period. Commercial growers must be knowledgeable about light to schedule bloom for seasonal sales, but most indoor gardeners don't have to be concerned with these technicalities. As a general guide, the normal light period for foliage plants is 12-14 hours per day; for flowering plants allow 16-18 hours per day.

An automatic timer is a useful item in the light garden. Timers are sold under various trade names. You can set them for a specific number of hours and know that the lamps will then turn off automatically. Timers are also valuable when you are away for a few days; with them the daily light period can be controlled.

Above: This orchid case is more than an excellent method of display. It also provides a controlled environment with timed lighting and stable temperature.

How much fluorescent light?

The intensity of fluorescent light given to plants must be tempered by common sense. Here are some guidelines: for germinating seeds and cuttings, allow 10 lamp watts per square foot (111 watts per m2) of growing area. For shelf-garden plants such as African violets, give 15 watts per square foot (167 watts per m2); and for high-energy plants such as orchids and roses, 20 lamp watts per square foot (222 watts per m2).

If you use incandescent light in shelf gardens to furnish the vital far red rays that are lacking in most fluorescent lamps, try the 4:1 ratio; it has worked well for me. For example, if you have 200 watts of fluorescent light, add 50 watts of incandescent light (five 10-watt bulbs). But don't confuse these low-light levels of incandescent light with accent lighting, which is different. Sometimes I increased the incandescent ratio, but I found that this created too much heat. The ratios given are the norms, but by no means infallible rules. Trial-and-error is part of the adventure of growing plants under artificial light.

If light intensity in shelf gardens proves too strong for some plants, move them away from the light to the end zones of the lamps, where light is less intense, or raise the adjustable reflector canopy. If light is not strong enough for some species, set them on inverted pots closer to the light or use a lattice support.

There is no exact measure for the distance a plant should be from fluorescent light. As a guide, plants such as geraniums and African violets will grow well with their tops set about 8-10in (20-25cm) from the lamps. Rather than use meters to measure lamp illumination, I prefer to observe the plants. If stems are spindly and foliage of poor color, I know the plants aren't getting enough light; if leaves are bleached or burned, I know the plants are getting to much light.

Fluorescent lamps

Fluorescent lamps come in a dizzying array of shapes, sizes, voltages, wattages,

37

and temperatures. Manufacturers give their lamps various trade names: cool white, daylight, warm white, natural white, soft white, and so on. These names can be misleading, however, because a natural white lamp does not duplicate the sun's rays, a daylight lamp does not duplicate daylight, and there is no difference to the touch between a cool white and warm white lamp.

Cool white lamps are closest to providing the red and blue light necessary for growth. Daylight lamps are high in blue,

but do not provide sufficient red light.

In addition to these standard fluorescents, several companies have designed lamps solely to aid plant growth. With these, supplemental incandescent light is probably not needed because the plant-growth lamps reportedly have both red and blue light.

Incandescent lamps

Some authorities claim that the major disadvantage of incandescent lamps in plant setups is that the heat they project

can be too hot and drying for plants. This is, of course, unrealistic because an 8- or 15-watt lamp at a distance of 10-12in (25-30cm) does not produce enough heat to harm plants in shelf gardens. And in accent lighting, where 150 watts may be used, the lamp is placed 30-36in (75-90cm) from plants, so again there should be no harm from the heat.

Incandescent lamps are more expensive to use than fluorescent lamps, for 70 percent of their power is wasted. However, when used as accent lighting incandescent

Above: A mobile light setup that is both efficient and practical. Gravel trays provide constant humidity under the drying effect of the lamps.

Above: This newly developed plant growth lamp can provide stylish and beneficial lighting for groups of plants in dim corners of the room.

lamps can keep a plant in a dim spot flourishing for years, whereas otherwise it would perish there. So if you have large ornamental speciments decorating your living room, incandescent floodlighting is well worth the extra cost. With this, the lamp-to-plant distance must be at least 24-30in (60-75cm)—36in (90cm) is an

Below: How the new plant lamp works: the peaks in its spectrum show that it supplies light in the color range that plants need for healthy growth.

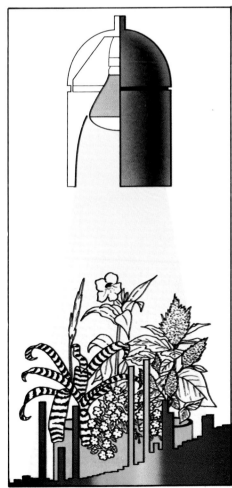

Wavelength (Nanometers)

300   400   500   600   700

even safer distance. Mercury vapor lamps can be placed even farther away—up to 6ft (1.8m) from plants—and still furnish adequate light.

Fixtures used with incandescent lamps for accent lighting include canopy reflectors and reflector floodlights. These give directional control of light to the plant and put it on display while supplying beneficial light without increase in heat. Such fixtures are attractive and even one 150-watt lamp can keep a plant in a shaded area handsome for months.

Mercury vapor lamps embody both fluorescent lamps and incandescent elements in the same housing. There are several kinds of mercury vapor lamps; the easiest to use is a self ballasting type. No additional equipment is needed, as in a fluorescent lamp installation. Mercury vapor lamps are available under various trade names, so check with your dealer.

Use mercury vapor lamps as you would incandescent floods. They diffuse light over a large area and from a considerable distance. Once 150-watt floodlight is suitable for an area up to 4ft (1.2m) in diameter; mount it 5-6ft (1.5-1.8m) away from the plants.

Whichever lamp you use, keep in mind that none is a miracle worker alone. Plants still need water, humidity, ventilation, feeding, and pest control. Some lamps may be better than others for plant growth, but plants will grow and prosper under any light provided there is enough illumination and sufficient day length.

Grow Your Own

There is a lot of fun in starting plants from seed, watching small specks growing into healthy young plants. And think of the money you save! If you have never tried growing houseplants from seed, or taken cuttings from your own plants, consider it now. Check the list at the end of this chapter for suitable varieties.

You can grow seeds in pots, but because a package contains many seeds, you really should use somewhat larger containers: shallow wooden fruit boxes and plastic storage boxes are good propagation containers. So are egg cartons (put a seed in each cup), frozen food trays, or almost any other container about 4-5in (10-12cm) deep. Just make sure you put small drainage holes at the bottom of any container so excess water can escape. Heat the end of an ice pick or skewer to make holes in rigid plastic containers.

You can also sow seeds in peat pots. Fill the pots with soil and insert a seed, and when the leaves are up, transplant pot and all. This saves some of the shock of moving the plants to fresh soil. Seed pellets or discs are also available. With these, insert seed and water: no other growing medium is needed. The pellet expands and becomes the container. When the leaves are up, plant the expanded pellet in soil.

Seed-starting materials

Years ago seed was started in any old soil, but often the soil was not sterile and contained fungus that caused young plants to develop a disease called 'damping-off' and to die young. So seed-starting materials that were sterile and porous were introduced. Today these 'starters' include a number of products, but vermiculite seems to be the most popular. Perlite, sand, sphagnum moss and sterile soil are also good starters.

Sowing seed

There is always a great deal of unnecessary discussion about how deep to plant seeds. Embed the seed about ¼in (6mm) into the starting medium if the seed is large. If the seed is small and specklike, sprinkle it on top of the medium and then add a thin layer of sterile soil over the seed. As a

Above: Streptocarpus 'Constant Nymph', an easily propagated indoor plant.
Right: Leaf cuttings of Streptocarpus with plantlets sprouting at soil level. They can be detached and potted up.

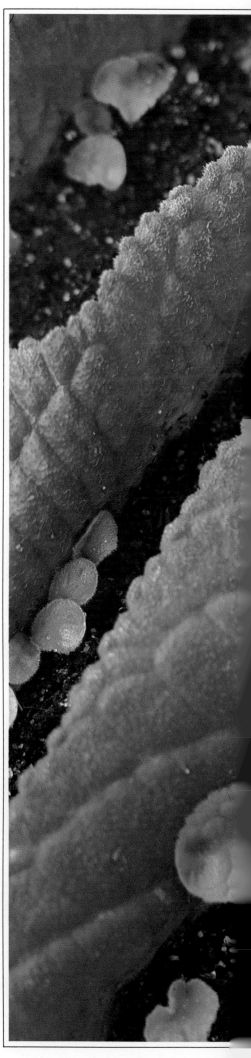

general rule, seed should not be covered more than its own depth.

To start, cover the bottom of your container with about ½in (1.25cm) of small stones or pieces of broken clay pots. Add the growing medium, and then moisten it a bit. (I usually spray the medium gently with water several times until all moisture is soaked up.) Now, depending on the size of the seed, scatter seed on top of the medium or embed the seed. Again spray the starter very gently, and place the container in a warm shaded place; the seed packet will give the recommended temperature. The whole process should not take more than 15 minutes.

Put a layer of transparent plastic or a bag propped on four sticks over the seed tray or box. This creates a tiny greenhouse that will provide adequate humidity to keep the growing medium moist, the essential part of germination. The medium *must* be constantly moist; even one drying out may be fatal. On the other hand, too

Above: Save seed and your own work by sowing thinly and evenly. Barely cover with soil and label before you have time to forget which pot is which!

Above: Some containers for sowing seed. From left: a plastic seed tray; a half-pot, or 'pan'; a plastic pot; a half-tray, and an egg carton. To prevent drying out during germination, use glass sheets or plastic film to keep the moisture level high.

Below: Seed sowing in trays. (1) Add drainage. Fill with sterile compost and level. (2) Sow seeds thinly in drills. (3) Barely cover with soil, water and cover with glass. (4) Transplant the seedlings when they have formed their first true leaves.

much moisture can cause damping-off disease, so check the medium daily; if too much moisture appears on the inside of the plastic, remove it for a few hours.

Germination

Seeds of most houseplants need warmth to germinate. Ideally, warmth should come from underneath the container. Put the container on top of a refrigerator; the ventilation grill provides constant, gentle heat. Do not use the tops of radiators, because this heat fluctuates and is liable to be either too intense or too low. You can also use low-voltage heating cables, which supply a constant heat of 70-78°F (21-26°C). Some containers come complete with cables.

Germination time is from several days to several months; it all depends on the plant and the cultural conditions. To be on the safe side, never throw away seeds before six months have elapsed. When the first tiny green shoots appear, give seedlings more air; that is, remove the plastic for most of the day. When the first true leaves sprout, the plastic can be discarded. Just remember that during the entire germination time the medium must be kept uniformly moist, never wet.

Dealing with seedlings

Often you will have more seedlings than you want. This is nothing to fret about; there are always friends to give them to. Once the seedlings get their second pair of

Above: These seedlings of tuberous begonias are at the right size for transplating from the seed tray to 3½ in (8.5cm) pots. Use a small spatula.

leaves, thin them out—that is, discard the weaker plants—so the stronger plants have space to grow. You can remove the excess plants with tweezers, or gently pick them out of the starting medium with the point of a pencil.

Leave the other plants in the container a few more days or until they are large enough to handle. Then remove the plants from the container and put each plant in a separate 2in (5cm) pot. Do this gently so the rootball is disturbed as little as possible. (This is why peat pots and cubes come in handy: they can be lifted out almost intact.)

Now be sure to put the pot in a protected area under stable conditions for several days so plants get over the shock of transplanting. Again, use transparent plastic to protect plants from fluctuating temperatures and drying out. And be sure the soil does not get too moist during this transplant time. Use a sterile packaged houseplant soil for transplants.

When the new seedlings are a few inches high, repot them into permanent containers. Do not put plants in very large pots because too much unused soil can become too dry or too wet. Generally, a 3 or 4in (7.5 or 10cm) pot suits seedlings very well for their first season of growth.

Cuttings and division

Sowing seed to get new plants is easy, although it does take some time and experience to get *everything* to grow. But

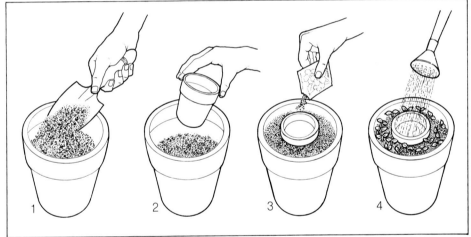

Above: How to sow very fine seed which otherwise floats away when watered. (1) Prepare a pot with drainage and sterile compost. (2) Insert a smaller pot. (3) Sow thinly on the compost surface and cover thinly. (4) Water into the pot—it will seep into the soil.

Below: 'Pricking out' seedlings. (1) When they have their first true leaves, thin out the weakest ones. (2) Lift the rest, holding them with finger and thumb. Place them in single pots. (3) Water with a fine rose. (4) The young plants will soon grow away.

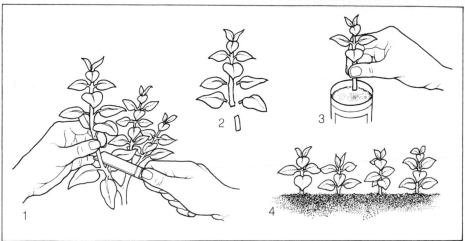

Above: Clump-forming plants like saintpaulias can easily be divided. This plant splits happily into four pieces, but if necessary use a knife.

taking cuttings of plants or dividing them to get new plants requires only a few minutes. If you want more plants of some particular species you already have, just snip a cutting or divide a mature plant to get two plants at no extra cost.

Stem cuttings
Some cuttings—such as those of the foliage houseplants *Tradescantia* or *Philodendron*—need only to be placed in water; wait for roots to form, then plant the cutting. But most cuttings need to be rooted in a growing medium. A stem cutting consists of 3-4in (7.5-10cm) from the top of a plant stem. The best time to start cuttings is in spring, the natural time of growing. You can use any kind of container—the same ones you used for seeds—and the same growing medium. Put 3 or 4in (7.5-10cm) of vermiculite or perlite in the bottom of the container. Dip the cut stem end in a rooting hormone and insert the cutting about 2in (5cm) into the medium. Because most cuttings need good humidity to form roots, place a transparent plastic bag over the container in tent fashion (on sticks) to trap humidity. Keep the bag clear of any leaves.

Keep the growing medium evenly moist, neither dry nor soggy, and place the cuttings in a warm—75°F (24°C)—location in a shady place. In a few weeks remove the plastic tent. Tug the cutting gently to see if it has roots. If it does, transfer the new plant to a 3in (7.5cm) pot

Above: Taking stem cuttings. (1) Using a sharp knife, remove a cutting with 2 or 3 pairs of leaves. Cut above a leaf. (2) Trim the cutting just below a leaf joint and remove the lower leaves. (3) Dip them in hormone rooting powder. (4) Insert them into sterile compost.

Below: (1) Take leaf cuttings of saintpaulias with a piece of stalk. Use a sharp knife. (2) Insert them into sterile compost, preferably around the edge of a pot for good drainage. (3) Plantlets will soon form. (4) Pot these up singly.

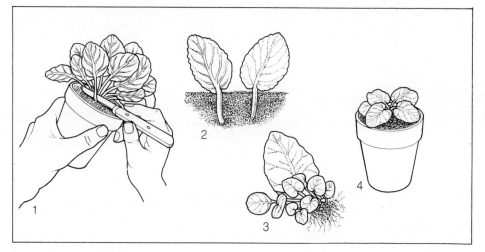

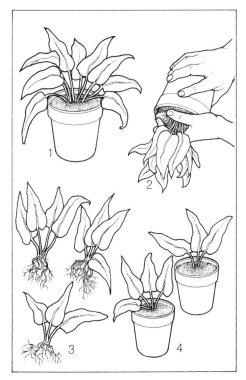

Above: Division. (1) This anthurium has filled its pot. (2) Hold the plant by its crown, invert it and knock the edge of the pot until the rootball comes out. (3) Divide the plant by hand or using a knife. (4) Pot up the divisions separately. Keep them warm.

Above: Hydrangeas root easily from stem tip cuttings, provided you trim off half the leaf area. This prevents the cutting drying out while it is rooting.

Below: Saintpaulias can be divided, grown from seed or from leaf cuttings, as shown below. As the plantlets grow the mother leaf will begin to shrivel.

of soil. If roots have not formed, leave the cutting under the plastic and wait.

Leaf cuttings

You can also get new plants from leaf cuttings. Take a leaf with a portion of stalk from a mature plant. Insert the leaf upright into a container of growing medium such as vermiculite and put a transparent plastic bag over it, or invert a glass jar over the container. Place the cutting in a shady place for a few weeks, and keep it moist.

You can also put leaf cuttings horizontally in a container of growing medium to get new plants. To do this, take leaves from a mature plant and first cut across the leaf veins in several places on the underside. Put the leaves right side up, flat on the medium in the container. Plantlets soon appear along the cut and draw nourishment from the mother leaf. When the new plants can be handled easily, cut them from the parent leaf and pot them separately in soil. Rex begonias, kalanchoes, and African violets can all be propagated from leaves.

Division

Division is pulling apart or splitting a large plant. By putting the plant on a low table and looking down at it, you can often see where a natural division takes place in the plant. The junctions are the places to perform the division, using a sterile knife if necessary. Put each plant in a pot of soil and allow them to grow on naturally.

Summary of Propagation Methods

Stem tip cuttings (eg *Beloperone guttata*)
In spring or summer, use a sharp knife to remove a young stem tip with three pairs of leaves. Never use a flowering shoot. Cut just above the fourth pair on the mother plant. Trim the cutting with a square cut just below the third pair of leaves. Remove these leaves, dip the cutting in rooting powder and pot in soil.

Leaf cuttings (eg *Streptocarpus hybrids*)
In summer, remove an entire leaf from the mother plant. Cut it off at soil level and lay it flat. Using a razor blade or sharp knife, slice the leaf in two along the length of the mibrib. Each leaf yields two long cuttings; you will need a seed tray rather than a pot to insert them edgeways into the soil. Young plantlets will grow up along the cut edge.

Leaf and stalk cuttings (eg *Saintpaulia*)
In spring or summer, use a razor blade or sharp knife to cut a mature leaf from the mother plant. Cut near the crown of the plant, leaving no snags which could set up rot. Insert the stalk into a pot so that the leaf itself rests at soil level. Plantlets will emerge at this point.

Basal shoot cuttings (eg *Sinningia*)
Wait until the young shoots are 2–3in (5–7.5cm) long in spring. Slice off a shoot, if possible with a sliver of the tuber. This sliver is just like a 'heel' of older growth and acts as a food supply while the cutting is rooting. Dust the cut surfaces with flowers of sulfur and pot.

Dividing a tuber (eg *Rechsteineria cardinalis*)
Just as the tuber is beginning to grow in spring, remove it from its pot and knock away the soil. Use a sharp knife to cut it into two or more pieces. Each piece must have at least one, preferably two or three, young shoots. Dust the cuts with flowers of sulfur and replant.

Dividing a rhizome (eg *Convallaria majalis*)
Do this in spring as growth commences. Remove the plant from its pot, knock away the soil and lay the rhizomes on a flat surface. Use a sharp knife to cut them up so that each piece has a shoot and roots attached. Dust the cuts with flowers of sulfur and replant them.

Root division (eg *Anthuriums*)
Do this in spring. Remove the plant from its pot and gently remove most of the soil. Use your fingers to prise the plant apart. It should fall naturally into several pieces with roots attached, but use a knife if necessary.

Separating bulbils (eg *Narcissus tazetta*)
Bulbils are small offset bulbs formed at the base of a mature bulb. Gently pull them away when repotting the parent bulbs in autumn and plant the bulbils in the garden. They will grow on for two years before reaching flowering size. Do not try to force them for Christmas flowering before this time.

Removing offsets (eg bromeliads)
Wait until the offsets are a third to one half the size of the adult plant, by which point they will have roots of their own. In spring or summer, remove the adult from the pot and gently pull away the rooted offsets. Use a knife if necessary. Pot the offsets separately.

Rooting stolons (eg *Episcia dianthiflora*)
Stolons are stems that produce young plants at intervals along their length. In spring or summer, use hairpins or bent pieces of wire to peg the plantlets into contact with the compost in pots or trays. Cut them from the parent only when they have rooted well.

Layering (eg *Aeschynanthus lobbianus*)
In summer, position a seed tray or pot of compost near to the parent plant. Take a non-flowering shoot and make a small cut just below a leaf joint and about 4–5in (10–12.5cm) back from the stem tip. Do not cut right through. Peg down this shoot so that the cut is covered. Roots will form at the cut.

Scale propagation (eg *Lilium auratum*)
When the bulbs are dormant in autumn or spring, remove them from their pots and carefully pull off a few plump scales. Insert these to half their depth in cutting compost. New growth will come from tiny bulbs at the base of the scales. Pot them on separately.

HOW TO PROPAGATE YOUR PLANTS

Abutilon hybrids
Stem tip cuttings. *Take these in midsummer.*
Acacia armata
Seed or stem tip cuttings. *Take the cuttings in midsummer.*
Acalypha hispida
Stem tip cuttings. *Take these in spring or summer.*
Acanthus mollis
Root division or seed. *Sow seed outdoors in March.*
Achimenes species and hybrids
By separating the tubers. *Do this in March after the foliage has died down.*
Adenium obesum
By seed. *Keep the seedlings warm.*
Aechmea species
By removing offsets. *Leave these until they are one third of the size of the parent and rooted.*
Aeonium tabulaeforme
By removing offsets. *Do this in spring.*
Aeschynanthus species
Stem tip cuttings or layering. *Use non-flowering shoots.*
Agapanthus africanus
Division of the rootstock or by seed. *Divide rootstock in April or May. Plants from seed take two or three years to flower.*
Allamanda cathartica
Stem tip cuttings. *Use non-flowering shoots.*
Allium neapolitanum
Division of the clumps of bulbs or seed. *Plants from seed take two to four years to flower.*
Alpinia purpurata
Division of the rhizomes. *Do this in spring.*
Angraecum species
Offsets from mature plants. *Difficult.*
Anguloa species
Division of the plants; three bulbs to a pot. *Do this in spring.*
Anthurium species and hybrids
Division of the rootstock. *Keep the divisions humid until established.*
Aphelandra species
Stem tip cuttings. *Prune the parent plant after flowering to promote the production of cuttings.*
Ardisia crispa/crenata
Seed or stem tip cuttings. *Cuttings need a heel.*
Ascocenda
From rooted side shoots. *Remove, pot in spring.*
Astrophytum asterias
Seed. *Sow in warmth in spring.*
Azalea indica
Stem tip cuttings. *Difficult to root. Wait until June and use a rooting hormone. Keep them humid.*
Begonia boweri
Stem tip cuttings. *Beware of fungal disease.*
Begonia 'Fireglow'
Stem tip cuttings. *Dust cuts with fungicide.*
Begonia 'Orange Rubra'
Stem tip cuttings. *Beware of fungal disease.*
Begonia semperflorens
Seed or stem tip cuttings. *Beware of fungal disease.*
Beloperone guttata
Stem tip cuttings. *Plants get leggy, so take cuttings yearly in spring.*
Billbergia pyramidalis
Offsets. *Wait until offset is half the size of its parent before separating. It should be rooted.*
Bougainvillea
Stem tip cuttings. *Take these in midsummer. They need bottom heat.*
Bouvardia x domestica
Stem tip cuttings. *Take these in spring and keep them warm.*
Brassavola nodosa
Division of the pseudobulbs. *Do this in spring.*
Browallia speciosa
Seed. *Sow in spring. For winter flowering, sow in autumn.*
Brunfelsia calycina
Stem tip cuttings. *Difficult to root. Use a rooting hormone.*
Calanthe vestita
Offset pseudobulbs. *Remove and pot them after the parent has flowered.*
Calceolaria hybrids
Seed. *As the seed is tiny sow it thinly.*

Callistemon species
Seed or stem tip cuttings. *Take cuttings in midsummer.*
Camellia japonica
Stem tip cuttings or layering. *Take cuttings in midsummer. Large plants are best layered.*
Campanula isophylla
Stem tip cuttings. *Take these in spring.*
Canna hybrids
Division of the rhizomes. *Wait until growth has started in spring. Each piece must have a bud.*
Capsicum annuum
Seed. *Sow seed in March.*
Catharanthus (Vinca) rosea
Seed or stem cuttings. *Sow seed in March.*
Cattleya hybrids
Division of rhizomes. *Do this in spring.*
Celosia argentea
Seed. *Sow seed in February.*
Chamaecereus silvestrii
Detach the short branches. *Allow them to dry for 24 hours before potting.*
Chrysanthemum
Stem cuttings. *Home propagated plants will not remain dwarf.*
Cineraria
Seed. *Keep seedlings cool and airy.*
Citrus mitis
Seed (pips) or stem tip cuttings. *Take cuttings in midsummer.*
Clerodendron species
Stem tip cuttings. *Take these in late spring.*
Clivia miniata
Division of offsets or seed. *Seed will produce plants that vary in quality.*
Cobaea scandens
Seed. *Sow seed in March.*
Coelogyne species
Division of the pseudobulbs. *Do this between March and May.*
Columnea species
Stem tip cuttings. *Do this in spring and use non-flowering shoots.*
Convallaria majalis
Division of the rhizomes. *Do this in winter.*
Costus igneus
Division of the roots. *Keep the divisions warm.*
Crassula falcata
Leaf cuttings. *Use the whole leaf and allow it to dry for 24 hours before potting.*
Crocus
Offset corms. *Remove these and grow them on separately to flower in two years.*
Crossandra infundibuliformis (C. undulifolia)
Stem tip cuttings or seed. *Take cuttings in late spring.*
Cuphea hyssopifolia
Seed. *Sow seed in January or February.*
Cuphea ignea
Seed or stem tip cuttings. *Sow seed in January or February.*
Cyclamen
Seed or division of the corms. *Keep the young plants cool and airy.*
Cymbidium species
Division of the pseudobulbs. *Do this in spring and keep the divisions dry for a week.*
Dendrobium 'Gatton Sunray'
Division. *Do this after flowering.*
Dipladenia species
Stem tip cuttings. *Take these in spring.*
Echeveria 'Doris Taylor'
Offsets. *Dry for 24 hours before potting.*
Echinocereus baileyi
Seed or offsets. *Sow seed in early spring.*
Echinopsis hybrids
Seed or offsets. *Offsets may be found to be already rooted.*
Epidendrum species
Division. *Do this between March and May.*
Epiphyllum hybrids
Stem tip cuttings. *Allow cuttings to dry for a few days before potting.*
Episcia cupreata hybrids
Division of clumps or stem tip cuttings. *Do this in spring.*
Episcia dianthiflora
From stolons. *Detach from the parent only when they are rooted.*

Erica species
Stem tip cuttings. *Root these in a pot covered with a plastic bag.*
Eucharis grandiflora
Offsets. *Remove and repot these in spring.*
Eucomis
Offsets. *Remove and repot these in autumn.*
Euphorbia fulgens
Stem tip cuttings. *Beware, the sap is irritant.*
Euphorbia milii/splendens
Stem tip cuttings. *Allow cuttings to dry for a few days before potting.*
Euphorbia pulcherrima
Stem tip cuttings. *Difficult. The roots are brittle and the sap is irritant.*
Exacum affine
Seed. *Seed is fine; sow it thinly in March.*
Freesia
Seed or offsets. *Seed needs 24 hours soaking in water to germinate successfully.*
Fuchsia
Stem tip cuttings. *Easy.*
Gardenia jasminoides
Stem tip cuttings. *Difficult to root. Use a rooting hormone.*
Gazania
Seed or stem tip cuttings. *Sow seed in January, take cuttings in midsummer.*
Gerbera jamesonii
Seed or division of the crowns. *Do this in March.*
Gloriosa rothschildiana
From offset tubers. *Seed is possible but the seedlings take two to four years to flower.*
Guzmania species
Offsets. *Wait until the offsets are rooted before removing them.*
Gymnocalycium mihanovichii
Seed followed by grafting onto *Trichocereus spachianus. Possible for an amateur to do.*
Haemanthus species
Offsets. *Remove these in March.*
Hedychium species
Division of the rhizomes. *Do this in spring.*
Heliconia species
Division of the rootstock. *Do this in spring and keep the divisions warm.*
Heliotropium hybridum
Seed. *Sow in spring.*
Hibiscus rosa-sinensis
Stem tip cuttings. *Take these with a heel.*
Hippeastrum
Seeds. *Plants of varying quality will be produced.*
Hoya species
Stem tip cuttings. *Take these in June.*
Hyacinthus orientalis
Bulbils or seed. *Sow seed as soon as it is ripe.*
Hydrangea macrophylla
Stem tip cuttings. *Take these in August.*
Hypocyrta species
Stem tip cuttings. *Keep the cuttings humid.*
Impatiens
Stem tip cuttings or seed. *The hybrids must be grown from cuttings, which root easily even in water.*
Ipomoea species
Seed. *Soak seed in water for 24 hours to ensure that it germinates. Do not let seedlings become chilled.*
Iris reticulata
Offsets. *Remove these when repotting.*
Ixia speciosa
Offsets. *Remove these when repotting.*
Ixora coccinea hybrids
Stem tip cuttings. *Bottom heat is needed.*
Jacobinia species
Basal shoot cuttings. *Prune the parent plant right down to make it produce young cuttings.*
Jasminum species
Stem tip cuttings. *Take cuttings in August and give them bottom heat.*
Jatropha podagrica
Stem tip cuttings or seed. *Allow cuttings to dry for 24 hours before potting.*
Kalanchoe species
Seed or stem tip cuttings. *Dry cuttings for a few days before potting.*
Kohleria amabilis
Divide the rhizomes or take stem tip cuttings. *Divide in spring or take cuttings in summer.*

Laelia species and hybrids
Division of the pseudobulbs. *Do this between February and May.*
Lantana species
Seed or stem tip cuttings. *Take the cuttings in August.*
Lapageria rosea
Seed or layering. *Do this in May. Layers may take two years to root.*
Leptospermum scoparium
Stem tip cuttings. *Take these in midsummer.*
Lilium auratum
Seed, division or scale propagation. *Propagate in autumn.*
Lithops species
Seed or division. *Allow divisions to dry for a few days before potting.*
Lobivia aurea
Seed or offsets. *Dry offsets for a few days unless they are already rooted.*
Lycaste aromatica
Division of the pseudobulbs. *In late spring.*
Mammillaria zeilmanniana
Seed or offsets. *Propagate in May.*
Manettia bicolor
Stem tip cuttings. *Give them bottom heat.*
Masdevallia coccinea
Division of the rhizomes. *Do this in spring.*
Medinilla magnifica
Stem tip cuttings. *Take these in early spring. Difficult to root.*
Miltonia species and hybrids
Division of the pseudobulbs. *Do this in spring or autumn.*
Narcissus tazetta
Offsets. *These will flower in two years.*
Neomarica caerulea
Division of the rhizomes. *Keep the divisions warm.*
Neoregelia species
Offsets or seed. *Wait until offset is rooted before separating it and potting.*
Nerine bowdenii
Offsets or seed. *Sow ripe seed in May.*
Nerium oleander
Stem tip cuttings. *These will even root in warm water.*
Nertera granadensis
Seed or division. *Easy.*
Nidularium innocentii
Offsets. *Wait until these are rooted before removing them and potting.*
Notocactus species
Seed or division. *Sow seed in spring.*
Odontioda species
Division. *Do this in spring.*
Odontoglossum grande
Division of the pseudobulbs. *Do this in autumn or spring.*
Oncidium species
Division. *Do this in spring.*
Oxalis rubra
Division of the tubers. *Do this in March.*
Pachystachys lutea
Stem tip cuttings. *Use non-flowering shoots in spring.*
Paphiopedilum species and hybrids
Division. *Do this in early spring.*
Parodia species
Seed. *Sow thinly because the seed is fine.*
Passiflora caerulea
Stem tip cuttings or seed. *Take cuttings in midsummer.*
Pelargonium types
Stem tip cuttings or seed. *Sow seed in early February.*
Pentas lanceolata
Stem tip cuttings. *Use non-flowering shoots in spring.*
Petrea volubilis
Stem tip cuttings. *Take these in spring or summer.*
Phalaenopsis hybrids
Divisions of the rhizomes. *Water sparingly at first.*
Pittosporum tobira
Stem tip cuttings. *Take these with a heel in midsummer.*
Pleione formosana
Offsets or bulbils. *Detach and pot these in spring.*

Plumbago capensis
Stem tip cuttings. *Take the cuttings with a heel.*
Primula species
Division or seed. *The seed must be sown fresh.*
Punica granatum 'Nana'
Seed or stem tip cuttings. *Cuttings need a heel.*
Rebutia species
Seed or offsets. *Easy.*
Rechsteineria cardinalis
Division of tubers, basal shoot cuttings or seed. *Propagate in March.*
Reinwardtia species
Basal shoot cuttings. *Cut back the parent plant in early spring to produce these cuttings.*
Rivina humilis
Seed, stem tip cuttings or leaf cuttings. *Propagate in spring.*
Rosa chinensis minima
Stem tip cuttings. *Use non-flowering shoots in late summer.*
Ruellia makoyana
Stem cuttings. *Take these in April.*
Russelia equisetiformis
Stem tip cuttings or division. *Easy.*
Saintpaulia
Leaf and stem cuttings or seed. *Seed produces plants varying in quality.*
Schizanthus pinnatus
Seed. *Sow seed in autumn.*
Schizocentron elegans
Division of rooted shoots. *Do this in spring.*
Schlumbergera species and hybrids
Stem tip cuttings. *Allow them to dry for a few days before potting.*
Sinningia
Seed or basal shoot cuttings. *Do this in spring.*
Smithiantha hybrids
Division of rhizomes or leaf and stem cuttings. *Divide in March, take cuttings in May or June.*
Solanum capsicastrum
Seed. *Sow in spring.*
Spathiphyllum species and hybrids
Division of the rootstock. *Keep the divisions humid and warm.*
Sprekelia formosissima
Offsets. *Remove these in autumn.*
Stanhopea wardii
Division of the pseudobulbs. *Do this in July or August.*
Stephanotis floribunda
Stem tip cuttings. *Use non-flowering shoots in late spring.*
Strelitzia regina
Division of the roots. *Do this when repotting and after the plant has flowered.*
Streptocarpus hybrids
Seed or leaf cuttings. *Take leaf cuttings in midsummer.*
Streptocarpus saxorum
Stem tip cuttings. *Do this in April.*
Thunbergia alata
Seed. *Sow seed in March.*
Tibouchina semidecandra
Stem tip cuttings. *Do this in March.*
Tillandsia cyanea
Offshoots. *Keep these warm until they are rooted.*
Trichopilia tortilis
Division of the pseudobulbs. *Divide after flowering.*
Tulipa
Offsets. *Remove these when repotting or after flowering.*
Vallota speciosa
Offsets. *Remove these in autumn.*
Vanda species and hybrids
From side shoots. *Remove and pot these in April.*
Veltheimia viridifolia
Offsets. *These take many years to flower.*
Vriesea splendens
Offsets. *Wait until the offsets are rooted before detaching and potting them.*
Zantedeschia species
Division of the rhizomes. *Do this when repotting.*
Zephyranthes species
Seed or offsets. *Easy.*
Zygopetalum crinitum
Division of the pseudobulbs. *Do this when repotting.*

Insects and Disease

I have a collection of more than 300 plants and they are rarely attacked by insects or disease. Only occasionally does trouble invade the growing area. But when it does, something must be done about it immediately. In this chapter we look at the common causes and effective remedies.

Even with the best of culture, plants will sometimes be attacked by insects. If you discover a light insect attack, do not worry about losing the plant; it can be saved by spraying with chemicals or by old-fashioned remedies such as a laundry soap and water spray. The main thing, however, is to know which insect you are fighting before you do battle. Most common inspects are recognizable on sight or with a magnifying glass, including aphids, spider mites, mealy bugs, scale, snails and slugs. If you cannot identify the insect, pick it off, kill it, and mail it to your local agricultural agency or department (listed in your local phone book), which may be able to identify it.

Aphids

If you cannot see aphids (plant lice), watch the plant: it may lose vigor and become stunted, and the leaves may curl or pucker as juices are drained out by the bugs. Because aphids are also carriers of mosaic and other virus diseases, you must get rid of them.

Aphids bear live young, generally hatching in the spring, although autumn is another spawning season. Typical aphids are small, pear-shaped, soft-bodied insects with a beak that has four needlelike stylets. Aphids use these daggers to pierce plant tissue and suck out plant sap. These insects also excrete honeydew or sugar; this excretion provides a great breeding ground for the growth of a black fungus known as sooty mold.

Aphids are variously colored black, red, green, pink, yellow, lavender or gray; the young aphids, or nymphs, may differ in color from the adult.

Mealy bugs

Mealy bugs are indicated by cottony accumulations in the leaf axils or on leaf veins. These insects have soft, segmented

Above: A single mealy bug on this nephrolepis fern looks like a speck of cotton wool. Right: A bad infestation of aphids and whitefly on a kalanchoe. Clear them with old-fashioned remedies.

bodies covered in cotton wax. Young mealy bugs are crawling, oval-shaped, light yellow, six-legged insects with smooth bodies. They have beaks that they insert into plant parts to get sap; as the sap leaves it, your plant wilts.

Once they start feeding, the youngsters develop the cottony, waxy covering. They move slower and slower day by day, but they do not really stop moving, although you may not be able to discern this.

Like aphids, mealy bugs produce a copious honeydew that forms a breeding ground for sooty mold fungus and attracts ants, which feed on it.

Red spider mites

The true red spider mites that attack plants are from the family Tetranychidae. As well as red, these tiny oval creatures are yellow, green or brown. They have long legs and are almost impossible to see on a plant, but they spin webs, which often advertise their presence.

Identifying and Tackling Insect Pests

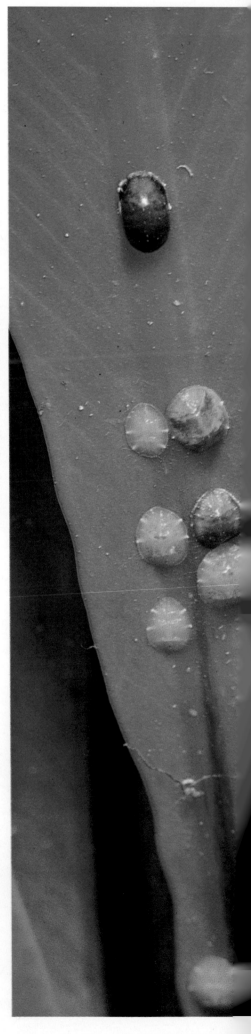

The two-spotted mite is the worst plant offender. Mites injure plants by piercing the leaves and sucking out the liquid content from the cells. Foliage turns pale and may become stippled around the injured parts. If the infestation goes untreated, the leaves become rust-red and die. The plants may become covered with the silken webs that the mites make as they move from area to area.

Scale insects
Scale insects are tiny, oval, but noticeable insects with an armored shell or scales covering their bodies. Once settled on a plant, scale (mainly the wingless females) insert their mouth parts into a leaf and start taking in sap. They stay in the same spot throughout their lives, molting twice, and laying eggs, or in many cases giving birth to live young. The males have elongated bodies and eventually develop wings, thus resembling gnats. They may attack leaves, although they prefer stems. Plants with scale insects usually show both leaf and stem damage.

Of all the insects mentioned, scale are the easiest to combat, because they are so easily recognized.

Thrips
Thrips are very small, slender chewing insects with two pairs of long narrow

Above: Red spider mites can barely be seen with the naked eye. A fine mottling on the leaves of this Impatiens identifies them as culprits.

wings. Their mouths are fitted with 'tools' that enable them to pierce or rasp leaves. Adults are generally dark in color and are active in late spring or summer. Some thrips are carnivorous and attack other thrips, and if the good ones overwhelm the bad ones, you can just sit back and watch the battle. Unfortunately, it is usually the bad ones that win.

Some thrips are active flyers; others just jump around; and still others do not move much at all. Thrips are indicated by a silver sheen among the leaves.

Preventatives
Because there are so many insecticides and so many trade names for these products, it is essential that you know something about them to avoid confusion and possibly killing your plants with chemicals. And of course there is the question of using poisons at all in the home; some people object to them because they are a hazard. For them we include natural preventatives. This section deals with specific poisons for specific insects.

Chemicals to kill bugs come in many forms, but perhaps the granular type is

Common insect pests

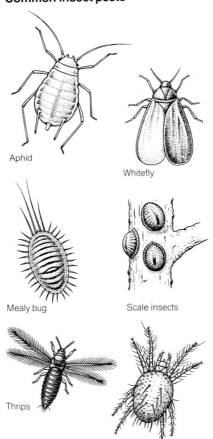

Aphid

Whitefly

Mealy bug

Scale insects

Thrips

Red spider mite

Chemicals for insect pests

The following chemicals are generally available for ridding plants of the common insect pests; trade names vary from country to country.

Malathion Broad-spectrum insecticide for aphids, red spider mites and scale insects. Fairly non-toxic to humans and most animals, but harmful to bees and fish. Do not use on *Crassula, Gerbera,* ferns or orchids.

Diazinon/Spectracide Good, but more toxic than malathion. Effective against aphids, red spider mites and scale insects. Do not use on ferns. Harmful to bees, fish, livestock, wild birds and animals.

Carbaryl Available in powder or dusts for general insect control. Harmful to bees and fish.

Nicotine Tobacco extract; relatively toxic but safe to eradicate aphids and other sucking insects from plants. Harmful to bees, fish, livestock, wild birds and animals.

Pyrethrum Botanical insecticide (made from certain kinds of chrysanthemum flowers); generally safe.

Derris/Rotenone A botanical insecticide generally used in combination with pyrethrum against aphids and flies. Safe except to fish.

Old-fashioned remedies

I have been indoor gardening for 20 years, long before modern insecticides hit the market, so I use old-fashioned methods of eliminating insects from plants. They are perhaps not as thorough as chemicals, but they are safe and avoid noxious odors.

Handpicking Hardly pleasant, but it can be done with a toothpick.

Soap and water For many insects, a solution of soap (no detergent) and water (½lb/6pts; 67gm/liter) works fine. Spray the mixture on bugs: repeat the dose every three to six days for three weeks.

Alcohol Alcohol on cotton swabs will effectively remove mealy bugs and aphids. Apply it directly to the insect.

Tobacco To get rid of scale, use a solution of old tobacco from a cigarette steeped in water for several days. Repeat several times.

Water spray This may sound ineffective, but it works if used frequently and with strong enough force to wash away insects.

Wipe leaves frequently This simple step goes a long way to reduce insect problems. It washes away eggs before they hatch.

Left: Appearing just like limpets, these scale insects suck from the fleshy midrib of a bird's nest fern. They may be found on both stem and leaves. Once settled, they remain stationary.

the most convenient to use. Merely sprinkle it on the soil and then apply water. Other chemicals are water soluble; mix them with water, and spray them on plants with special sprayers (always a bother). There are also powders or dusts, which to my way of thinking are not necessary.

Systemic insecticides are gaining popularity, and are very convenient to use. They are available in granular or liquid form. Sprinkle the granules on the soil, and then thoroughly water the plant.

Through the roots, the insecticide is drawn up into the sap stream, making it toxic. Thus, when sucking and chewing insects start dining on the plant, they are poisoned. Liquid systemics should be diluted with water and sprayed on the plant.

Systemics protect plants from most, but not all, sucking and chewing pests for six to eight weeks, and so in general they need be applied only three or four times a year to protect plants.

How to use chemicals
No matter what poison you use (if any), do follow the directions on the package to the letter. In most cases repeated doses will be necessary to eliminate insects fully. Also, keep poisons out of the reach of children

Fighting Plant Diseases

Above: Fungal growth on a pelargonium. Fungal diseases are most likely to occur where plants are grown in damp, poorly ventilated conditions. Many remedies are available.

and pets. For a good, general chemical that does not have a cumulative effect, use malathion. If that does not work and you want to use other poisons, always follow these rules:

1 Never use a chemical on a plant that is bone dry.
2 Never spray plants in direct sun.
3 Use sprays at the proper distance marked on the package.
4 Try to douse insects if they are in sight.
5 Do not use chemicals on ferns.
6 Always use chemicals in well-ventilated areas; outdoors is best.
7 Never use a spray anywhere near food.
8 Wash hands thoroughly afterwards.

Plant diseases

Diseases sound formidable. However, if plants are well cared for they rarely develop diseases. Still, just in case, it is wise to know what to do; no one wants a costly plant ruined by fungus or botrytis, and a little knowledge can help you save infected plants. Again, most diseases will

Above: Mosaic virus revealing itself by the mottling on the petals of this Cymbidium. Viruses are a mystery and are incurable. In plants they can lead to streaking, stunting and weak growth.

be minor, but if left unchecked they can become major concerns.

Ailments that strike plants are manifested by visible symptoms—spots, rot, mildew, and so on. Many plant diseases may cause similar external symptoms, so it is important to identify the specific disease to ensure positive remedies.

Unfavorable growing conditions—too little or too much humidity, or too much feeding—can help contribute to disease, but diseases are mainly caused by bacteria

and fungi. Bacteria enter the plant through minute natural wounds and small openings. Inside, they multiply and start to break down plant tissue. Animals, soil, insects, water and dust carry bacteria that can attack plants. And if you touch a diseased plant, you can carry the bacteria to healthy ones. Soft roots, leaf spots, wilts and rots are some diseases caused by bacteria.

Fungi, like bacteria, enter a plant through a wound or a natural opening or by forcing their entrance directly through plant stems or leaves. Spores are carried by wind, water, insects, people and equipment. Fungi multiply rapidly in shady, damp conditions rather than in hot, dry situations; moisture is essential in

Chemicals for plant diseases

Benomyl A systemic used against many bacterial and fungal maladies.

Captan An organic fungicide that is generally safe and effective for the control of many diseases. Harmful to fish.

Karanthane Highly effective for many types of powdery mildew.

Sulfur This is an old and inexpensive fungicide and still good; it controls many diseases.

Zineb Effective against many bacterial and fungal diseases. Can irritate the skin, eyes and nose.

their reproduction. Fungi cause rusts, mildew, some leaf spot and blights.

Fungicides

Fungicides are chemicals that kill or inhibit the growth of bacteria and fungi. They come in dust form, ready to use, or in wettable powder. Soluble forms that can be mixed with water and used as a spray are also available.

As with all chemicals, use as directed on the package and always keep containers out of the reach of children and pets.

Virus disease

Virus disease is indicated in plants by concentric rings on leaves, spotted areas or striations of various colors on blooms.

The first step in an attempt to save a plant with virus disease is to remove the infected leaf or area and dust the wound with powdered charcoal. However, in most cases, if one part of the plant is affected, it follows that the entire plant may harbor a virus. Thus, I generally recommend that the plant be discarded—this procedure prevents the disease from spreading in the growing area to other plants.

There are some chemicals that reportedly do help to prevent or thwart virus diseases and, while I do not suggest using poisons at home, if a plant is a particularly rare one, you might want to administer a remedy. The product most often used is called zineb. Be sure to use this chemical exactly as prescribed on the package.

The Plant Groups

Our houseplants come from all over the world and in this chapter we take a look at the various groups, such as orchids, bromeliads, begonias, gesneriads, succulents and bulbs. In the descriptions that follow you will find suggestions on how to grow these plants. We start with the orchid family.

Orchids, more than 35,000 species, grow wild all over the world from Alaska to the Himalayas. The *Pleione* orchid can break through snow to bloom, and some species of *Angraecum* become giants in the steaming East African jungles. Perhaps the greatest number are found in New Guinea, but Africa, Borneo, Central and South America also have vast orchid areas.

Most orchids are epiphytes, treetop dwellers, living in rain forests at altitudes of some 5,000 feet (1524m), but some species, the terrestrials, grow in the ground. The epiphytes cling to the branches of trees but derive no nourishment from the host; they simply grow where they can find a foothold. Some even grow on roofs or on other plants, but they are never parasitic. Most of them have an extensive root system in which dead leaves, twigs, and insects collect. Rain eventually dissolves this miscellaneous matter, which furnishes the nutrients for the plant.

Most orchids have pseudobulbs—swollen stems—that store water for use in times of drought. Because many orchids come from regions where there are sharply defined seasons—quantities of rain for five months and then no moisture for many more—nature has equipped the plants with these storage receptacles. So in your home, if you forget to water your orchids, most of them will survive for weeks without moisture.

There are two patterns of growth among orchids. The sympodial type produces a new growth each year from the base of the existing growth and this bears flowers, makes its own roots, and so repeats the cycle. The monopodial type has one stem that grows taller each year, and there is no new shoot from the base. Flower spikes and roots grow from the leaf axils.

The world of flowers is tremendous but only in the orchid family do we find the

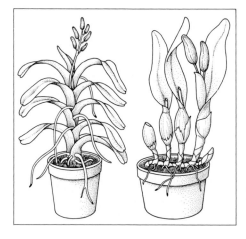

Above: Monopodial orchids (left) make growth upwards on a single stem. Sympodial orchids (right) produce a new growth every year from the base. Right: A beautiful and varied display of orchid flowers—a small sample from this large and exciting family.

beauty and drama, the color and form that make this group unique. Blooms may be small, about ½in (1.25cm) as in some species of *Pleurothallis* or as large as 7in (18cm) in certain stanhopeas. With the exception of true black, all colors and combination of colors occur. Bright yellow, vivid pink, red, and pure white are often seen, and most orchids have fragrance; some are heavily scented, others delicately.

The flowers that have opened on a plant stay fresh an incredible length of time, for more than a month on some oncidiums. As cut flowers orchids last in water for at least two weeks.

They have been called 'flowers of the four seasons' because there are species that bloom in spring, many in summer, and a vast number in autumn and winter. Indeed, only half a dozen well-chosen pots of orchids at your window will provide color throughout the year.

Bromeliads and Begonias

Above: Begonia 'Orange Glow' will give a vibrant show in an airy room. Right: The eyelash begonia, Begonia boweri, receives its name from the small hairs and the black markings at the margins of the leaves.

Bromeliads

Of the 2000 bromeliads, most come from South America, the greatest number from Brazil, and many are native to Mexico and Central America. In nature they are mainly epiphytes that grow in treetops along with orchids; here they receive partial sunlight. There are also some kinds—*Cryptanthus*, for example—that are terrestrial, growing in shaded ground. Others cling to rocks, and a few grow in full sun in the desert.

Bromeliads are almost always found in areas of good air circulation and this is vital to their growth. In a stagnant atmosphere they soon become spindly and unattractive. Some have a vase or bowl formation of leaves recurved to form a receptacle for food and water. In the jungle, organic matter drops into this reservoir; sometimes small tree frogs live and make their home there and, once dead, decomposition of their bodies furishes food for the plant.

It is the vase or bowl that makes bromeliads so popular as houseplants. They are easy to grow because if you forget to water them for several days the water in the natural plant reservoirs sustains them. Indeed, as long as the vase holds water bromeliads can live a long time without more moisture.

The circular rosette of thick leaves is most common among aechmeas. Nidulariums and neoregelias have flattened tops like a pressed fan. Vertical and tubular growth is prevalent among billbergias.

Above: Guzmania lingulata 'Minor Orange', a popular and beautiful bromeliad. As with other bromeliads, attention focuses on the colored bracts rather than the small flowers.

Bromeliad flowers range from tiny, almost microscropic, blooms as in some *Hohenbergia* species to the 2in (5cm) blossoms of *Tillandsia lindeni*. Although most species have small blooms that last only a few days, the floral bracts and berries provide color for weeks. In many bromeliads the true flowers are hidden in the bracts, creating the charming effect of a miniature bouquet.

Most blooms are red or pink, lavender or blue, sometimes white, yellow, and green too. Few have scent. Bromeliads are valued for their brilliant bracts rather than for their true flowers. On most the bracts are generally large and vibrantly colored in pink or coral.

Begonias

The *Begonia* genus contains some 400 species of succulent herbs or small shrubs that are native to all moist tropical countries except Australia. They are versatile plants, including small ones for window growing, and medium and tall growers for room accent. There are compact rex varieties with exquisite leaf coloring, the everblooming wax or semperflorens, the angelwings that are continually bright with color, and dramatic trailers with elegant cascades of bloom.

The flowers usually grow in branching clusters, upright or pendent. Some produce tall airy sprays, others, such as 'Orange Rubra,' have a colorful pendent inflorescence. The peak of bloom generally occurs in spring and summer but there are also some autumn- and winter-flowering varieties. Blooms range in size from insignificant to large and handsome. Some are brilliant red or orange, others subdued white or pink. Usually bracts match the color of the bloom.

Begonias are generous with flowers and a dozen kinds can bring color to the window garden throughout the year. Usually flowers last only a few days but a mature plant will bear for several weeks.

Authorities used to classify begonias according to root structure. For years there were four groups: bulbous, rhizomatous, tuberous, and fibrous. In time these categories proved inadequate, for many kinds fall into two of the groups, and others fit none of them. A newer classification specifies eight, sometimes nine groups. Begonias are usually listed as:

Semperflorens, or wax
Hirsute, or hairy-leaved
Angelwing
Rhizomatous
Rex
Tuberous
Fibrous-rooted
Basket

Begonias make wonderful houseplants because so many bloom on and off throughout the year. Angelwings are laden with flowers from March to May. Some rhizomatous types open from December to February; others are at peak production in April and May. In the hirsute group there are plants for autumn, and others for summer display.

Gesneriads, Cacti and Succulents

Gesneriads

Gesneriads—some 1,500 of them, mainly from South America—have only recently been appreciated as houseplants. One group of gesneriads, the saintpaulias, or African violets, has been popular for decades, and now columneas and kohlerias, rechsteinerias and smithianthas are also taking their place at our windows.

Most gesneriads are small to medium-sized plants, making them ideal for the home. In nature, the plants usually grow in bright to shaded locations where there is plenty of moisture. Dry, hot sun will desiccate them quickly; if any plants can be called forest dwellers, it is these. In the home they do well in a bright airy place where there is adequate (40 percent) humidity.

Most gesneriads bloom in summer but there are some for autumn and winter flowering as well. Flowers may be tubular and large, such as the 6in (15cm) long blooms of some gloxinias (*Sinningia*), or small and delicate at 1in (2.5cm) across, as in some varieties of African violets. Colors range from white through orange,

red, and pink to rich purples and blues—a vast array depending on the species grown. Many have somewhat hairy leaves, so misting is not advisable. Gesneriads are classified as:

Achimenes
Aeschynanthus
Columnea
Episcia
Kohleria
Rechsteineria
Saintpaulia (African violets)
Sinningia (Gloxinias)
Smithiantha
Streptocarpus

Cacti and succulents

All cacti are succulents but not all succulents are cacti. Within these groups we find an incredible number of attractive houseplants—literally thousands. Most, but not all, succulents are native to deserts. Those that are not adorn the trees in rain forests, grow on mountainsides, near the sea, or in the semiarid regions of North and South America. Most cacti come from

Above: A pale pink African violet, one of the many different colors now available from this most popular of all gesneriads. Hybrids with bicolored flowers and some with variegated foliage have also been bred.
Above right: Smithiantha cinnabarina, or temple bells, is another fine gesneriad that can be relied upon to bring rich color to the indoor garden.

Mexico but some grow in the western deserts of the United States and high in the Cordilleras of Peru, Bolivia, and Argentina. Cacti such as *Rhipsalis* and the Christmas cactus (*Schlumbergera*) inhabit the rain forests of Central America; a few even grow under the snow in British Columbia.

The shapes of succulents and cacti are marvels of the plant world. Euphorbias have bizarre contorted forms, the leaves and rosettes of echeverias appear carved from stone. Cacti are columnar or barrel-shaped—an infinite array.

Cactus blooms are sometimes called 'silk flowers' because they resemble bright

fabrics. Colors are vibrant—vivid pinks and reds, blazing yellows, also white. Perhaps they are so blatantly colorful because they are destined to last so short a time. The average life is about two days, but a healthy plant bears several flowers in succession, so bloom continues for a week or more. Most flowers are large for the size of the plant—parodias and lobivias have 2in (5cm) blooms on plants that are only 3-4in (7.5-10cm) across.

As a rule, succulents other than cacti do not have such startling flowers; most of the agaves and aloes bear small- to medium-sized blossoms. Poinsettias (*Euphorbia pulcherrima*) are no exception; it is the large colorful bracts that make them so pretty. Succulent plants are generally larger than the cacti, but there are some exceptions.

Right: The brilliant blue-pink blooms of Mammillaria mollendorffiana reward the grower's care and patience. With over 225 species to choose from, mammillarias are the most popular of all dwarf cacti for home cultivation.

Beautiful Bulbs to Grow Indoors

Bulbs

Too often the many fine flowering bulbous plants are overlooked, yet they offer an immense selection for the home and they grow and bloom readily with little care. Mainly from South Africa, they are well worth your attention because nature does most of the work for you—the bulb contains next year's flowers. Even the novice gardener is assured of a display of color when planting bulbs.

Most of the bulbs described in the second part of the book are tender types

Above: Eucharis grandiflora is an unusual bulb from Colombia with dramatic flowers. The blooms have the bonus of a fine fragrance.

that can be carried over year after year. Generally, they require a rest period after bloom. Some must be stored in a dark place for a few months to regain vigor for next year's production; others keep growing through the year.

In addition to the familiar hardy narcissus, crocus, hyacinth and tulip, there

Top: You can plant bulbs in bowls with no drainage if you use a bulb fiber containing charcoal. Do not use fiber dry; wet it and squeeze out the excess moisture.
Center. For the best flowering effect, place the bulbs (here crocus) close together but not touching.
Bottom: Most bulbs need covering with fiber or compost. A few need to protrude and some need deep planting. Check this for each species in the second part of the book.

are the lesser know tender bulbs such as *Eucharis, Eucomis,* and *Vallota* that produce exquisite blooms. The glory lily (*Gloriosa rothschildiana*) and *Veltheimia* are others that give splendid color.

The secret of successful growing is to start the bulbs into growth slowly. Right after potting, set them in a shaded place and water sparsely until you see signs of growth. When the leaves are 5-6in (12.5-15cm) high, move the plants to a bright location and increase the amount of water. After a few more weeks, set the

Above: Yellow crocuses are usually the earliest to bloom of the large-flowered varieties. Bring them into the warm only when the buds show color.

pots in the sun and keep the soil evenly moist. Most bulbs do not need feeding; they already have a store of nutrients, so this is one chore you can omit.

An important aspect of bulb growing is the rest period after bloom. When flowers fade, continue watering until leaves die down naturally. Then store the bulbs—pot

and all—in a cool (50°F, 10°C), dark place. Don't water. Allow sufficient resting time, as indicated in the descriptions that follow. Then repot in fresh soil and start growth for another season of bloom.

Some of the unusual bulbs are difficult to find, because they are not yet readily available in the trade. However, specialty suppliers have most types, so persevere.

Bulbs can make an indoor garden colorful indeed; don't miss them. In the second section of the book I include more than a dozen excellent ones for you to try.

Part Two

Having considered the techniques of indoor gardening, we come now to the raw material: a recommended selection of 200 flowering houseplants that will bring color to your windowsills throughout the year. These are arranged in alphabetical order of Latin name and each entry contains the following information: the common names you are likely to encounter; temperature requirements (see code below); ease of growth (For beginners, For everyone, For a challenge); willingness to flower (Easy to bloom, Difficult to bloom); notes on how to grow the plant throughout the year; advice on propagation; and a special tip, where appropriate, on how to encourage the plant to bloom.

Temperature code
- Cool conditions 55-65°F (13-18°C)
- Intermediate conditions 65-75°F (18-24°C)
- Warm conditions 75-80°F (24-27°C)

Left: Plant shops and nurseries are a storehouse of color and vitality. Choosing plants from this stunning array would be a positive pleasure.

Abutilon hybrids

(Bellflower; flowering maple)
● **Intermediate temperature**
● **For everyone**
● **Easy to bloom**

This is an amenable houseplant that has treelike growth to about 48in (120cm). Related to hollyhocks, abutilons have maplelike leaves and bear paper-thin, 2in (5cm) bell shaped flowers in early spring; they last for 2 days. There are many hybrids with flowers in delicate shades of yellow, orange and red.

Grow these plants in equal parts of potting soil and sand at a south or west exposure; water heavily in warm weather and feed every third watering with plant food. Do not feed in the winter. Repot yearly in early spring and be sure abutilons have at least two to three hours of sun daily. Plants have a tendency to legginess so must be cut back at least once a year to encourage bushiness. These plants require no special care.

To encourage bloom:
Keep plants in small pots – a 5–6in (12.5–15cm) clay container is fine.

Above: **Abutilon 'Boule de Neige'**
Well known for their paper-thin orange, yellow or red flowers, abutilons are decorative plants where a vertical accent is necessary. Do stake plants so they do not become unwieldy.

Acacia armata

(Kangaroo thorn; wattle)
● **Cool conditions**
● **For everyone**
● **Difficult to bloom**

A thorny shrub, the kangaroo thorn has flattened leaf stalks as simple leaves; in spring globular heads of rich yellow flowers are produced. It makes a small and attractive treelike plant indoors, reaching a height of about 48in (120cm).

Grow the kangaroo thorn in full sunlight in a rich mix of equal parts of potting soil and humus. Keep soil evenly moist all year but take care not to overwater; provide good ventilation to keep growing conditions cool. After flowering allow the plant to rest at 50°F (10°C). Prune back to 6–10in (15–25cm). Fertilize mildly 3 times a year during warm months, not at all the rest of the year. Rarely bothered by insects. Propagate by seeds in spring or from stem cuttings in the summer.

To encourage bloom:
Keep in full sun with good air movement.

Right: **Acacia armata**
Grown more outdoors than indoors, this beautiful yellow flowering plant is a happy choice if you have space for it. Flowers appear in early spring and assure color at the window.

Acalypha hispida
(Chenille plant; foxtails; red hot cat's tail)
- **Intermediate conditions**
- **For beginners**
- **Easy to bloom**

This is a showy plant with attractive, hairy green leaves and strings of red flowers that resemble a chenille texture. The flowers spring from leaf axils and may grow to 20in (50cm) in length. The chenille plant grows to a height of about 30in (75cm); flowers appear at intervals during summer.

Grow the chenille plant at a sunny window in a rich mix: use equal parts of soil and humus. Water heavily during warm weeks and keep humidity at about 40 percent for best growth. Fertilize every second watering during spring and summer but not at all the rest of the year. Start new plants from cuttings in autumn. For a handsome pleasing display grow several plants together in a 6in (15cm) container.

To encourage bloom:
Give plenty of water and sun.

Right: **Acalypha hispida**
The long chenillelike red catkins make A. hispida a popular house-plant. The large leaves are decorative as well, and when young this is a fine plant for limited space.

Acanthus mollis
(Bear's breeches; Grecian urn plant)
● Cool conditions
● For beginners
● Easy to bloom

The leaves of this plant are a popular floral motif in art and architecture; the foliage is ornamental, lush and green, and spires of showy pink and white flowers appear in summer on the 48in (120cm) plant.

For best results, grow in bright light in large tubs using a porous standard houseplant soil mix; water heavily – these are thirsty plants. Do not feed.Keep humidity at about 40 percent and mist leaves frequently. After blooming, allow the plant to die down naturally with the soil kept barely moist. Propagate by seed or division of rhizomes in early spring. An excellent patio or terrace plant.

To encourage bloom:
Give plenty of water; crowd plants in tubs, repotting only rarely.

Left: **Acanthus mollis**
The large glossy green scalloped leaves and showy white and pink flowers make this a popular patio plant. Especially suited where vertical accent is needed, provides good garden room decoration.

Adenium obesum 'Multiflorum'

(Desert rose; impala lily)
● **Warm conditions**
● **For a challenge**
● **Difficult to bloom**

An East African plant, the impala lily is an attractive shrubby plant up to 24in (60cm) tall, with dark green fleshy leaves arranged spirally. Its lovely 1in (2.5cm) funnel shaped white flowers edged with crimson blaze with color in spring.

Grow this succulent plant in a sunny window – an east or south exposure is fine. Use equal parts of sand and humus for potting. Water judiciously, never allowing the soil to become waterlogged; this plant prefers dryness. In early spring feed about 3 times at 2-week intervals. Do not feed during the rest of the year. In winter the plant loses its leaves; keep soil barely moist then. Adeniums appreciate heat – up to 78°F (26°C) during the day, 10°F

(5.6°C) less at night. Plant can be obtained from specialty suppliers.

To encourage bloom:
Observe winter rest.

Below: **Adenium obesum 'Multiflorum'**
An extraordinary succulent with rosettes of leaves and large white, crimson-edged flowers. The stems eventually become woody trunks of a sculpturesque form.

Achimenes hybrids

(Cupid's bower; hot water plant)
● **Warm growing conditions**
● **For a challenge**
● **Difficult to bloom**

Offering a superb summer display of color, these members of the gesneriad family have been highly hybridized and there are dozens of varieties in a rainbow of colors available for summer blooming. Not to be missed.

Plants need full sun for bloom and a rich soil and humus mix. Start from tubers in early spring in 6–8in (15–20cm) pots; when 4–5in (10–12.5cm) high repot in separate containers. Some of the hybrids are compact, others make excellent basket plants, growing to 20in (50cm). Keep soil evenly moist at all times, using lime-free water, and when bloom is over, store pots indoors in a dim cool place. Repot in early spring in fresh soil. Keep plants misted to avoid red spider.

To encourage bloom:
Must have at least 4 hours of sun daily; keep humid.

Photo above: **Achimenes hybrids 'Paul Arnold'**
Dozens of attractive varieties come from this large gesneriad group, and all offer a wealth of colorful flowers for summer show.

Aechmea chantinii

(Amazonian zebra plant; queen of the bromeliads)

● **Intermediate conditions**
● **For everyone**
● **Easy to bloom**

One of the most glamorous bromeliads, *A. chantinii* grows to about 40in (1m) with green and white banded leaves and a branched spike of fiery red bracts crowned in yellow — a stunning inflorescence, especially as bloom occurs in winter. Color remains until April.

Grow at a south or west exposure in 4–5in (10–12.5cm) pots of medium-grade fir bark. Water moderately all year and keep 'vase' of plant filled with water; do not feed. Mist leaves with water occasionally. Plants are relatively free of insects and grow with little care.

Start new plants from offshoots; when they are 3–4in (7.5–10cm) high and fully rooted, cut them off and pot individually in fir bark.

To encourage bloom:
Use the 'apple-in-the-bag' method. Place the plant in a plastic bag with some ripening apples; the gases given off by the apples will encourage the plant to bloom. Alternatively, place a ripening apple in the central funnel of the plant.

Right: **Aechmea chantinii**
Called the 'Queen of the Bromeliads', A. chantinii has handsome broad leaves, rosette growth and an inflorescence that seems artificial, it is so vividly colored. Floral bracts last for months.

Aechmea fasciata
(Exotic brush; silver vase; urn plant; vase plant)
● **Intermediate conditions**
● **For everyone**
● **Easy to bloom**

The most popular plant of the bromeliad group, this plant grows to 30in (75cm) with wide leathery leaves of green and frosty white. Tufted blue and pink flower heads appear in spring and last until summer, or even longer. Plants are compact, vase shaped, beautiful.

Grow the urn plant at a south or west window in 3–4in (7.5–10cm) clay pots filled with medium-size fir bark. Water moderately all year but keep 'vase' of plant filled with water at all times, except when the temperature falls below 55°F (13°C). Do not feed. Mist foliage occasionally; plants are almost pest-free – the leaves are too tough.

Start new plants from rooted offshoots; when they are 3–4in (7.5–10cm) high cut them off and pot in individual containers of bark.

To encourage bloom:
Use the 'apple-in-the-bag' method.

Right: **Aechmea fasciata**
Perhaps the most popular bromeliad, A. fasciata, with silver-banded green leaves and a beautiful tufted pink inflorescence, will bloom readily and the color lasts for months. Highly recommended.

Aeonium tabuliforme
(Saucer plant)
● **Cool conditions**
● **For everyone**
● **Easy to bloom**

This striking 20in (50cm) plant has a flat rosette of overlapping leaves making a handsome picture; flowers in summer are bright yellow and bloom on tall stalks. The plant dies down somewhat in winter but is still worth space indoors. Unusual.

The saucer plant likes all the sun it can get so grow it at a south window; use equal parts of sand and humus. Water thoroughly and then allow to dry out before watering again. Feeding is unnecessary. Provide ample ventilation and humidity of about 30 percent. Overwatering can cause stem rot. This plant is generally not bothered by insects. New plants are grown from leaf cuttings in spring. Rosette dies once it has flowered.

To encourage bloom:
Give plenty of sun.

Left: **Aeonium tabuliforme**
A fine succulent with bright yellow flowers, this aeonium is sometimes grown indoors. Leaves overlap in a beautiful pattern; a worthy plant for the indoor garden.

Aeschynanthus lobbianus

(Basket vine; lipstick vine)
- **Warm conditions**
- **For a challenge**
- **Difficult to bloom**

This summer-flowering gesneriad is a trailing plant up to 36in (90cm) long, with dark green leaves and clusters of brilliant red flowers at the tips of the stems – very colorful for basket growing.

Plants need bright light but no sun, which can scorch leaves; a northerly exposure is fine. Grow in a porous mixture of equal parts of soil and humus. In active growth give plants plenty of water and mist them to keep humidity high (about 50 percent). Feed only once a month with plant food. Occasionally attacked by mealybug; use old-fashioned methods to eradicate. New plants from cuttings taken in early spring.

To encourage bloom:
Keep humidity high. Rest the plant at 55°F (13°C) during the winter, keeping it rather dry.

Below: **Aeschynanthus lobbianus**
Brilliant red flowers in tubular 'lipstick cases' adorn this plant in midsummer – a mature specimen may have over 50 flowers. The plant has pendent growth and is best grown in a basket container.

Agapanthus africanus

(Blue African lily; lily of the Nile)
- **Cool conditions**
- **For everyone**
- **Easy to bloom**

This plant grows from a bulb and has handsome strap shaped dark green leaves, and fine clusters of blue flowers in summer. Plants grow to about 40in (1m) and make a handsome display grouped together in large tubs.

Grow the lily of the Nile in a south or west window; use 10in (25cm) tubs and a rich potting soil – standard houseplant mix is fine. Be sure drainage is good. Water heavily during the warm months; when flowering is over, reduce watering and allow the plant to rest almost dry during the cool months. Do not feed. Get new plants from seed or division of roots in early spring.

To encourage bloom:
Leave undisturbed in the same pot for many years. They flower better when allowed to become rather rootbound. Observe resting time.

Right: **Agapanthus africanus**
With long stalks of blue flowers in handsome clusters and long strap-like green leaves, the lily of the Nile is as exotic as its name. A good tub plant for indoor beauty.

Aeschynanthus speciosus

(Basket vine)
- **Warm conditions**
- **For a challenge**
- **Difficult to bloom**

This gesneriad has spectacular orange-red flowers in midsummer; it trails to about 36in (90cm) and makes a handsome basket plant. Leaves are glossy and paler green than those of *A. lobbianus*. A very pretty plant, but somewhat finicky.

A. speciosus needs a west or east exposure, and a porous growing medium of equal parts of soil and humus. In active growth give the plant plenty of water and mist it to keep humidity high (about 50 percent). Feed only once a month. Watch for mealybug, which occasionally attacks. New plants from cuttings taken in spring. Hard to beat for summer color.

To encourage bloom:
Keep humidity high. Rest the plant in winter, keeping it rather dry.

Right: **Aeschynanthus speciosus**
(Hybrid x A. parasiticus)
The basket vine offers orange-red color on and off through the warm months. This fine gesneriad is best grown in hanging containers.

Allamanda cathartica
(Common allamanda; golden trumpet)
- **Warm conditions**
- **For a challenge**
- **Difficult to bloom**

If you have room, this tropical evergreen climber up to 15ft (4.6m) has tubular waxy golden-yellow giant flowers in late spring and early summer that dazzle the eye. Puts on a spectacular display at any window.

The golden trumpet needs sun, so a south window is necessary; pot in large tubs of rich soil; a standard houseplant soil is fine, with added humus. Flood plants and then allow to dry out before watering again. Feed every second watering (these are greedy plants) except in autumn and winter. Rest after flowering and in December cut back by one third and repot. Take stem cuttings in early spring for new plants.

To encourage bloom:
Repot annually to next pot size.

Below: **Allamanda cathartica**
A tropical vine from Guyana, allamanda bears 5in (12.5cm) yellow flowers in spring and summer. It is a large plant that needs space, but is well worth the effort.

Allium neapolitanum
(Flowering onion)
- **Cool conditions**
- **For everyone**
- **Easy to bloom**

A member of the lily family, this is a bulbous plant with green strap leaves, and lovely umbels of white flowers in summer. Plants grow to 40in (1m) and need space. Dramatic as cut flowers, which last for days in a vase of water. A very rewarding plant, requiring little work.

Grow at a sunny window and use a mixture of equal parts of soil and sand; drainage must be perfect. Keep the soil evenly moist, and rest plants somewhat in winter with scant watering. Feed monthly. Propagate by offsets separated in early spring.

To encourage bloom:
Give plenty of water.

Right: **Allium neapolitanum**
If you don't think an onion can be pretty, grow this fine bulbous plant with its large white star shaped flowers; the blooms are beautiful cut and placed in a vase.

Alpinia purpurata
(Red ginger)
● **Warm conditions**
● **For a challenge**
● **Difficult to bloom**

From the ginger family, this showy 5ft (1.5m) plant with large leaves and boat shaped red bracts makes a brilliant summer display at the window. The tiny white flowers are hidden in the bracts. A fine addition to the indoor garden if you have space, and of good color.

Grow ginger at your sunniest window; plants need 3 hours of sun a day to bear flowers. Pot in a loose mix of equal parts of soil and humus that drains readily. Flood plants with water during warm weather; allow to rest slightly at other times, with less moisture. Use large tubs. Feed twice weekly; these are greedy plants. They need a good amount of heat during the day to prosper. New plants from division of rhizomes.

To encourage bloom:
Give plenty of water and sun.

Below: **Alpinia purpurata**
A fine ginger plant – though somewhat large – with dense clusters of red bracts; an excellent touch of tropical atmosphere for a spacious window.

Angraecum eburneum
(Comet orchid)
- Intermediate conditions
- For everyone
- Easy to bloom

A large orchid up to 36in (90cm), this fine plant has long leathery dark green leaves and large crystalline white to pale green flowers with spurs on tall scapes. Plants may have as many as 20 flowers in the autumn, an excellent addition to the indoor garden. Does best in a hanging container where there is a good circulation of air.

Grow the comet orchid in a bright but not sunny window; sun may harm this plant. Use large-grade fir bark for potting mix, and clay pots (plastic ones hold moisture too long for these orchids, which are sensitive to overwatering). Do not feed, but repot every second year in fresh bark. Provide good humidity – at least 30 percent.

When flower scapes appear in autumn be careful not to wet them, because rot can occur; and keep plants out of drafts. Leaves occasionally form patches of black but this will not harm the plant; trim away dead tissue. New plants can be obtained from offshoots.

To encourage bloom:
No special requirements.

Below: **Angraecum eburneum**
Large white to pale green crystalline flowers in autumn make this orchid highly desirable for indoor accent, and the evergreen straplike leaves are attractive as well. Blooms readily indoors. Very handsome.

Anguloa clowesii
(Yellow tulip orchid)
- Intermediate conditions
- For everyone
- Easy to bloom

This spectacular 20in (50cm) orchid has papery green leaves, and tulip shaped vivid chrome yellow flowers in summer – as many as 5 or 6 fragrant blooms per plant. This very handsome orchid is easy to bring into bloom indoors.

Grow the yellow tulip orchid at a north exposure – bright light is needed but no sun. Use clay pots and medium-grade fir bark. Water evenly throughout the year; too much water can harm the plant. Do not feed. Provide ample ventilation and humidity. Temperature fluctuations can harm the plant. New plants from suppliers.

To encourage bloom:
Do not overwater.

Right: **Anguloa clowesii**
The yellow tulip orchid is aptly named. Its fragrant blooms cluster at the base of the plant, but are never hidden from view because the leaves are upright.

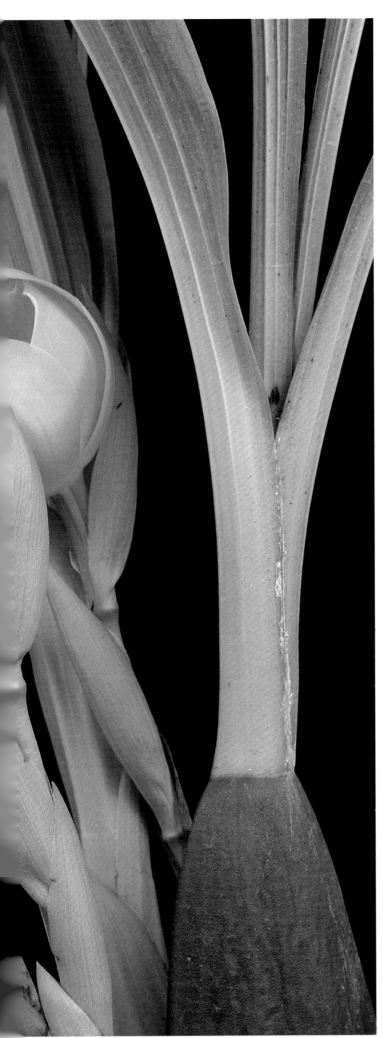

Anguloa ruckeri
(Tulip orchid)
- ● **Intermediate conditions**
- ● **For everyone**
- ● **Easy to bloom**

This handsome 20in (50cm) plant has broad dark green papery leaves, and fleshy waxy pink-brown tulip shaped flowers in spring that last for several weeks – it is a grand sight in bloom. This plant brings a touch of the exotic to the indoor garden.

Grow the tulip orchid at a north exposure – sun will harm this plant. Use a potting mix of medium-grade fir bark in a clay pot. Provide ample ventilation and humidity of at least 20 percent. Water judiciously all year; too much water can cause rot. Protect the foliage from water. Do not feed. Temperature fluctuation can harm the plant. Rarely bothered by insects. New plants from suppliers.

To encourage bloom:
Do not overwater.

Below: **Anguloa ruckeri**
The tulip orchid is well known by enthusiastic indoor gardeners for its waxy pink-brown flowers, perhaps the most exotic orchid grown indoors. Leaves are dark green and leathery. A beautiful plant.

Anthurium andreanum

(Flame plant; flamingo flower; painter's palette, pigtail plant; tail flower)

● **Warm conditions**
● **For beginners**
● **Easy to bloom**

This very popular plant grows up to about 24in (60cm) and has rich green elongated heart-shaped leaves and waxy white or coral colored flower spathes.

Anthuriums need a shady location — place them at a north or east window. Use a potting mix of equal parts of soil and humus that drains readily. Apply water so that the soil is evenly moist all year, but take care as overwatering can harm plants. Adequate humidity (60 percent) is necessary for good growth, so mist plants frequently during warm weather. Feed about once a month during the growing season, not at all in winter. Provide warmth — at least 75°F (24°C) by day. Propagate from seeds or by dividing plants.

To encourage bloom;
No special requirements.

Photo left:
Anthurium andreanum
An exotic anthurium from Central America, with its glossy green leaves this is a glamorous subject for a shady part of the indoor garden. It bears large flower spathes throughout the summer, and comes in white or shades of pink and red.

Anthurium scherzerianum

(Flame plant; flamingo flower; pigtail plant; tail flower)
● **Warm conditions**
● **For beginners**
● **Easy to bloom**

From Central and South America, these 20in (50cm) plants have a flower spathe of brilliant red, which appears lacquered and lasts for weeks. Flower spathes may appear throughout the year. A striking display.

Grow the flamingo flower in a shady place – a north window is fine. Use a porous mixture of equal parts of soil and humus, and keep the soil quite moist in the warm months and, somewhat drier in winter months, but never bone dry. Plants need higher than average temperatures – at least 78–82°F (26–28°C) to thrive – and sufficient humidity (50 percent). Mist

with water frequently. Start new plants from offsets or seed.

To encourage bloom:
Keep humidity high.

Photo left:
Anthurium scherzerianum
Almost artificial in appearance, the brilliant red spathes of anthuriums make them a popular indoor plant. Miniature varieties are now available.

Aphelandra squarrosa 'Louisae'

(Saffron spike; zebra plant)
● **Warm conditions**
● **For a challenge**
● **Difficult to bloom**

This is certainly a beautiful aphelandra, with shiny corrugated leaves, and yellow bracts in summer. The plant grows to about 20in (50cm) – a good small subject for the window garden.

Aphelandras need a sunny window – a south or east exposure is fine. Grow in small pots of rich soil; use equal parts of humus and packaged soil. Keep evenly moist all year; feed every 2 weeks in warm weather. Plants grow rapidly and are quite thirsty; they wilt severely if not given enough water so care is necessary to grow them properly. In winter they tend to get leggy, so start new ones from cuttings each spring.

To encourage bloom:
Rest for 4 to 6 weeks in a cooler temperature after flowering.

Photo above:
Aphelandra squarrosa 'Louisae'
This fine houseplant from South America has stellar yellow flowers – a brilliant display at any window. A good plant for limited space.

Ardisia crispa/crenata
(Coral berry; spear flower)
● **Intermediate conditions**
● **For everyone**
● **Easy to bloom**

This showy 20in (50cm) plant has small berries following tiny sweet-scented white or rose flowers in summer. Leaves are scalloped and dark green. It is very ornamental in its season and easy to grow indoors.

In summer protect *Ardisia* from strong sun but in winter the plant can be grown at a south window. Use a rich potting soil of equal parts of soil and humus. Drainage must be almost perfect. Give plenty of moisture all year except in winter. Feed monthly during the warm months. Do not feed when flowers appear; this will discourage the formation of berries. After a few years, start new plants from cuttings; the old ones get straggly.

To encourage bloom:
Give plenty of water.

Below: **Ardisia crispa/crenata**
An ardisia covered with red berries makes a fine winter gift. Leaves are dark green and handsome. This plant from the East Indies is always welcome in window gardens.

Ascocenda
● **Intermediate conditions**
● **For everyone**
● **Easy to bloom**

A group of fine hybrids (*Ascocentrum* × *Vanda*) that bear flowers usually twice a year, in spring and then again in early autumn. These plants are very desirable for the window garden. Compactness is another advantage for people with limited space; plants rarely grow over 16in (40cm). Many fine varieties.

Grow in a south window – they need good sunlight. Plant in medium-grade fir bark; small containers are best. Water evenly all year; do not feed. Provide good humidity (40 percent); spray plants with tepid water in warm weather and be sure they are in an area of good air circulation. They are especially good under artificial light. Get new plants from suppliers.

To encourage bloom:
Use small pots.

Right: **Ascocenda 'Orange Gem'**
This beautiful orchid often flowers twice yearly. There are many hybrids available from the parents _ Ascocentrum and Vanda. All have neat, compact growth.

Astrophytum asterias
(Sand dollar cactus; sea urchin cactus; star cactus)
- **Intermediate conditions**
- **For beginners**
- **Difficult to bloom**

Easy to grow, this almost spineless star shaped cactus has 2in (5cm) yellow flowers with red centers in spring or summer. Growing only 3in (7.5cm) across and 1in (2.5cm) tall, it is a fine plant if space on your windowsill is limited.

The star cactus needs sun, so place it at a south exposure. Grow in equal parts of sand and soil, and be sure drainage is perfect. Keep evenly moist all year except in winter, when plants can be grown somewhat dry but not bone dry. Do not feed or mist. *A. asterias* is one of the most attractive astrophytums. Propagate by seed in the spring.

To encourage bloom:
Give plenty of sun and a cool resting period in winter.

Photo above:
Astrophytum asterias
Commonly known as the sea urchin cactus, probably because of the unusual marking on the plant body.

Azalea indica
(Rhododendron simsii)
(Indian azalea)
- **Cool conditions**
- **For a challenge**
- **Difficult to bloom**

A fine small-leaved evergreen shrub, *Azalea indica* makes a handsome tub plant, with brilliant white, pink, red or purple flowers from midsummer to Christmas. The plant will eventually grow to about 30in (75cm) — a handsome accent for cool indoor gardens.

Grow this plant at a bright window — sun is not necessary. Use a rich potting soil of equal parts of humus and standard houseplant mix. Water heavily most of the year with lime-free water, but after bloom taper off moisture and keep the soil just barely moist. Cut back to 4–6in (10–15cm) and resume watering when growth starts. Feed every 2 weeks during growth; not at all the rest of the year.

Azaleas require the coolest place at your window and need frequent misting to keep humidity high (about 40 percent). New plants should be bought from suppliers.

To encourage bloom:
Observe resting time. Never allow soil to dry out. Put plant outside in a cool, moist place through the warm summer months.

Right: **Azalea indica**
Here is a plant that can brighten any autumn day. A compact shrub, it can be in flower at Christmas.

Begonia boweri
(Eyelash begonia; miniature eyelash begonia)
- **Warm conditions**
- **For everyone**
- **Easy to bloom**

This charming miniature, up to 14in (35cm) tall, bears lovely white or pink flowers, but is best known for its exquisite foliage — delicate green leaves edged with black markings like an eyelash. Of the rhizomatous group, *B. boweri* is sure to please any gardener.

Grow the eyelash begonia at a west or east window — bright light is fine; sun is not needed except in winter. The potting mix should be porous and rich — use standard houseplant soil and add half a cup of humus for a 5in (12.5cm) pot. Let soil dry out thoroughly between waterings and give less moisture in winter. Feed in active growth.

Above: **Begonia boweri**
Long a favorite, the eyelash begonia has spectacular foliage and white or pale pink flowers that are a delight throughout summer and autumn.

Rhizomatous begonias are food storehouses, so this plant can tolerate some drought if necessary. Propagate by division or cuttings.

To encourage bloom:
Allow to grow potbound.

Begonia 'Orange Rubra'
(Angelwing begonia)
- **Intermediate conditions**
- **For everyone**
- **Easy to bloom**

This angelwing begonia with pretty orange flowers and wing shaped leaves bears flowers in spring. The fibrous rooted plant grows to 36in (90cm) and can reach to 6ft (1.8m) if conditions are ideal. Very pretty.

For angelwings, a sunny location is needed – a south window preferably. Grow in equal parts of soil and humus kept well watered during the warm months – less water in winter is fine. Feed every month. Prune occasionally to keep plants within bounds – cut back to about one third original size in late autumn. Cuttings can be taken in early spring for new plants.

To encourage bloom:
Give at least 4 hours of sun a day, and keep well ventilated.

Below: **Begonia 'Orange Rubra'**
A fine angelwing begonia with handsome leaves spotted in white, and cascades of orange flowers.

Begonia 'Fireglow'
- **Intermediate conditions**
- **For a challenge**
- **Difficult to bloom**

One of the newer begonias, this plant blooms over a long period of time in summer and autumn with handsome red flowers. Leaves are bright green and plants grow to about 16in (40cm). For all its beauty however, this can be a temperamental plant. Needs care.

Grow this begonia at a bright location where there is neither too much sun nor too much shade. Use a potting soil of equal parts humus and soil that drains readily. Feed every 2 weeks in the growing season – not at all rest of year. To keep plant in fine stead, dry off slightly after bloom time for about 3 to 5 weeks with just scant moisture; then resume watering. Do not mist or get water on the leaves. New plants from cuttings.

To encourage bloom:
Observe resting time after flowering period, with little moisture.

Photo left: **Begonia 'Fireglow'**
Splendid red flowers adorn this modern hybrid begonia in summer and autumn. Beautiful, but needs coaxing through the winter.

Begonia semperflorens
(Wax begonia)
- **Intermediate conditions**
- **For beginners**
- **Easy to bloom**

These small plants make a handsome accent in the window garden. Growing to 14in (35cm) tall, wax begonias are available in several colors, white and red being the most popular. Leaves are dark green or mahogany colored. Nice small plants for colorful summer flowers.

Grow wax begonias in filtered sun. Use a potting mix of equal parts of humus and houseplant soil that drains well. Small pots are best for these plants. Although the plants require copious watering in their growing season (warm months) they must never become waterlogged. Feed every 2 weeks while plants are in active growth; in late autumn and winter allow the plants a rest, and to dry out somewhat.

Provide good air circulation and keep a lookout for thrips, which sometimes attack begonias – use appropriate remedies when necessary. Prune back tops when plants get leggy. Propagate by cuttings or seed.

To encourage bloom:
Give plenty of light.

Below: **Begonia semperflorens**
Long an outdoor favorite, the wax begonia is small and pretty. The flowers appear on and off for many months, making it a valuable asset in the indoor garden.

Beloperone guttata (Drejella)

(Shrimp plant)
- **Intermediate conditions**
- **For beginners**
- **Easy to bloom**

Paper-thin, flesh-colored bracts that overlap like a shrimp's body give this plant its common name; the leaves are dark green. The shrimp plant grows to about 36in (90cm) and makes a handsome display in early spring. The white flowers, almost hidden by the bracts, do not last long but bloom occurs over a long period of time, well into autumn.

You can grow the shrimp plant at almost any window and it will still bloom. It is not fussy about soil, but needs even moisture all year. Plants do not need feeding – they grow by themselves, practically. Prune back leggy growth in early summer – remove the top 8–10in (20–25cm) of the plant to encourage bushiness. Propagate by stem cuttings. A yellow variety has recently been introduced, and is quite stunning.

To encourage bloom:
Good light and some sun produces richer colored bracts.

Right: **Beloperone guttata**
Flesh-colored overlapping bracts give this plant its common name of shrimp plant. Leaves are papery in texture, and dark green. Blooms at intervals for most of the year.

Billbergia pyramidalis

(Queen's tears; summer torch)
- **Intermediate conditions**
- **For everyone**
- **Easy to bloom**

A 30in (90cm) popular bromeliad with golden-green leaves, and orange-pink bracts and red and blue flowers in midsummer – a treat at any window. Flowers are short lived but a mature plant bears several spikes.

Grow *B. pyramidalis* at a west or east window. Use a potting mix of equal parts of lime-free soil and medium-grade fir bark, packed tightly. Clay pots are best – plants become top heavy in plastic ones. Keep 'vase' of plant filled with water, and the bark moderately moist all year. Use lime-free water. Feeding is unnecessary. This plant is rarely bothered by insects and requires repotting every second year. New plants from offshoots in spring.

To encourage bloom:
Use the 'apple-in-the-bag' method. Place the plant in a plastic bag with some ripening apples; the gases given off by the apples will encourage the plant to bloom. Alternatively, place a ripening apple in the central funnel of the plant for the same effect.

Photo left: **Billbergia pyramidalis**
Golden-green leaves and orange-pink flower bracts make this easy to grow bromeliad a favorite.

Bougainvillea
(Paper flower)
● **Warm conditions**
● **For a challenge**
● **Difficult to bloom**

Bougainvillea indoors? Why not. This climbing plant bears handsome red or purple bracts in midsummer (the flowers are insignificant) and needs space, for it grows to 6ft (1.8m) or more if conditions suit it. It responds well to pruning to size, however; this should be done immediately after flowering. The leaves are handsome, mid or dark green in colour. A great basket plant. Difficult but worth the trouble.

Grow bougainvillea at the sunniest window you have and use a rich potting soil. Add one cup of humus to an 8in (20cm) pot. Plants are greedy and need plenty of water and feeding every 2 weeks while in active growth, but no feeding in cool weather when the plant slows down; water sparingly then. The plants should be rested throughout the winter.

Be alert for red spider, which occasionally attacks plants – use a suitable chemical preventative or mist thoroughly to discourage infestation. Grow new plants from stem cuttings.

To encourage bloom:
Provide at least 4 hours of sun daily.

Left: **Bougainvillea**
This popular red or purple flowering climbing plant is perfect for the sunny window. With careful culture it will bloom freely throughout the summer. Needs support; very tropical and pretty.

Bouvardia×domestica

(Jasmine plant; trompetilla)
- Cool conditions
- For everyone
- Easy to bloom

A shrub to 40in (1m), *B.×domestica* has oval leaves in twos or threes and clusters of brightly colored tubular fragrant flowers from summer to late autumn, making it a valuable asset in the window garden. Flower color is generally white, pink or red; there are many varieties.

Bouvardia needs a sunny window to bloom; pot in packaged soil that drains readily. Water freely in the warm months, but not so much the rest of the year. Feed monthly. Provide adequate humidity by misting the plant with tepid water. Easily grown. Propagate by stem cuttings in spring.

To encourage bloom:
Prune in late spring or early summer. Raise new plants every 2 years.

Left: **Bouvardia x domestica**
A desirable plant for the indoor garden because of its many color varieties. Bouvardia requires space, but makes a handsome display.

Brassavola nodosa
(Lady of the night)
● **Intermediate conditions**
● **For beginners**
● **Easy to bloom**

Producing an exquisite 3in (7.5cm) dazzling white heavily scented flower, *B. nodosa* grows only 10–14in (25–35cm) tall, and has terete type (pencil-like) leaves. The plant puts on its show in autumn, one flower following another for several weeks. The flowers are particularly fragrant at night.

Grow the lady of the night at an east or west window; use medium-grade fir bark and 4–5in (10–12.5cm) pots. Keep the plant moderately moist at all times and be careful to ensure that air circulation is good. Mist occasionally. Do not feed. Be sure drainage is good and do not pamper this plant – it grows almost by itself. Propagate by division.

To encourage bloom:
Dry out slightly for about 3 weeks in early October to encourage buds.

Right: **Brassavola nodosa**
Small but with charm, this orchid has needlelike leaves and heavenly scented white flowers that perfume the whole room at night.

Left: **Browallia speciosa**
This delightful plant is now available in compact hybrids that flower freely. They can be placed outdoors during the summer months.

Browallia speciosa
● **Intermediate conditions**
● **For a challenge**
● **Difficult to bloom**

Glossy leaves, and violet funnel shaped flowers in summer, make this plant a joy to have indoors. Pinching the growing tips out will keep the plant to about 14in (35cm); otherwise it will grow to 24in (60cm). It takes some coaxing, but is not impossible to bloom. Worth a try. Best grown several to a tub for a handsome display. Many brightly colored hybrids are available.

Grow *Browallia* in a shady place; sun harms these plants. Use a potting mix of equal parts of humus and houseplant soil. Be sure drainage is good. Keep soil evenly moist – plants should never dry out. Feed every 2 weeks in summer months. Provide good air circulation and never allow temperatures to fall below 50°F (10°C). Propagate by seed in spring. Discard plants once flowering has finished.

To encourage bloom:
Keep soil evenly moist. Stick to the summer feeding program.

Brunfelsia calycina
(Chameleon plant; yesterday, today, and tomorrow)
● **Cool conditions**
● **For a challenge**
● **Difficult to bloom**

An outdoor shrub that can grow indoors, this 40in (1m) plant has fragrant purple flowers that turn white and then pink; foliage is dark green and bushy. The flowers appear from late winter until autumn. Plants require large tubs and – where space is no problem – can make a valuable and attractive addition to the window garden.

Grow *Brunfelsia* at a sunny window; use a porous soil mix of equal parts of soil and humus. Keep evenly moist and feed twice weekly. Mist plants with tepid water occasionally and pinch shoots back when young to promote bushiness. Provide good ventilation. Difficult to grow but worth the time because the flowers are so handsome. Grow new plants from cuttings in spring.

To encourage bloom:
Pinch back – remove tips, about 2in (5cm), when growth is halfway mature. Give dry, cool rest period before and after flowering.

Right: **Brunfelsia calycina**
A pretty tub plant giving a glorious display of purple flowers in the summer. Lovely fragrance.

Calanthe vestita
● **Intermediate conditions**
● **For everyone**
● **Easy to bloom**

This 10in (25cm) orchid grows from a bulb and, if planted in spring, bears pink-purple and white flowers in mid-December – quite a treat. Once established the plant is really undemanding and grows easily.

Plant bulbs in equal parts of soil and fir bark in spring in 4in (10cm) clay pots; place at a west window until growth starts. Water judiciously at first. Increase watering as growth matures, then move to an east or south window. Do not feed; do not spray with water. When leaves mature in autumn allow the plant to dry out somewhat but do not keep bone dry; reduce the temperature by 10°F (5°C) if possible. When buds form resume watering. After the flowers fade, let it dry out naturally and store pot and bulb in a dry shady place. Start plant again in fresh growing medium in spring.

To encourage bloom:
Follow rest periods.

Right: **Calanthe vestita**
Do not let the fact that this orchid is deciduous deter you; it makes up for its bareness in winter with dainty and showy pink-purple and white blooms.

Calceolaria hybrids
(Lady's pocketbook; lady's slippers; pocketbook plant; pouch flower; slipper flower; slipperwort)
● **Cool conditions**
● **For everyone**
● **Easy to bloom**

Though short lived – only a few months – these colorful 10in (25cm) annuals are popular and add a note of festivity to the window garden. Many hybrids are available in a variety of stunning colors from dark yellow to brilliant reds.

Grow at a sunny but cool window in a rich soil; keep moderately moist at all times. Do not feed. Sow seeds in April or August for new plants. Try to maintain cool temperatures: 55°F (13°C) for best growing. Will not succeed in heat. When flowering is over, discard plants.

To encourage bloom:
No special requirements.

Above: **Calceolaria hybrids**
An annual garden plant, calceolarias are frequently grown indoors for their abundance of slipper-shaped highly colored flowers. Many hybrids.

Callistemon citrinus/ lanceolatus
(Bottlebrush plant; crimson bottlebrush)
● **Cool conditions**
● **For everyone**
● **Easy to bloom**

This slender shrub reaches 60in (1.5m), and has slender leaves and stunning red or yellow spikes of flowers with no petals, but long stamens. The brilliant red flowers appear in summer and autumn. Makes a handsome indoor subject grown in large tubs, if you have space for it.

Grow *Callistemon* in full sun – a south window is best. Use a standard packaged houseplant soil that drains readily. Allow to dry out between waterings and feed every 2 weeks in warm weather. Keep slightly dry in winter, but never bone dry. Spray occasionally with tepid water to maintain good humidity. This plant can tolerate heat or cold, but prefers a rest in winter at 50°F (10°C). New plants from stem cuttings in spring.

To encourage bloom:
Ensure good ventilation in summer.

Photo above: **Callistemon citrinus/lanceolatus**
Brilliant color makes Callistemon a popular plant, but it is large and requires space. Blooming in summer or autumn and rather unusual, it adds interest to the indoor garden.

Camellia japonica
(Common camellia; tea plant)
● **Cool conditions**
● **For a challenge**
● **Difficult to bloom**

For cool locations, camellias are worth their weight in gold because they bear handsome flowers – pink, white or red – and the season of bloom lasts from midwinter to spring. Plants will grow to 10ft (3m) or more.

Grow camellias in a bright window – east or west exposure – and use equal parts of garden loam, peat moss and sand for the soil mix. Acidity to pH 5.5 is essential. Give plenty of water; the soil should never dry out. Mist foliage every day in summer, about every other day the rest of the year. Use tepid, lime-free water for watering and misting. Apply an acid fertilizer during active growth in spring and keep humidity at about 50 percent. Repot only when absolutely necessary.

Watch for occasional attacks of red spider – grow with good air circulation to avoid pests. Bud drop is a common complaint indoors: too much water in cool weather hinders bud opening and too little water causes buds to drop. Grow new plants from tip cuttings in spring.

To encourage bloom:
Ensure coolness: 50°F (10°C).

Right: **Camellia japonica**
Many varieties of fine flowering evergreens for that cool location. Flower colors range from white to red. Outstanding for a large window.

Campanula isophylla

*(Bellflower; Italian bellflower;
star of Bethlehem;
trailing campanula)*

● **Cool conditions**
● **For beginners**
● **Easy to bloom**

These plants are rewarding for
basket growing, with trailing stems
up to 20in (50cm) long, covered with
white or blue flowers from August
until December. A mature plant has
hundreds of flowers.

Campanulas need plenty of light
and require good circulation of air to
thrive. Shade from direct sun in
summer. Use standard potting mix;
be sure drainage is perfect. Water
heavily and then allow soil to dry out
between waterings. In winter, when
growth is slow, cut back to about 5in
(12.5cm); keep on dry side and cool
− 55°F (13°C). In spring, repot in
fresh soil and increase moisture.
New plants from cuttings.

To encourage bloom:
Pick off flowers as they fade; seed
formation reduces bloom. Old plants
decline in flowering vigor; replace
with young cuttings.

Right:*'**Campanula isophylla
'Star of Italy'**
*If you want a basket of heavenly blue
flowers, here is your plant. A
rewarding indoor subject, easy to
grow and certain to please. A white-
flowering cultivar is available.*

Canna hybrids
(Indian shot)
● **Intermediate conditions**
● **For everyone**
● **Easy to bloom**

Garden plants up to 30in (75cm) tall, these fine tuberous-rooted plants have long bright green leaves carried on erect stalks, and showy spikes of colorful flowers – red, pink or yellow – in summer. There are several varieties, some with brown/purple leaves. Grown in tubs cannas make very satisfactory indoor subjects. Good accent for the indoor garden.
  Grow cannas in full sun – a south window is necessary for bloom. Use a potting mix of equal parts of soil and humus that drains readily. Water freely – these are thirsty plants – and feed every 2 weeks except in winter. Plants like warmth but will tolerate some cool nights (50°F, 10°C). Propagate by division of the rootstock in spring.

To encourage bloom:
Provide necessary sun. Rest at 45°F (7°C) throughout winter.

Left: **Canna hybrids**
Long-popular in the garden, Canna can also be grown in tubs indoors. There are many color varieties of both leaves and flowers.

Capsicum annuum
(Christmas pepper; ornamental chilli; red pepper plant)
● **Cool conditions**
● **For beginners**
● **Easy to bloom**

This is a delightful Christmas plant with small summer flowers followed by red autumn fruits shaped like miniature peppers that last through the cold months. Plants grow to 9–14in (23–35cm) tall – fine small companions for larger houseplants at windows. Many hybrids are available with different colored fruits.
  Give the red pepper plant a window where there is full sun – it needs all the light it can get. Grow in standard packaged houseplant soil kept evenly moist all year. Grow cool (60°F, 16°C) or the ornamental fruit drops. Do not feed. This plant lasts only one year, but it is worth its space at the window because of its good

color and handsome foliage. Start
new plants from seed in spring;
warmth is needed to germinate them.

To encourage bloom and fruit:
Give ample sun and ventilation.
Spray flowers with water once a day
to help the fruit to set.

Right: **Capsicum annuum**
*This lovely decorative plant has
handsome brilliant red, yellow or
purple pepper shaped fruit in winter.*

Catharanthus roseus
(Vinca rosea)
(Madagascar periwinkle)
● **Intermediate conditions**
● **For beginners**
● **Easy to bloom**

This 14in (35cm) plant has dark
green glossy leaves, and rose-red or
red-centered white flowers in
summer, making it a handsome
addition to the indoor garden.
Excellent seasonal color.
  Grow the Madagascar periwinkle
in full sun – it likes a west or south
window. Use standard houseplant
soil kept evenly moist all year. Be
sure drainage is good. Feed every
2 weeks during warm months. Use
small pots for best results – grow
several to a tub for a handsome
display. Never allow temperature to
go below 55°F (13°C). Start new
plants every year from tip cuttings
taken in spring or raise from seed.

Above: **Catharanthus roseus**
*Rose red flowers in summer make
this a fine seasonal plant for indoors.
New plants are best started from
cuttings or seed each year. Unusual
and worth the space.*

To encourage bloom:
Ensure good ventilation.

Cattleya hybrids

(Corsage flower)
- Intermediate conditions
- For everyone
- Easy to bloom

These are a large and popular group of orchids, with leathery strap shaped leaves and exquisite flowers well known to the florist. Plants do bloom indoors and there are thousands of hybrids to choose from, in colors from white to pink and red. Great for that special place at the window. Flowering time depends on the variety. Superlative in the home.

Cattleyas need sun – indeed they must have a southern or eastern exposure to bloom. Use a medium-grade fir bark or osmunda fiber for potting. Keep plants evenly moist all year – there is no specific drying out time necessary. Do not feed, as this can prevent blooming. Provide ample humidity (40 percent) and be sure there is a good circulation of air in the growying area. These are epiphytic plants and need a buoyant atmosphere to prosper. Plants are rarely bothered by insects. Blooming times depend on specific hybrids, with plants for all seasons. New plants from suppliers or division.

To encourage bloom:
Provide ample sun.

Right: **Cattleya
Bob Betts 'Mont Millais'**
Known as the corsage flower, cattleyas are always sure to please the indoor gardener. The flowers are large and generally fragrant. C. Bob Betts 'Mont Millais' is a fine white and a parent of many cattleyas.

Right: **Cattleya porcia**
A delightful free-flowering species, with clusters of pretty pink flowers in early autumn. Resting the plant during the winter will encourage bloom for the next year.

Cattleya skinneri

- Intermediate conditions
- For everyone
- Easy to bloom

One of the showiest and easiest indoor orchids, this plant bears several rose purple flowers, 3in (7.5cm) across, in late summer. Plants grow to about 30in (75cm) and flowers are colorful for 2 to 3 weeks.

Place this plant at a bright window – an east or west exposure is fine. Grow in large-grade fir bark kept evenly moist all year. Spray with tepid water to maintain humidity. Do not feed. A good circulation of air is necessary to keep plants healthy. Rarely bothered by insects. Repot every third year in clay pots.

To encourage bloom:
Keep humidity high.

Right: **Cattleya skinneri var. alba**
An elegant white variety of C. skinneri, its abundant long-lasting large flowers make the plant especially worthy of a place at the window. Easy to grow.

Chamaecereus silvestrii
(Gherkin cactus, peanut cactus)
● **Warm conditions**
● **For beginners**
● **Easy to bloom**

Growing to 10in (25cm), this cactus has narrow cylindrical green branches with white spines. The flowers are 2in (5cm) across, brilliant orange-red and stunning, but last only a few days. Easy to grow, this is a good pot plant for beginners.

Grow the peanut cactus in full sun – without adequate sun the bloom will be sparse. Use a potting mix of equal parts of soil and sand that drains readily. Water sparingly – allow soil to dry out between waterings; overwatering will kill the plant. Do not feed. Keep in a well-ventilated place. Remove small branches and use as cuttings in spring for new plants.

To encourage bloom:
Give plenty of sun. Keep the plant very cool in winter (40°F, 4°C).

Below: **Chamaecereus silvestrii**
Here is a fine complement to leafy green plants. This cactus has cylindrical branches and bears beautiful red flowers. A good pot plant and highly recommended.

Celosia argentea
● **Intermediate conditions**
● **For beginners**
● **Easy to bloom**

This plant is available in two forms: 'Cristata' (cockscomb) with comblike crested flower heads in various colors, and 'Pyramidalis' (plume celosia, Prince of Wales' feathers) with plumed flowers in brilliant red or yellow. Both types have pale green leaves. 'Cristata' and the dwarf varieties of 'Pyramidalis' reach 12in (30cm) in height; other varieties of 'Pyramidalis' are larger and may reach 36in (90cm).

Grow *Celosia* in your sunniest window; use a standard packaged houseplant soil that drains well. Water freely most of the year except in winter, when moisture can be somewhat less. Feed monthly in warm weather. In winter allow to die back, and repot in fresh soil in spring. Otherwise, discard old plants and start afresh from seed.

To encourage bloom:
Always provide good ventilation.

Photo above: **Celosia argentea 'Pyramidalis'**
The red or yellow flowers resemble plumes. An ideal plant for the windowsill, as dwarf varieties grow to only 12in (30cm). Generally pale green, the leaves of some varieties are a beautiful bronze.

Chrysanthemum
(Florist's mum)
● **Cool conditions**
● **For beginners**
● **Easy to bloom**

Potted chrysanthemums of yellow, bronze, white, or red make beautiful plants at windows. There are many hybrids of these plants that make fine temporary seasonal plants for the home. The most popular types are the dwarf 'all the year round' chrysanthemums that reach 6–10in (15–25cm) and can provide flowers at any season.

Grow chrysanthemums at a bright but not sunny window; keep them as cool as possible: 60°F (16°C) is ideal. Use a rich soil and keep quite moist throughout blooming. After flowers fade, cut back to 2–4in (5–10cm) and set plants in a frost-free garage or cold frame with soil kept barely moist until spring; then set them in the garden. They can be potted and used again indoors the following season, although dwarfed varieties will grow to their usual height of up to 30in (75cm). Stem cuttings can be taken but, again, new plants may be larger and the compactness of dwarf varieties lost.

To encourage bloom:
Keep plants well watered.

Right: **Chrysanthemum**
Always beautiful in the garden, chrysanthemums are just as welcome indoors. Many colors are available, and plants make fine indoor subjects in small tubs.

Cineraria
● Cool conditions
● For a challenge
● Difficult to bloom

Officially called *Senecio cruentus,* these are difficult plants to resist – they have flowers in vibrant shades of red, blue and purple in very early spring and bloom for about 2 to 3 weeks indoors. After flowers fade, they must be discarded; still they are worth their price for providing a stunning seasonal display.

Keep plants at a bright but not sunny window and soil should be watered evenly at all times. To keep plants blooming, maintain cool temperatures of, say, 55–60°F (13 – 16°C). Sun and warmth will desiccate cinerarias. Be careful of the cineraria mite, which is prevalent on plants – use any of the suitable pesticides with caution.

To encourage bloom:
Grow in coolness (45–50°F, 7–10°C) until flower buds form.

Right: **Cineraria**
One of the finest gift plants, this well-known favorite has daisylike flowers in brilliant colors; well worth growing from seed if you want a challenge.

Citrus mitis
(Calamondin orange)
● Warm conditions
● For everyone
● Easy to bloom

This popular 30in (75cm) pot plant from the Philippines has small orange fruits and dark green oval leaves. Flowers are white and fragrant. Both flowers and fruit appear throughout the year, with the best display in winter.

Grow the calamondin orange in a sunny location. Use a potting mix of equal parts of humus and houseplant soil. Allow soil to dry out between waterings and feed every 2 weeks in the summer months. In winter allow soil to dry out somewhat and keep cooler (55°F, 13°C). Provide a buoyant atmosphere and mist leaves with water frequently to deter spider mites, which adore this little orange tree. Cut back each year to about 10in (25cm) to encourage new growth and a bushy habit. Get new plants from pips or cuttings.

To encourage bloom and fruit:
Give ample sun or plunge outdoors in full sun from June until September. Plants need pollinating by hand to set fruit if you are unable to put them outdoors.

Photo above: **Citrus mitis**
A handsome small tree, C. mitis bears tiny oranges in winter, making it a decorative windowsill plant. Ideal for small spaces. Easy to grow.

Clerodendrum speciosissimum
(Glory bush; Java glorybean)
● Intermediate conditions
● For everyone
● Easy to bloom

Here is a 60in (1.5m) plant with lovely long-lasting scarlet flowers – and many of them – in summer. In habit it is somewhat vining but bushy and plants need little care. A wealth of color for little effort.

Give full sun – a south exposure is ideal – and grow in porous soil of equal parts of humus and soil. Be sure the drainage is good. Keep soil evenly moist except in winter, when plants rest somewhat – water sparsely then. Feed only when in active growth. Occasionally prune to keep the plant attractive; pinch off errant stems. Do not try to force plants into late growth in resting time. Cuttings root easily for new plants.

To encourage bloom:
Dry out occasionally. Prune after blooming to encourage young growth on which the next year's flowers will be borne.

Right:
Clerodendrum speciosissimum
Large and suitable for tubs, with a little encouragement this very showy plant produces fine scarlet flowers.

Clerodendrum thomsoniae
(Bleeding heart vine; glory bower)
- Intermediate conditions
- For everyone
- Easy to bloom

True to its name this is a glory of a plant with large leaves and small but striking flowers – they are white and deep crimson, and appear in early spring and may last until September. Overlooked by most growers, this climbing plant is a fine addition to the window garden. Unpruned it will grow to 10ft (3m) in height. Very decorative as pot or basket plants.

Grow the glory bower in a bright window – east or west exposure. Use a porous soil of equal parts of humus and soil. Keep the soil evenly moist except in winter, when plants lose some leaves naturally and need little water. Feed every 2 weeks when in active growth. Cuttings root easily and bloom the first year. An outstanding plant.

To encourage bloom:
Prune after blooming to encourage young growth on which the next year's flowers will be borne.

Below:
Clerodendrum thomsoniae
A striking plant with large leaves and stellar red and white flowers. A large plant but very attractive, and certainly worth space indoors.

Clerodendrum ugandense
(Blue glory bower)
- Intermediate conditions
- For everyone
- Easy to bloom

For winter bloom, it is hard to beat the blue flowers of *C. ugandense*. The shrublike plants are handsome at windows, given space, as they grow to about 48in (120cm).

Grow this winter-blooming plant in a sunny place – a south or west window is fine. Use a porous soil: standard houseplant soil is suitable, but be sure drainage is near perfect. Feed every 2 weeks but only when the plant is in active growth. In winter allow it to dry out slightly but never let the soil get bone dry. Trim and groom occasionally to keep within bounds. Start new plants each year from cuttings in early spring.

To encourage bloom:
Provide rest period of 3 to 5 weeks with little water after plant blooms.

Photo above:
Clerodendrum ugandense
If you want blue flowers in winter and spring, this is the plant to grow – a large handsome species.

Clivia miniata
(Kaffir lily)
- Intermediate conditions
- For everyone
- Easy to bloom

A fine bulbous plant, *C. miniata* has dark green straplike leaves, and handsome clusters of orange flowers in early spring that last for several days. Mature plants are a splendid sight in bloom. Many new hybrids are available.

Grow *Clivia* in a shady place – a north or west window is fine; sun will harm the plants. Use a growing medium of equal parts of sand and soil. Keep soil evenly moist all year except in winter, when soil can be somewhat dry. Feed every 2 weeks in very early spring – not at all during the rest of the year. Leave bulbs in pots for several years – plants react adversely to repotting. New plants by division of bulbs in late winter.

To encourage bloom:
Grow potbound in 6 or 7in (15 or 18 cm) containers. Keep dry during the winter months.

Right: **Clivia miniata**
If you can't grow anything, this plant will make you a gardener. Easy to bloom each spring with magnificent clusters of orange flowers. Handsome straplike dark green leaves. Highly recommended.

Cobaea scandens

(Cathedral bells; cup and saucer vine)
- Intermediate conditions
- For a challenge
- Difficult to bloom

Handsome large tubular purple flowers make this vine worth its space in the window garden. In midsummer the plant, a mass of bloom, is a sight indeed.

This plant needs a very sunny place – a south window is essential for bloom. It requires a humus-rich soil and buckets of water when once established. Feed weekly – this is a greedy species. Provide suitable supports, because the plant climbs quickly. Although *Cobaea* will survive the winter provided the temperature does not fall below 45°F (7°C), it is advisable to grow new plants from seed every year. It is worth growing, however, for its short highly colorful display.

To encourage bloom:
Water, water, water. If the plant is making more leaf than flower, stop feeding at once.

Below: **Cobaea scandens**
A vine, usually grown as an annual. The cup-shaped purple flowers are unusual and stunning. The plant grows quickly and needs support.

Coelogyne cristata
- Cool conditions
- For everyone
- Easy to bloom

From the mountains of the Himalayas comes this fascinating 20in (50cm) orchid with grasslike leaves and dazzling showy white 4in (10cm) fragrant flowers. In midwinter the display is a beautiful sight.

Grow *C. cristata* at an east or west window and use medium-grade fir bark. Keep the bark moderately moist all year except after flowering, when a short 3 to 5 week rest with little water is advisable. Mist to keep humidity high and grow as cool as possible: 60°F (16°C) at night is fine. Do not feed. Rarely bothered by insects. New plants from suppliers.

To encourage bloom:
Observe rest after blooming time. Grow the plant in a cool place.

Right: **Coelogyne cristata**
One of the cool growing orchids from the Himalayas, this fine plant bears crystalline white flowers in winter. A sight to behold and not to be missed.

Coelogyne ochracea
- Warm conditions
- For everyone
- Easy to bloom

A springtime beauty, this 20in (50cm) orchid bears delicate yellow and white flowers in clusters; they are scented and beautiful. This is an easy orchid to grow and highly recommended; it should be grown more widely.

The plant will do well at a west or east exposure; grow in medium-grade fir bark, kept evenly moist all year. Needs some warmth: 75°F (24°C). Do not feed but mist with tepid water occasionally to maintain good humidity. New plants can be obtained from orchid suppliers.

To encourage bloom:
See that the plant has some sunshine during winter months.

Below: **Coelogyne ochracea**
Pretty as a picture, this dainty harbinger of spring has yellow and white flowers. A fine orchid.

Columnea×banksii
● **Warm conditions**
● **For a challenge**
● **Difficult to bloom**

This beautiful trailing gesneriad to 36in (90cm) has small oval green leaves, and lovely two-lipped scarlet flowers with yellow markings in summer. Ideal for basket growing.

Grow this plant at a bright window – sun is not necessary. Use equal parts of soil and humus and be sure the medium drains readily. A stagnant soil can cause harm to the plant. Water judiciously all year, keeping the soil just moist to the touch but never too dry or too wet. Feed during growth at every other watering. Adequate humidity is necessary for best growth – maintain 40 percent. Mist the plant with tepid water in hot weather. Grow new plants from tip cuttings.

To encourage bloom:
No special requirements.

Below: **Columnea×banksii**
A mass of blooms in summer, this plant is ideal for basket growing. Easy to propagate from cuttings.

Columnea microphylla
(Goldfish vine; small-leaved goldfish vine)
● **Warm conditions**
● **For a challenge**
● **Difficult to bloom**

With tiny leaves and bright red and yellow flowers this trailing gesneriad can make any window a garden. The colorful display occurs in winter and spring and plants may have as many as 100 flowers. Grows to 48in (120cm).

A west or east exposure and a growing medium of equal parts of soil and humus are fine. Keep evenly moist all year and grow in warmth – 75°F (24°C). Coolness can inhibit growth. Feed every 2 weeks when in active growth and maintain a humidity of about 50 percent. Shade from summer sun. Propagate by taking tip cuttings in spring.

To encourage bloom:
Keep warm and humid; slightly drier in winter. Remove spent flowers to prevent berries forming, which waste the plant's energy.

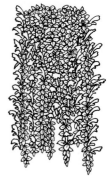

Right: **Columnea microphylla**
With tiny leaves and bright scarlet and yellow flowers, this trailing gesneriad creates a sensation.

Convallaria majalis
(Lily of the valley)
● **Cool conditions**
● **For beginners**
● **Easy to bloom**

These popular garden flowers are grown for their sweet fragrance and lovely little bell shaped white flowers. Excellent for forcing indoors for winter bloom. Take up little space; only 8in (20cm) tall. Pleasant additions to the indoor garden and excellent for cut flowers.

Grow lily of the valley by starting rhizomes in the autumn. Plant in shallow bowls of sphagnum moss and soil and grow shaded in a cold greenhouse until January. Then gradually bring to light and sun and the warmth of the house. Keep the soil evenly moist. Flowers open in about 3 weeks. Keep plants somewhat cool while growing (never above 60°F, 16°C). Start new plants from rhizomes each year. Handle with care as plant is poisonous.

To encourage bloom:
Start in a cool shady place. Never allow soil to dry out.

Below: **Convallaria majalis**
The old favorite, lily of the valley is as delightful and easy to grow indoors in pots as it is outside. Flowers are guaranteed, and can be cut and used for decoration in the home.

Costus igneus
(Fiery costus)
- Intermediate conditions
- For everyone
- Difficult to bloom

From Central and South America comes this charming 15in (38cm) plant with succulent stems and spectacular, large, paper-thin 3in (7.5cm) orange flowers in spring or summer. A truly delightful and ideal houseplant, sure to please.

Grow *C. igneus* at a sunny exposure – it needs all the light it can get. Use a well-drained growing medium of one part sand, one part humus and one part soil. Keep moderately moist all year. Plants are temperamental – drafts will quickly harm them. Propagate by dividing clumps in spring.

To encourage bloom:
Give plenty of sun.

Above: **Costus igneus**
Paper-thin brilliant orange flowers create a sensation in bloom in autumn, and the attractive upright growth makes this a valuable indoor plant. Not to be missed.

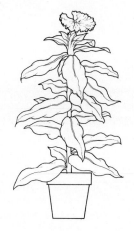

Crassula falcata
- Warm conditions
- For beginners
- Easy to bloom

A large group of succulents originating from South Africa, most crassulas make excellent houseplants and this is no exception. With thick gray sickle shaped leaves and scarlet flowers this plant grows to about 30in (75cm). Not spectacular, but handsome. A very amenable plant and sure to please.

You can grow this plant in full sun. Provide a well-drained potting soil: use equal parts of humus, soil, and perlite or gravel. Allow to dry out between waterings. Feed every 2 weeks in summer; not at all the rest of the year. Provide good air circulation – do not mist the leaves. Rarely bothered by insects. New plants can be started each year from stem or leaf cuttings or seed.

Right: **Crassula falcata**
Here is an overlooked beauty, with firm clusters of brilliant red flowers that are excellent for cutting. A good succulent and easy to grow.

To encourage bloom:
Provide full sun and keep cooler (55°F, 13°C) in winter.

Crocus
● Cool conditions
● For beginners
● Easy to bloom

The crocus, long a favorite houseplant with its brilliant flowers, is a harbinger of spring, only 6in (15cm) tall. There are a variety of hybrids to brighten indoors with early spring color.

Give crocuses a bright exposure – a west or east window is fine. Plant the small corms as soon as you get them; put 6 or 8 corms in a 10in (25cm) pot filled with standard houseplant soil. Keep plants in a cool – 50°F (10°C) – location out of the light until leaves are up 3–4in (7.5–10cm), then move them to a bright place. Keep the soil evenly moist; apply plant food after the leaves have formed and then again when plants are in bud. Allow plants to die back naturally and then store in a shady

Above: **Crocus 'Striped Beauty'**
The lovely white-striped purple flowers of the Dutch crocus are well known and provide a colorful accent in spring. For the most effective display grow several together.

place – pot and all – for 6 to 8 weeks. After this rest repot in fresh soil.

To encourage bloom:
Give plenty of water when leaves are fully expanded. Keep plants cool (50°F, 10°C) until buds show color.

Crossandra infundibuliformis
(C. undulifolia)
(Firecracker flower)
- **Intermediate conditions**
- **For everyone**
- **Easy to bloom**

A mass of orange flowers in springtime, *Crossandra* has shiny green leaves and grows to about 16in (40cm). Plants require little care. For a lavish display grow several plants in one container.

Grow at a sunny window, in equal parts of soil and humus. Keep evenly moist all year and feed every 2 weeks. Be sure plants have a good circulation of air – they do not respond in stagnant conditions. Even small plants bear handsome orange flowers and many times there is a second blooming at midsummer. New plants from seed started in spring or from stem cuttings.

To encourage bloom:
Be sure plants have good air circulation at all times.

Below:
Crossandra infundibuliformis
From India and the East Indies, this rather small plant boasts fine orange flowers at intervals during the year.

Cuphea hyssopifolia
(Elfin herb; false heather)
- **Intermediate conditions**
- **For beginners**
- **Easy to bloom**

This is a small 12in (30cm) herb with wiry branches and heatherlike leaves. The star shaped flowers are purplish red, and abundant in spring and summer. A very pretty pot plant, providing a dainty display and good color through the warm months. Worth its space at the window.

Grow false heather in sun – a south or west window is fine. Use standard packaged houseplant soil. Water freely all year except in winter, when moisture can be reduced. Provide good ventilation. Do not feed. Pot in fresh soil yearly. For more plants propagate by seeds or cuttings in summer.

To encourage bloom:
Give plenty of sun.

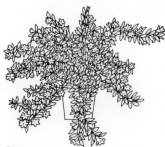

Right:
Cuphea hyssopifolia var. alba
This white-flowering variety has tiny blooms that appear at intervals throughout the year. A welcome addition to the indoor garden.

Cuphea ignea
(Cigar flower; firecracker flower; Mexican cigar plant)

● **Intermediate conditions**
● **For beginners**
● **Easy to bloom**

A shrubby plant up to 12in (30cm) tall, with bright red, black and white tubular flowers in the warm months. A pretty little pot plant for windows and easy to grow indoors.

Grow at a sunny window; use standard houseplant soil but be sure drainage is good. Keep soil evenly moist all year and provide good ventilation for plants. Feed every 2 weeks when in active growth. Spray with water occasionally to provide good humidity. Check plants for insects; mealy bugs attack sometimes – use appropriate remedies. Start new plants each year

Above: **Cuphea ignea**
The black and white ashlike tips of the red tubular flowers give this abundantly blooming plant its common name of cigar plant.

from seed in spring or from stem cuttings taken in summer.

To encourage bloom:
No special requirements.

Cyclamen

(Alpine violet; poor man's orchid; shooting star)

● **Cool conditions**
● **For a challenge**
● **Difficult to bloom**

Grown from a tuber, this is a charming plant up to 16in (40cm) tall, with flamboyant flowers in red, pink or white. The pretty heart shaped leaves are dark green or silver, and the single, double or fringed flowers start appearing in late winter and continue for 2 or 3 months.

Keep the cyclamen out of the sun – a north window is fine. Start tubers, one to a 5in (12.5cm) pot, in late summer in a rich potting mix of equal parts of humus and soil. Set the top of the tuber slightly above the soil surface; otherwise, water may collect in the crown and cause rot. Keep the soil moist and the plants in coolness, 55–60°F (13–16°C): and feed every 2 weeks while in growth. Inspect frequently for mites; use a hard spray of water to eradicate them. When flowers fade in March, let the plants rest by gradually withholding water until the foliage dies. Keep nearly dry, the pot on its side in a shady place in coolness, until September. Then remove dead foliage and repot in fresh soil mix.

To encourage bloom:
Give plenty of water. Keep the plants cool and humid (but do not spray the flowers). Observe the resting period.

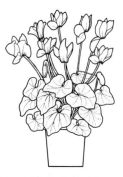

Right: **Cyclamen**
Cyclamen grow wild in Greece and along the eastern shores of the Mediterranean. Hybrids from these are highly prized indoor flowering plants. They come in beautiful pastel shades, and are always desirable.

Cymbidium hybrids
● Cool conditions
● For everyone
● Easy to bloom

Here is a large group of grassy leaved orchids with magnificent flowers; a mature plant can have over 100 blooms. There are hundreds of hybrids and bloom can occur in any season depending upon the individual plant. Both standard and miniature varieties are available. Lovely accent for the indoor garden.

Cymbidiums needs a bright or sunny place – good light is essential for bloom. Use fir bark for potting and keep the medium quite moist all year. Do not feed. To make plants bloom, subject them to a cool period (55–60°F, 13–16°C) for about 6 weeks and then return to average home temperatures. Always provide good air circulation and adequate humidity (about 40 percent). Rarely bothered by insects. New plants from division of rhizome in spring.

To encourage bloom:
Provide cool period. Give as much sun as possible in autumn.

Right: **Cymbidium hybrids**
This large group of orchids offers handsome long-lasting flowers in an array of colors. Plants come in standard sizes up to 48–60in (120–150cm) or in miniature (up to 24in, 60cm) for those with limited window space. C. Elmwood (top) and C. Excalibur (bottom) are both miniature varieties. Easy to grow, they contribute elegant sophistication to any indoor garden.

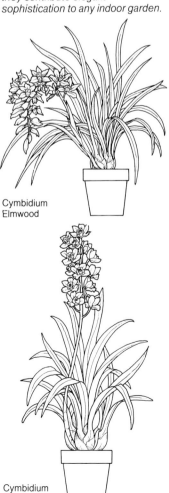

Cymbidium
Elmwood

Cymbidium
Excalibur

Dendrobium 'Gatton Sunray'
- **Warm conditions**
- **For everyone**
- **Easy to bloom**

A spectacular orchid hybrid growing to 48in (120cm) this cane type dendrobium has dark green leaves and masses of bright yellow and red flowers in summer – as many as 50 to a plant. Needs space but worth it – a truly lovely orchid for indoors.

Grow in sun. Pot in medium-grade fir bark kept evenly moist all year except in winter. Do not feed. Provide adequate humidity (30 percent) and good ventilation. After flowers fade allow plant to rest a little, with less moisture; when new growth starts, increase watering. Rarely bothered by insects. New plants from suppliers or division.

To encourage bloom:
Give plenty of sun.

Below:
Dendrobium 'Gatton Sunray'
This colorful dendrobium is hard to resist. With a little extra care the plant will bloom twice a year.

Dipladenia 'Amoena'
(Mexican love vine)
- **Warm conditions**
- **For a challenge**
- **Difficult to bloom**

A climber to 7ft (2.1m), this lovely plant from Brazil has leathery leaves and beautiful pale pink funnel shaped flowers in early spring until summer, sometimes into autumn. Ideal for basket growing. Delightful plant for all occasions.

Place this plant at your sunniest window. Pot in equal parts of soil and humus and be sure drainage is almost perfect. It will not succeed in waterlogged soil. Water evenly while in growth, but not so much during the rest of the year. Feed every 2 weeks except when the plant is resting. Propagate by stem cuttings or by sowing seed in spring.

To encourage bloom:
Give plenty of sun. Keep humid.

Below: **Dipladenia 'Amoena'**
This attractive climber will bloom beautifully when only 12in (30cm).

Dipladenia splendens 'Rosea'
(Pink allamande)
- **Warm conditions**
- **For a challenge**
- **Difficult to bloom**

Similar to *Dipladenia* 'Amoena' this fine climber up to 15ft (4.6m) has leathery leaves and fine pink flowers in summer – dozens to a plant. It can be pruned to be a small pot plant and will still flower. Ideal for basket growing and a beautiful addition to the indoor garden.

Grow at your sunniest window – without good sun it will not bloom. Pot in equal parts of soil and humus and be sure drainage is perfect. Water evenly while in growth; not so much the rest of the year. Feed every 2 weeks except when the plant is resting in winter. It is occasionally attacked by red spider mite; use appropriate remedies. Mist with water to provide the humidity essential for health. You can start new plants from stem cuttings or by sowing seed in spring.

To encourage bloom:
Provide ample sun. Keep slightly cooler (55–60°F, 13–16°C) in winter.

Right:
Dipladenia splendens 'Rosea'
This fine rose-pink flowering Dipladenia hybrid creates a fountain of color in the summer months.

Echeveria 'Doris Taylor'

- ● **Warm conditions**
- ● **For beginners**
- ● **Easy to bloom**

A fine 20in (50cm) succulent with deep green spoon shaped leaves covered with white hairs. Flowers are red and yellow, borne in clusters from the centre of the plant in spring. An attractive indoor plant.

Grow *Echeveria* at a sunny window – good light is essential for bloom. Use a potting mix of equal parts of sand and soil that drains readily. Water sparsely, allowing the soil to dry out between waterings. Feed monthly during warm weather. Do not get water on the leaves, as rot will result. Keep this plant in an airy position. New plants from seed, leaf cuttings or offsets in spring.

To encourage bloom:
Give plenty of sun. Keep cool in winter (45°F, 7°C).

Below: **Echeveria 'Doris Taylor'**
Perhaps the best known of the echeverias, the handsome spoon shaped foliage and red and yellow flowers of this fine plant make a most attractive indoor display.

Echinocereus baileyi
(Rainbow cactus)

- ● **Warm conditions**
- ● **For a challenge**
- ● **Difficult to bloom**

This is a small desert cactus that grows to about 8in (20cm) and requires little attention. It is light green in color and has spines. Flowers are a beautiful pink, and there are many to a plant in summer. This is a very good plant for growing under artificial lights.

Grow the rainbow cactus in your sunniest window – without good sun there will be sparse bloom. Use a potting mix of equal parts of sand and soil, and cover the top with some chipped gravel. Water and then allow to dry out before watering again. Feed every month except in winter, when plants like a 6 week rest with little water – move to a cooler location then if possible. Propagate by seed or offsets in spring.

To encourage bloom:
Give plenty of sun. Keep at 40°F (4°C) in winter.

Right: **Echinocereus baileyi**
A lovely 8in (20cm) cylindrical cactus with violet-pink flowers. Amenable, but needs coaxing into bloom.

Echinopsis hybrids
(Sea urchin cactus)
- **Warm conditions**
- **For beginners**
- **Easy to bloom**

Their beautiful large flowers make these cacti impossible to resist. They are breathtaking in summer in bloom. The body of the plant is dark green with spines and, depending on the particular hybrid, grows to 6–30in (15–75cm) in height. A lovely desert cactus for the home.

Grow at a sunny window – a south or east exposure is fine. Use a potting medium of equal parts of sand and soil, and cover the top with some chipped gravel. Water freely in spring and summer, not so much the rest of the year. Feed every 2 weeks in warm weather. In winter move to a cool bright place and keep somewhat dry. Grow new plants from offsets in spring.

To encourage bloom;
Provide winter rest at 36°F (2°C) and keep rather dry.

Photo left: **Echinopsis hybrid**
Certainly one of the most dazzling of the cacti. The large impressive flowers are often fragrant and are red, white or pale lilac. Very elegant.

113

Epidendrum stamfordianum
- Warm conditions
- For everyone
- Difficult to bloom

This pretty orchid, growing to 36in (90cm), has long dark green leaves, and sprays of hundreds of small but pretty yellow and red flowers in spring or summer. Not easy to bloom but not impossible, and very impressive when it does. Only mature plants bear flowers.

Grow in a bright location – some sun is fine but not direct light. Pot in large-grade fir bark with excellent drainage. Overwatering can cause harm to the plant. Water heavily and then allow to dry out before watering again. Provide ample ventilation. Rarely bothered by insects. Get new plants from suppliers.

To encourage bloom:
Secure mature plants.

Below:
Epidendrum stamfordianum
For a cascade of flowers – as many as 100 to a plant – this orchid excels.

Epidendrum cochleatum
(Clamshell; cockleshell orchid; shell flower)
- Cool conditions
- For everyone
- Easy to bloom

An amenable orchid up to 30in (75cm) tall, with light green leaves, and unusual shell shaped purple and yellow flowers in summer. Nice pot plant that blooms yearly with the minimum of care.

Grow the shell orchid in a bright location – a west or east window is fine. Use medium-grade fir bark for potting; water freely in warm months, not as much the rest of the year. Do not feed. Provide good ventilation. Rarely bothered by insects. Get new plants from suppliers.

To encourage bloom:
No special requirements.

Photo above:
Epidendrum cochleatum
The clamshell orchid is easy to grow and a favorite for unusual flowers.

Epiphyllum
(Epicactus; leaf cactus; orchid cactus)
- Warm conditions
- For everyone
- Easy to bloom

A cactus, but descended from the jungle dwellers, epiphyllums are generally large plants up to 30in (75cm) with dramatic 6–7in (15–18cm) flowers in red, pink, purple, yellow or white. Peak bloom season is midsummer and there are dozens of fine hybrids for windowsill beauty.

Grow in a bright window – an east or west exposure is fine, although epiphyllums need less light than other cacti. Use a potting mix of equal parts of small-grade fir bark and soil. Keep quite moist during the growing times, April to September; the rest of the year, keep evenly moist. Feed with every other watering through the warm weather only. Plants are large and sprawling and need support – a small trellis is fine. Recently, miniature epiphyllums have been introduced, about 20in (50cm) high, and these make ideal houseplants. Take cuttings in spring for new plants.

To encourage bloom:
Observe the resting times. Keep at 50°F (10°C) during the months of the winter rest period.

Right: **Epiphyllum 'Ackermannii'**
Large flowers of deep hues make epiphyllums popular. Many varieties are available, in gorgeous colors.

Episcia cupreata
(Flame violet)
● **Warm conditions**
● **For everyone**
● **Easy to bloom**

This fine plant from the gesneriad family grows to 16in (40cm) with exquisite foliage – bright silver and green – and vivid red flowers in May or June. It makes a fine hanging plant for indoor decoration.

Place episcias at a bright window but where they are protected from direct sun. Grow in a rich mix of equal parts of soil and humus. Water heavily during the growing times but be sure drainage is perfect. Provide humidity of 40 percent but do not mist leaves. Plants like warmth – about 70°(21°C),with a 5°F (3°C) drop in temperature at night. New plants can be grown from seeds, cuttings or offshoots.

To encourage bloom:
Provide adequate humidity.

Below: **Episcia cupreata**
This is one of the popular episcias, with fine scarlet flowers and leaves that look sugar-coated.

Episcia dianthiflora
(Lace flower)
● **Warm conditions**
● **For everyone**
● **Easy to bloom**

This 14in (35cm) plant from the gesneriad group is a trailer with green velvety leaves and tufted white flowers. Bloom is in summer. Makes a very pretty show when grown as a basket plant.

This plant needs a bright but not sunny location. Grow in a mix of equal parts of soil and humus that drains readily. Plants are subject to rotting if overwatered. Use lime-free water. Provide suitable humidity of about 40 percent but do not mist foliage. Plants like warmth – about 70°F (21°C) during the day with a 5°F (3°C) drop in temperature at night. Propagate by rooting plantlets that develop on stolons.

To encourage bloom:
Provide adequate humidity.

Right: **Episcia dianthiflora**
From tropical Mexico, this white flowering episcia is a favorite houseplant; decorative foliage adds to its appeal. Use it in hanging containers for maximum display.

Erica
(Heath)

- **Cool conditions**
- **For a challenge**
- **Difficult to bloom**

Heaths make lovely indoor plants, growing up to 24in (60cm), with narrow hard leaves and bell shaped or tubular flowers in clusters; they are generally summer blooming, although some winter-flowering species are popular at Christmas. Many varieties and species. Fine outdoor plants that can make the transition into the home if given a little extra care.

Grow heaths and heathers in full sunlight – a south window is best. Use a standard houseplant soil that drains well; never allow soil to become waterlogged and always use lime-free water. Feed moderately during warm months. For success with these plants grow cool (72°F, 22°C maximum) and be sure ventilation is good in the growing area – the plants succumb in a stagnant atmosphere. New plants from cuttings in spring.

To encourage bloom:
Give full sun.

Below: **Erica x hyemalis 'Ostergruse'**
Who can resist the heaths with their lovely tubular flowers? A fine addition to the window garden.

Eucharis grandiflora
(Amazon lily)
● **Intermediate conditions**
● **For beginners**
● **Easy to bloom**

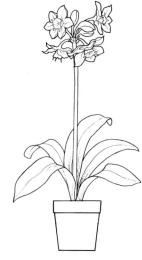

This fine amaryllis plant grows to 30in (75cm), and has large, shiny green leaves, and lovely glistening white flowers usually in spring and again in early autumn. A must for every indoor garden.

Grow the Amazon lily at a bright window but be sure there is protection from direct sun. Use a potting soil of equal parts of soil and humus, kept quite moist in early spring and late summer – the rest of the time it should be only slightly moist. Provide ample humidity (40 percent is fine). Feed moderately about once a month during growth, but not at all during resting times. Get new plants by division of clumps.

To encourage bloom:
Be sure to allow the plant to rest at proper times, with scanty water.

Below: **Eucharis grandiflora**
Bright white glistening flowers and large dark green leaves combine to display nature at her best. Highly recommended for indoor gardens.

Eucomis bicolor
(Pineapple lily)
● **Cool conditions**
● **For beginners**
● **Easy to bloom**

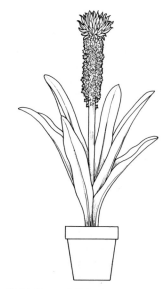

This bulbous lily grows to about 30in (75cm), with shiny green foliage, and handsome crowns of green purple-edged flowers in July or August. It is called the pineapple lily because the inflorescence resembles a tiny pineapple at the apex of the plant.

Provide bright light for the pineapple lily – a west or east window is fine. Use a standard houseplant soil mix. Keep evenly moist all year except in winter, when the plants can be grown somewhat dry. Do not feed. Provide good humidity; spray with tepid water in warm weather. Get new plants by removing small bulbs that develop next to the parent bulb, or sow seeds during the spring.

To encourage bloom:
Observe the winter resting time.

Right: **Eucomis bicolor**
A bulbous plant with shiny green leaves and a handsome cone of green purple-edged flowers in summer. Lovely for indoor accent.

Euphorbia fulgens
(Scarlet plume)
● **Intermediate conditions**
● **For everyone**
● **Easy to bloom**

A fine shrub, up to 30in (75cm), with slender leaves. The tiny yellow flowers, borne in clusters, are surrounded by bright scarlet bracts and appear in winter. Some plants grow into handsome specimens for indoor decoration.

Grow the scarlet plume in full light – a west or east window is fine. Use a potting mix of equal parts of sand and soil. Water freely most of the year – only in winter should the soil be somewhat dry. Feed every 2 weeks in warm months, but not at all the rest of the year. Mealy bugs may attack the plant if it is grown without ample humidity: use appropriate remedies. Start new plants from cuttings taken in spring.

This plant is poisonous; the sap is irritant and should be washed off the skin immediately with cold water.

To encourage bloom:
Grow in good light.

Below: **Euphorbia fulgens**
A fine shrub with bright scarlet bracts, this is a good winter blooming plant. Slender dark green leaves enhance its attraction.

Euphorbia milii
(Crown of thorns)
● **Cool conditions**
● **For everyone**
● **Easy to bloom**

Well known and well liked, this 30in (75cm) plant with dark green leaves bears small vivid red bracts surrounding insignificant flowers in winter. The stems have prickles, but the plant is very amenable to indoor culture, and worth its space.

Grow the crown of thorns in a bright sunny window. Pot in equal parts of standard houseplant soil and sand, that is kept evenly moist all year except in winter and early spring, when a slight drying out is beneficial. Feed monthly in summer and autumn, but not at all the rest of the year. Plants resent drafts but like good air circulation. Take new plants from cuttings in spring.

This plant will exude a poisonous sap from cut surfaces and should be handled with gloves.

To encourage bloom:
Be sure this plant has a slight rest after blooming has finished.

Right: **Euphorbia milii**
The stems of this small shrub are covered in sharp prickles. Bright red bracts give the plant popular appeal.

Euphorbia pulcherrima
(Poinsettia)
● **Intermediate conditions**
● **For a challenge**
● **Difficult to bloom**

This highly prized Christmas plant grows up to 30in (75cm). (Pot plants are chemically dwarfed and will revert to tall shrubs unless they are well pruned after flowering.) Leaves are scalloped and mossy green, and the 'flowers' are actually leafy bracts turning fiery red, white or pink. Recently some fine hybrids have been developed that hold their color for months at a time!

The poinsettia needs a bright but not sunny location and intermediate temperatures about 65°F (18°C) or a little above. Grow in a rich porous houseplant soil. Drainage must be perfect. In winter when the plant is in bloom, keep soil evenly moist. Reduce moisture when the leaves start to fall, and move the plant to a cooler place.

In spring put the plant in the garden but leave it in its pot. Cut back and replace in fresh soil. In September bring the plant back into the house, and in October provide a period of uninterrupted darkness – at least 14 hours a day – to initiate flower buds for Christmas. (Put under a bench or in a closet where no artificial light reaches the plant.) Get new plants from suppliers.

This plant is poisonous and should be handled with gloves.

To encourage bloom:
Keep humid and avoid drafts. Be sure a dark period is given – every day for at least 40 days. Start this in early October for Christmas bloom.

Left: **Euphorbia pulcherrima**
This popular Christmas plant is tough to beat for midwinter color with its large showy bracts in shades of red, pink or white. This photograph shows several individual plants grouped together, each one of which produces bracts of a single color. The bracts do not change from white through pink to red as the plants become fully grown.

Exacum affine
(Persian violet)
● **Cool conditions**
● **For everyone**
● **Easy to bloom**

Small fragrant violetlike flowers and shiny green leaves make this plant a beauty for indoors. New varieties grow up to 9in (23cm); older ones up to 18in (45cm). Plants can bloom from summer well into winter, when color is so needed at the windows. A real find.

Grow the Persian violet in full sun – a south window is best. Use a potting soil of equal parts of humus and soil, and be sure drainage is perfect. Feed every 2 weeks when in active growth, and water evenly all year. Provide somewhat cool temperatures – about 60°F (16°C) – and good ventilation. Treat as an annual and raise new plants from seeds each year.

To encourage bloom:
No special requirements.

Below: **Exacum affine**
Not spectacular but certainly worth space in the indoor garden, Exacum has small fragrant flowers that may last well into the winter months.

Freesia

- Cool conditions
- For a challenge
- Difficult to bloom

These fragrant flowering bulbs of the iris family are hardly easy to grow indoors, but not impossible. The trumpet-shaped flowers, 2in (5cm) long on stems up to 18in (45cm), come in many colors – white, yellow, pink, purple – and make excellent cut flowers for the living room.

Pot 6 corms, 1in (2.5cm) deep and 2in (5cm) apart, in a 6in (15cm) pot of two parts sandy loam, one part leafmold and one part old manure. Plant from August to November for January to April bloom and give full light (no sun). Keep plants moist and cool, 60°F (16°C). Do not feed. After the flowers fade, gradually dry the soil, shake out the corms, and keep them dry for repotting in fresh mix for beautiful flowers next year.

To encourage bloom:
Ensure cool growing conditions.

Right: **Freesia**
Available in many different colors, the graceful flowers of freesias are exquisitely scented. Beautiful for indoor display as cut flowers.

Fuchsia

(Lady's eardrops)
- Cool conditions
- For everyone
- Difficult to bloom

These handsome plants, up to 36in' (90cm) tall, bear pendent red, white, pink or purple flowers (or combinations of these colors) and dark green leaves. The plants are bushy, and excellent for hanging baskets or tubs.

Grow fuchsias in bright light but out of the sun, and keep the temperature between 55–60°F (13–16°C). Use a rich, well-drained potting soil of equal parts of humus and soil. Flower buds are set in spring and summer; feed every 2 weeks. Flood the plants while they are growing, and pinch at early stages to encourage branching. Mist foliage frequently and provide a buoyant atmosphere. Watch out for white fly. Take cuttings in February for new plants. Difficult but worth the effort for their elegant display.

To encourage bloom:
Mist frequently; give plenty of water. Provide cool growing conditions and good ventilation. Give a cool period during the winter months at 45°F (7°C) with much less water.

Photo above: **Fuchsia 'Snowcap'**
Lovely plants with pendent flowers in various colors, fuchsias can be difficult but worth the trouble. Highly regarded as an indoor plant where growing conditions are suitable.

Gardenia jasminoides

(Cape jasmine)
- ● Warm conditions
- ● For a challenge
- ● Difficult to bloom

These are evergreen shrubs up to about 30in (90cm) tall, with waxy dark green foliage and scented white flowers. They are well known and well loved, but difficult plants to achieve success with indoors, though not impossible. They are best suited to a conservatory or garden room.

Grow gardenias in bright light in summer and in a sunny place in winter. Use a well-drained, lime-free potting mix of equal parts of humus, soil and peat moss. Keep evenly moist with lime-free water. Be sure the plants have adequate humidity – about 40 percent. From spring to autumn, feed once a month with an acid fertilizer. Mist foliage frequently to avoid red spider infestations. Give a deep soaking in a sink or pail once a month. Buds may drop or fail to open if night temperature is above 70°F

Above: **Gardenia jasminoides**
Very popular but difficult to bloom, with lovely scented white flowers.

(21°C) or below 60°F (16°C). Propagate by cuttings in spring.

To encourage bloom:
Mist with tepid water frequently. Keep out of drafts and fluctuating temperatures, but always provide good ventilation for the plants.

Gazania hybrids

(Treasure flower)
- ● Warm conditions
- ● For everyone
- ● Easy to bloom

These outdoor, 10in (25cm) plants adapt to indoors with few problems. Flowers are 2in (5cm) across, and orange, yellow, brown, pink and red; the plant has woolly, gray-green foliage. Flowers open in the sun and close at night. Daisylike, long-lasting and very pretty, they provide indoor color from spring to autumn.

Give these your sunniest window and a rich soil of equal parts of humus and soil. Plants are thirsty and need buckets of water to prosper. Feed every 2 weeks. Keep humidity at about 40 percent. Start new plants each year from seed sown in late winter or early spring, or from cuttings taken in mid to late summer for flowers the following year.

To encourage bloom:
Give plenty of sun.

Above: **Gazania 'Monarch mixed'**
This outdoor ground cover plant does beautifully in shallow pots of rich soil indoors. Splendid colors.

Gerbera jamesonii
(Barberton daisy; Transvaal daisy)
- **Cool conditions**
- **For everyone**
- **Easy to bloom**

The 20in (50cm) Transvaal daisy has lobed leaves and 4in (10cm) daisylike flowers in summer. Many varieties are available but flower color is usually in the red to orange range. They make fine houseplants, but have to be replaced every second year. Cut flowers are excellent for decoration.

Grow at a sunny window – a south exposure is fine. Use a potting mix of equal parts of soil and humus that drains readily. Water when the soil feels dry to the touch – too much water can hinder the plants. Feed every 2 weeks when in growth. Do not mist the plants but provide an airy place for them. New plants by division or from seed in spring.

To encourage bloom:
Grow in full sun.

Right: **Gerbera jamesonii**
Outdoors the Transvaal daisy is well known and the lovely red, yellow or orange flowers can be grown indoors too in small tubs. Not often grown but certainly desirable for the home.

Gloriosa rothschildiana
(Glory lily)
- ● **Intermediate conditions**
- ● **For beginners**
- ● **Easy to bloom**

This is a splendid tuberous plant of the lily family that grows to 6ft (1.8m) and has bright green foliage and exquisite 3in (7.5cm) orange and yellow flowers edged with crimson. Tubers started in very early spring bear flowers in midsummer that last for over a week. A showy plant, and easy to grow.

Grow the glory lily in sun – it likes heat. Use a loose potting mix of equal parts of houseplant soil and humus. Pot one tuber to a 5in (12.5cm) pot; set the tuber about 1in (2.5cm) below the surface of the soil; growth starts in a few days. Provide a bamboo stake or other support, as this is a climbing plant. Water heavily while in growth and feed every 2 weeks. When the flowers fade, let foliage die naturally; then store the plant in its pot in a cool dry place at 55° (13°C) for 6 to 9 weeks. Repot in fresh soil and start again.

Above: Gloriosa rothschildiana
A fine tuberous plant with narrow leaves and showy orange, crimson and yellow flowers in summer. Start tubers in spring. A fine indoor plant.

To encourage bloom:
Give plenty of water. Observe the cool resting period.

Guzmania lingulata
(Orange star; scarlet star)
- ● **Intermediate conditions**
- ● **For beginners**
- ● **Easy to bloom**

A fine bromeliad growing to 30in (75cm), with apple green straplike leaves and star shaped inflorescence. The orange or scarlet bracts are impressive, but the flowers are insignificant in the center of the bracts. Bloom varies but generally occurs in summer.

Grow in sun or bright light – the more sun, the brighter the bracts. Use equal parts of fir bark and lime-free soil; do not firm the growing medium too much. Keep moderately moist all year with lime-free water and make sure the vase of the plant is filled with water from spring to autumn. Do not feed. Provide good ventilation and humidity of about 30 percent. Rarely bothered by insects. Grow new plants from offsets at the base of the mother plant; repot in bark and soil when 3–4in (7.5–10cm) high, usually in autumn or spring. Make sure the offsets are rooted before detaching them.

Above: Guzmania lingulata 'Minor Orange'
A fine small bromeliad, this guzmania has a rosette of apple green leaves. A spectacular orange inflorescence that lasts for several months puts this plant high on anyone's list for indoor color.

To encourage bloom:
Do not feed. Keep warm and humid.

Gymnocalycium mihanovichi
- **Warm conditions**
- **For everyone**
- **Easy to bloom**

This is a 3in (7.5cm) globular cactus with pale yellow spines; it has abundant flowers in summer with outer petals varying in color from pink through red to purple and with a whitish center. This is a good houseplant that grows with little care. Valued for its small size, fascinating flowers and ease of culture.

Many varieties are available, including cultivars in which the body of the cactus is colored red, pink, yellow or black. These do not contain chlorophyll and must be grafted onto a green rootstock in order to survive; they will flower in ideal conditions.

Grow this cactus in sun – a south or east window is fine. Use a potting medium of equal parts of soil and sand. Be sure the drainage is good. A thin layer of gravel on top will help to prevent crown rot if too much water is given. Water moderately all year except in winter, when the plant can be kept somewhat dry but never

Right:
Gymnocalycium mihanovichi
Cultivars of the pretty globular cactus are available in a variety of colors, but without chlorophyll they cannot survive on their own. They are grafted onto a green rootstock – Trichocereus spachianus (top). The original species (bottom) is green and will flower on its own roots.

bone dry. Do not feed. Rarely bothered by insects. New plants from seed. An easy plant to grow under artificial light.

To encourage bloom:
Observe winter dormant season at low temperature: 50°F (10°C).

Haemanthus albiflos
(Elephant's ears; white paintbrush)
- **Cool conditions**
- **For everyone**
- **Difficult to bloom**

Growing to 12in (30cm) in height, this fine bulbous plant from South Africa has fleshy dark evergreen leaves and a head of greenish white flowers with orange-tipped stamens – very handsome. Bloom occurs in summer and autumn. A very attractive plant, still somewhat difficult to find but worth the search.

This plant needs a bright exposure but no direct sun – a west or east window is fine (it will also bloom in north light). Use a potting mix of equal parts of soil and sand that drains readily. Do not bury bulbs; allow the tip to protrude above the soil line. Water scantily at first; then increase watering as leaves mature. Do not feed. After flowering allow the plant to be somewhat dry for about 6 weeks – then resume the watering schedule. Obtain new plants by dividing mature bulbs.

To encourage bloom:
Observe dry periods. Repot only every 3 years; plants flower better when potbound.

Left: **Haemanthus albiflos**
White orange-tipped flowers within a cup of creamy white bracts make this plant a showy specimen indoors

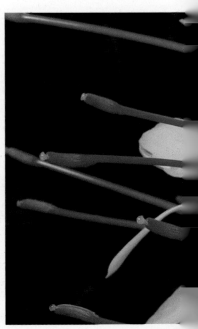

Haemanthus katharinae
(Blood flower; blood lily)
● **Cool conditions**
● **For a challenge**
● **Difficult to bloom**

This deciduous bulbous plant grows to 16in (40cm), with bright green leathery leaves. The plant bears a salmon red sphere of small flowers after the leaves have developed; bloom time is midsummer. Lovely, but a bit temperamental.

Provide a sunny place for *H. katharinae.* Pot one bulb to a 5in (12.5cm) clay pot; use equal parts of soil and sand. Leave the tip of the bulb protruding. Water carefully – very little moisture until the leaves start to grow, then increase watering. Do not feed. After flowering reduce the moisture, but never let soil get bone dry. Do not repot – instead topdress the soil every year. Be alert for crown rot if too much water gathers at the base of the plant. New plants from bulbs started in spring.

To encourage bloom:
Repot only every third year.

Left: **Haemanthus katharinae**
Once coaxed into bloom, the rewards are certainly worth the effort – the bright red flower head will certainly dazzle the eye.

Hedychium gardnerianum
(Kahili ginger)
● **Warm conditions**
● **For a challenge**
● **Difficult to bloom**

A large tropical lily up to 6ft (1.8m) tall, this plant has glossy green canelike leaves, and bears exotic red and yellow flowers in summer. Grows like a weed once started.

Put this ginger at your sunniest window – it needs lots of light. Grow in large tubs – about 10in (25cm) in diameter – in equal parts of sand, humus and soil. Water heavily during growth but reduce watering after the plant blooms. Mist occasionally with tepid water. Excellent terrace or patio plant where climatic conditions allow. Protect from cold in winter. New plants from rhizomes in spring.

To encourage bloom:
Give plenty of sun and water.

Left: **Hedychium gardnerianum**
Tropical and pretty is this red and yellow flowering ginger. Difficult to bloom but well worth a try indoors.

Heliconia angustifolia
- Warm conditions
- For a challenge
- Difficult to bloom

This member of the banana family is large, growing to 60in (1.5m) so you will need adequate space to grow it. The plant has big glossy green leaves and showy flower bracts, orange-red, edges lined green. Flowers are dramatic and appear in summer.

H. angustifolia needs a sunny window. Pot in equal parts of soil and humus and be sure drainage is good. Water heavily in summer but reduce watering in winter, when plants should be allowed to rest with less moisture and in coolness (about 55°F, 13°C). Feed every two weeks during growth and spray plant with tepid water in warm months; these plants require excellent humidity. Difficult but not impossible to bloom, and plants make handsome accents for patio or terrace where the climate allows. Propagate by dividing root-stock when growth starts in spring.

To encourage bloom:
Provide warmth – 75°F (24°C) – and ensure position in full sun.

Right: **Heliconia angustifolia**
Very tropical in appearance, with orange bracts and green-white flowers. Different, and one of the best heliconias for indoors.

Heliotropium hybrids
(Cherry pie; heliotrope)
- Intermediate conditions
- For beginners
- Easy to bloom

Heliotrope is an old favorite, a 30in (75cm) plant, with oval wrinkled dull green leaves, and clusters of fragrant blue-purple flowers that open from summer to winter. As pot plants they are best raised annually or every second year, because they get straggly (although they can be pruned hard in early spring with success). A plant that gives a nice touch of outdoors for indoors.

Grow heliotrope at a bright window – a west or east exposure is fine. Use equal parts of humus and soil for potting, and water copiously. These are thirsty plants. Feed every 2 weeks during growth. They can tolerate coldness (45°F, 7°C) if necessary and are rarely bothered by insects in the home. New plants from seed or stem cuttings in spring.

Above: **Heliotropium hybrid**
The fragrant purple flowers of heliotrope bloom from May to October. A fine gift plant.

To encourage bloom:
Water freely while in growth. Rest in winter and provide good ventilation during the summer months.

Hibiscus rosa-sinensis

(Chinese hibiscus; Chinese rose; rose mallow)

- Warm conditions
- For everyone
- Easy to bloom

A large 48in (120cm) free-flowering plant, hibiscus grows well in tubs in a porch or garden room. Plants have lush green foliage and bear mammoth, paper-thin, red, pink, orange, white or yellow flowers that each last only a few days, followed by more flowers – bloom continues for about 6 weeks in midsummer.

Sun is the key to success with hibiscus so put them at your sunniest window. Grow in equal parts of soil and sand, and be sure drainage is perfect. Flood with water during growth; these are thirsty plants. Feed every 2 weeks. Spray foliage with tepid water. Prune back small specimens to 4in (10cm) in early spring; large plants by one third. Watch for spider mites, which like

these plants. Propagate by taking cuttings in spring.

To encourage bloom:
Provide ample sun and water. Drafts and fluctuating temperatures may cause the buds to drop before opening. Rest the plant during the winter at 50°F (10°C).

Below: **Hibiscus rosa-sinensis**
Many varieties grow and bloom indoors, with large colorful flowers. Try them in tubs in a garden room.

Hippeastrum hybrids

(Amaryllis)

- Intermediate conditions
- For beginners
- Easy to bloom

These striking bulbous plants with strap foliage bear large flowers in white, pink, red, rose or violet, with the petals sometimes banded in a contrasting color; the stalks are up to 26in (65cm) long. A colorful display in early spring, the flowers appearing before the leaves are fully developed. Many hybrids are available including *H.* 'Claret', 'Giant White' and 'Scarlet Admiral'.

Buy good quality bulbs in autumn and start in growth from January to March; use one bulb to a 6–7in (15–18cm) clay pot; allow 1in (2.5cm) space between the walls and the bulb. Let the upper third of the bulb extend above the soil line. Use any standard houseplant soil. Set the pot in a cool shady place and grow almost dry until the flower bud is 6in (15cm) tall. Then move the pot into a sunny window and water heavily. From planting to blooming is usually 3 weeks or more.

After the plant blooms, keep it growing so the leaves can make food for next year's flowers. When foliage

Above: **Hippeastrum hybrid**
The favorite amaryllis with huge flowers. With many varieties in different colors, these showy plants are always welcome indoors.

browns let the soil go dry for about 10 to 12 weeks or until you see new flower buds emerging; then replant in fresh soil. Propagate by seeds or by removing offsets when repotting.

To encourage bloom:
Feed after flowering until the leaves die down. Observe the rest period.

Hoya australis

(Porcelain flower; wax plant; wax vine)
● **Intermediate conditions**
● **For a challenge**
● **Difficult to bloom**

This robust 30in (75cm) plant from Australia has shiny green leaves, and clusters of small white waxy flowers in summer or autumn. This species is somewhat easier to grow than the old-fashioned *Hoya carnosa.* It is best grown in a hanging container.

Grow the porcelain flower in a sunny place – a south or west window is fine. Use a potting soil of equal parts of soil and humus; drainage must be perfect. Water heavily during warm months but never allow soil to become soggy. In autumn and winter allow to dry out between waterings. Feed every 2 weeks in summer. The plant blooms off old wood so do not prune. Repot only when necessary; the roots resent disturbance. Topdress every few months using fresh soil. New plants can be grown from cuttings taken in spring or autumn.

To encourage bloom:
Do not overwater. Keep cool in winter at 50°F (10°C).

Below: **Hoya australis**
Similar to Hoya carnosa this plant from Australia has small white waxy flowers, red at the center. Ideal for growing in hanging baskets.

Hoya bella

(Miniature wax plant)
● **Intermediate conditions**
● **For a challenge**
● **Difficult to bloom**

This 12–24in (30–60cm) vining plant resembles its larger cousin *Hoya carnosa.* It is excellent for small window gardens and hanging baskets. Leaves are small and dark green, and it has waxy purple-centered white fragrant blooms.

Grow the miniature wax plant in bright light. Use a well-drained potting soil of equal parts of humus and houseplant soil. Grow in small pots for best results. Give plenty of water in spring, summer, and autumn; in winter let the soil go almost dry. Feed monthly during warm weather. Mist the foliage frequently and check for mealy bugs, which adore wax plants. Do not remove stems on which flowers have been produced; they are also the source of next season's bloom. Propagate by cuttings in spring.

To encourage bloom:
Grow in small well-drained clay pots; crushed brick can be added to the bottom of the pot to improve drainage. Do not prune or move the plant once in bud. Keep cooler (55°F, 13°C) during winter months.

Right: **Hoya bella**
This fine plant has waxy clusters of fragrant white-purple flowers that perfume a room. Especially rewarding in hanging baskets.

Hoya carnosa
(Wax plant)
- **Intermediate conditions**
- **For everyone**
- **Easy to bloom**

Above: **Hoya carnosa**
The popular wax plant is noted for its fragrant waxy flowers. Mature specimens bloom for months.

These attractive vines, with leathery leaves and charming clusters of fragrant white flowers, are old favorites. They can reach up to 20ft (6m), and make magnificent showy plants for summer bloom. Only mature plants are likely to bloom; young ones (2 years or under) seldom do. Best grown on a trellis or support, but is also handsome in hanging baskets.

Grow in bright light; use a standard houseplant soil and grow potbound. Give plenty of water during growth but in winter let the soil go almost dry. Do not remove the stem or spur on which flowers have been produced – this is the source of next year's bloom. Do not feed. Mist foliage frequently to ward off mealy bugs. Propagate by taking stem cuttings in spring.

To encourage bloom:
Buy mature plants. Do not prune at all – this will check flowering. Maintain good light as buds form.

Hyacinthus orientalis
(Hyacinth)
- **Cool conditions**
- **For beginners**
- **Easy to bloom**

Erect bulbous plants with 10in (25cm) stems, hyacinths have long narrow leaves. Flower spikes are closely packed with waxy, very fragrant flowers available in shades of red, blue and yellow and white. Can be forced to bloom in spring or winter but only once – then they should be planted outside. Many varieties are available.

Grow at a bright window – sun is not necessary. Use a potting mix of equal parts of soil and humus that drains readily. Water freely when the plant is growing. Pot bulbs in September for Christmas flowering; keep cool (50°F, 10°C) and in a dark place until growth is under way, then bring out into the light. Rest for 8 weeks after flowering; leave in the pot in a cool (50°F, 10°C) place. Do not feed. Grow new plants from offsets. Can also be grown over water.

To encourage bloom:
The cool, dark period of 8–10 weeks after the bulbs have been potted is vital for forcing bulbs for Christmas; without it the plants will not make sufficient root to support tall flowers.

Photo left: **Hyacinthus orientalis**
The very fragrant packed flower spikes make hyacinths an indoor favorite. Varieties are available in many colors. Take your pick from white, yellow, pink or blue.

Hydrangea macrophylla

(Common hydrangea; house hydrangea; snowball flower)

- **Cool conditions**
- **For beginners**
- **Easy to bloom**

Hydrangeas are large-leaved shrubs with showy clusters of white, blue or pink flowers. They are bushy, grow to about 24in (60cm) and bloom in spring and summer.

Grow in sun; use a rich potting mix of equal parts of soil and humus. Water freely when in growth and feed every 2 weeks. Keep cool (65 °F, 18°C), and be sure there is good circulation of air. After plants bloom, cut back shoots to 2 joints; repot in slightly acid soil and set outdoors; feed and keep the soil moist.

After the first frost, store indoors in a shady, cool place, and water about once a month. In January increase warmth, light and water. When the plant is actively growing, move to a window. The degree of soil acidity determines the coloring of the pink and blue varieties. A pink plant can be made blue by changing the soil to an acid pH 5.5. New plants from suppliers or take stem cuttings.

To encourage bloom:
Observe cool growing conditions and winter rest period.

Below: **Hydrangea macrophylla Lacecap type**
Shrubby plants with fine clusters of pink, blue or white flowers; a traditional and successful houseplant for cool rooms.

Hypocyrta glabra

- **Intermediate conditions**
- **For everyone**
- **Easy to bloom**

This very popular 15in (38cm) plant, related to *H. strigillosa*, has small leathery bright green leaves, and fascinating orange flowers in summer. Very easy to grow, this pleasing little plant adds a touch of the unusual to the indoor garden. Not to be missed.

Grow in a bright but not sunny window all year except in winter, when some sun is necessary. Use equal parts of small-grade fir bark and soil. Water, allow to dry out, and water again. Feed every 2 weeks except after bloom; then allow to rest a few months with no feeding. After bloom, pinch back plants by about 4in (10cm) to encourage new growth. Provide additional misting in summer. Grow new plants from tip cuttings in spring.

To encourage bloom:
Provide good sun in winter.

Below: **Hypocyrta glabra**
Known for their goldfish shaped orange flowers, hypocyrtas are compact plants; the leathery shiny leaves of this species makes it handsome even when not in bloom.

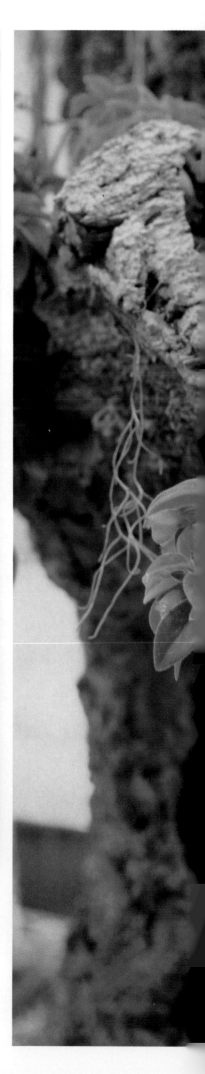

Hypocyrta nummularia
(Goldfish plant; kiss me plant)
- **Warm conditions**
- **For everyone**
- **Difficult to bloom**

Similar to *H. strigillosa,* this epiphytic species grows to 30in (75cm). It has small dark green leaves, and reddish orange flowers in spring. It blooms more freely than most hypocyrtas.

Grow in bright light all year except in winter, when sun is essential. Plant this epiphyte in equal parts of small-grade fir bark and soil. Keep the soil evenly moist all year, and feed every 2 weeks in the warm months. Prune back slightly after blooming to encourage new growth. The plant has a branching habit. Propagate from tip cuttings taken in early spring. It is best to root several cuttings in one pot.

To encourage bloom:
Give winter sun.

Above: **Hypocyrta nummularia**
A mass of reddish-orange flowers in spring, this is the most free-flowering of all the hypocyrtas.

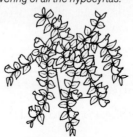

Hypocyrta strigillosa
((Kiss me plant)
- **Warm conditions**
- **For everyone**
- **Easy to bloom**

This trailing epiphyte from Central America grows to 24in (60cm). It has small leathery glossy green leaves, and goldfish-shaped reddish orange flowers in spring. Unusual; good for growing in hanging baskets.

Place the goldfish plant at a bright window all year except in winter, when sun is essential. Grow in equal parts of small-grade fir bark and soil. Water, allow to dry out, and water again. Feed every 2 weeks when in growth. After bloom, pinch back the plant slightly to encourage new growth. Flowers appear on new growth in very early spring.

Propagate by tip cuttings of new growth in spring.

To encourage bloom:
Give winter sun. Rest during the winter months at 60°F (16°C).

Photo left: **Hypocyrta strigillosa**
A trailing plant with small leaves and oddly shaped orange-red flowers.

Impatiens walleriana
(Busy Lizzie; patience plant; patient Lucy; snap weed; sultana; touch-me-not)
- **Intermediate conditions**
- **For beginners**
- **Easy to bloom**

This shrubby plant grows to 24in (60cm) and is an excellent indoor subject. Leaves are dark green and flowers generally in shades of red, also white. Many hybrids are available. Flowers appear on and off throughout the year, and first begin to open in midsummer.

Grow in a bright window, but sun is not needed. Use a loose houseplant soil – drainage must be perfect or plants suffer. Water heavily during growth (allowing soil to dry out between waterings), but keep barely moist in winter and move to a cool place, 60°F (16°C). After blooming, cut back the plant to about 4in (10cm) and topdress with soil and grow on again. Propagate by taking cuttings or sowing seed in spring.

Above: **Impatiens walleriana**
One of the easiest houseplants to grow, busy Lizzie produces red or white flowers throughout the year. Easy to propagate from cuttings.

To encourage bloom:
Do not pamper – allow soil to dry out between waterings. Young plants often produce the most flowers – keep a supply of young plants coming along from cuttings.

Ipomoea violacea
(Morning glory)
- **Intermediate conditions**
- **For a challenge**
- **Difficult to bloom**

An outdoor climber, morning glory can be grown in tubs indoors for beautiful flowers all through the warm months. Plants can grow up to 8ft (2.4m) and need support; leaves are large and glossy, and flowers brilliant blue-purple in color. Beautiful accent for indoors.

Grow morning glories in your most sunny window – without good light they will not bloom. Use a rich mix – equal parts of soil and humus – and be sure drainage is almost perfect. These are thirsty plants that need copious watering. Feed weekly during growth; not at all the rest of the time. Plants die down somewhat in winter – allow to rest with little water in a cooler location (50°F, 10°C). Resume watering with warm weather; it is best to repot at this time. Grow new plants from seed started in spring; soak for 24 hours before sowing to aid germination.

To encourage bloom:
Give ample sun and good ventilation.

Left: **Ipomoea violacea**
Beautiful violet-blue flowers create a sensational display at windows in summer when you grow the morning glory. Provide a suitable support.

Iris reticulata
- **Cool conditions**
- **For a challenge**
- **Difficult to bloom**

These outdoor irises can be grown indoors in small pots. Plants are 6in (15cm) high and have grassy foliage, and beautiful violet purple flowers in early spring. Unusual, and worthy of any indoor garden. They are not easy to grow, but not impossible – give them a try.

Irises need a bright window with ample light – in shade they will not prosper. Use a potting medium of equal parts of sand and soil. Keep quite moist all year except after bloom – then allow to die down naturally by reducing water. Store in a dark place for a few months and then repot in fresh soil for a new growing season. Do not feed. New plants from offsets when repotting bulbs in spring or autumn.

To encourage bloom:
Observe resting times. Keep really cool (00°F, 00°C) until buds color.

Right: **Iris reticulata 'Harmony'**
Best known as an outdoor plant, this iris can also decorate your rooms. Vividly colored flowers make it a must for the adventurous gardener.

Ixia speciosa
(Corn lily; grass lily)
- **Cool conditions**
- **For a challenge**
- **Difficult to bloom**

This bulbous plant is lovely, with grassy green foliage up to 24in (60cm), and large clusters of deep crimson flowers in late spring; hybrids extend the color range into white, cream, yellow, blue, and purple. Generally an outdoor plant, it does well in pots and makes a colorful statement at the window.

Grow at a west or east window; use a potting mix that drains well – standard houseplant soil is fine. Plants do best in small clay pots, 4–5in (10–12.5cm), planting 2 corms to a pot. Water sparsely at first, but when foliage starts to grow increase the watering. Do not feed. After it blooms, allow the plant to die back naturally; store in a cool dry place for 8 to 10 weeks. Repot in fresh soil. A truly handsome plant, and the flowers are excellent for cutting.

To encourage bloom:
Observe resting time and grow in really cool conditions (50°F, 10°C).

Left: **Ixia speciosa**
The rich crimson blooms of the corn lily provide dazzling indoor color in late spring. Very free-flowering, but it must be kept cool all the time.

Jacobinia carnea

(Brazilian plume; king's crown)
- **Intermediate conditions**
- **For everyone**
- **Easy to bloom**

This 30in (75cm) plant from Brazil
has downy green leaves, and
plumes of pink flowers that last a few
days. Hardly a spectacular plant, but
pleasing for the indoor garden if you
have extra space.

Grow in a sunny window. Pot in
standard houseplant soil. Keep
evenly moist all year; feed every
2 weeks. Plants suffer from lack of
water, so keep well watered.
Ventilate when the temperature
exceeds 70°F (21°C). Most plants
last only a year or so and then
decline. Take tip cuttings in spring for
new plants; discard the old ones.

To encourage bloom:
Provide plenty of sun.

Below: **Jacobinia carnea**
*A handsome Brazilian plant with dark
green leaves and plumes of pink
flowers. Nice amenable plant for a
sunny window, not spectacular.*

Ixora coccinea

(Flame of the woods; Indian jasmine)
- **Cool conditions**
- **For beginners**
- **Easy to bloom**

This robust houseplant grows to 30in
(75cm), and has bright green
rounded leaves, and clusters of
brilliant red flowers in early summer.
Easy to grow and very rewarding, as
even young plants will bloom.

Grow in sun. Use a potting mix of
equal parts of lime-free soil and
humus. Keep quite moist during
growth but barely wet in winter. Feed
every 2 weeks during growth. Group
several plants together for a lovely
show. Some plants bloom on and off
throughout the year if conditions are
good. Prefers a cool environment—
60°F (16°C). Outstanding hybrids
include *Ixora* 'Super King' and 'Peter
Rapsley'. Start new plants from
cuttings taken in spring.

To encourage bloom:
Give plenty of sun and humidity. Do
not move plants or buds may drop.

Above: **Ixora 'Peter Rapsley'**
*An undemanding plant with upright
growth and beautiful clusters of red
flowers in early summer. A charming
plant, not to be missed.*

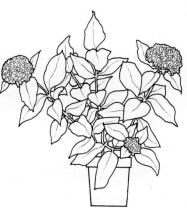

Jasminum polyanthum

(Pink jasmine)
- **Intermediate conditions**
- **For everyone**
- **Easy to bloom**

This beautifully fragrant jasmine has
mid-green leaves and white and pale
pink flowers from autumn to spring.
Plants climb to 10ft (3m) or more and
need support. This is a good offbeat
plant for the indoor garden.

Grow jasmine in sun – otherwise it
will not do well and will not flower.
Use a rich potting mix of equal parts
of humus and soil. Feed with acid
fertilizer every month during growth.
Mist foliage occasionally and give
pots a deep soaking in the sink once
a month. Provide ample humidity (50
percent). Repot every second year.
New plants from cuttings in spring.

To encourage bloom:
Provide ample sun and very good
ventilation. Keep cooler in winter
(55°F, 13°C) during flowering.

Right: **Jasminum polyanthum**
*A splendid climbing plant from China
with fragrant white and pale pink
flowers. It grows to a large size and
needs support for good display.*

140

Jatropha podagrica
(Guatemala rhubarb)
● **Intermediate conditions**
● **For a challenge**
● **Difficult to bloom**

Above: **Jatropha podagrica**
*A tropical evergreen shrub with
unusual clusters of scarlet flowers
borne on long stalks. A stimulating
addition to any indoor garden.*

A succulent plant of the euphorbia
family, *J. podagrica* has dark green
leathery leaves, and small scarlet
flowers in long red-stalked clusters
in mid-spring — a brilliant display at
any window. It grows up to 40in (1m)
tall. Not easy to grow, but an
excellent garden room subject for
the more adventurous..

Grow in sun; it needs plenty of
light to bear flowers. Use a potting
mix of equal parts of houseplant soil
and humus. Plants require copious
watering during growth; in winter,
allow to dry out somewhat. Be sure
drainage is perfect; waterlogged soil
is harmful to this plant. Feed every 2
weeks during growth only. Start new
plants from cuttings in spring.

To encourage bloom:
Give plenty of water when growing,
but ensure drainage is perfect.

Kalanchoe blossfeldiana
(Flaming Katy; Tom Thumb)

● **Intermediate conditions**
● **For beginners**
● **Easy to bloom**

This 12in (30cm) succulent has leathery green leaves, and bright red flowers in winter, making it especially appealing. Bloom sometimes occurs again in spring. Hybrids are available with pink, white or yellow flowers.

Grow at a bright window, but sunlight can scorch this plant. Use a standard houseplant soil – add one cup of sand to a 6in (15cm) pot. Do not feed. Allow soil to dry out between waterings. Do not mist plants, as the succulent leaves will be harmed. Any water on the base of the plant or foliage can cause rot. Provide good ventilation. Trim back bottom leaves when they become too thick. Repot every second year. New plants from seed in spring or stem cuttings in summer.

To encourage bloom:
Do not overwater at any time, but especially in winter.

Left: **Kalanchoe blossfeldiana**
Beautiful clusters of bright red flowers make this a stunning addition to the indoor garden.

Kalanchoe pumila
● **Intermediate conditions**
● **For beginners**
● **Easy to bloom**

This dwarf plant, up to 6in (15cm) high, is valued for its winter blooming red-purple flowers. The leaves are gray with a waxy bloom. It is a good basket plant.

Grow in bright light – sun is not needed. Use a potting mix of equal parts of sand and soil, and be sure drainage is good. Water freely during most of the year except in February, when watering can be tapered off slightly. Do not feed. Avoid getting water on the fleshy leaves, or they might rot. New plants from cuttings in summer or seeds in spring.

To encourage bloom:
Give plenty of sun.

Above: **Kalanchoe pumila**
Here is a plant that can take almost any indoor situation and survive – with beauty. Flowers are reddish purple, small leaves oval. Makes an excellent basket plant.

Kohleria amabilis
(Tree gloxinia)

● **Warm conditions**
● **For a challenge**
● **Difficult to bloom**

This fine 16in (40cm) gesneriad has bright green leaves, and pink flowers in spring and summer. It is best grown in a hanging basket, where it makes a lovely show.

Grow in bright light, but sun is not necessary. Use a rich soil mix of equal parts of humus and soil. Drainage must be good. Water heavily during growth, much less the rest of the time – about once a week – but never allow the soil to become bone dry. Do not mist plants, as this can rot the hairy leaves. Take tip cuttings for new plants, or large rhizomes may be separated and single scales planted like seeds.

Above: **Kohleria amabilis**
A gesneriad with lovely green leaves and beautiful pink flowers.

To encourage bloom:
Grow warm and humid.

Laelia anceps
● **Intermediate conditions**
● **For everyone**
● **Easy to bloom**

This is a showy orchid, with leathery leaves, and fine 4in (10cm) fragrant pink flowers in summer or autumn. It makes a handsome plant and the flowers last for weeks. It is generally an amenable houseplant, a sterling orchid for the beginner, and sure to please in any indoor garden.

Grow in full sun, as it needs really good light. Use a potting mix of medium-grade fir bark. Keep moist all year. Do not feed, but mist this plant with tepid water to promote good humidity. Repot only every third year. Rarely bothered by insects – leaves are too tough. Buy new plants from specialists or divide mature plants (with over 7 growths).

Above: **Laelia anceps**
A large orchid but well worth its space; bears 4in (10cm) pink flowers that last for two months or more on the plant. Very showy in bloom.

To encourage bloom:
Give plenty of sun, and a winter resting period with slightly cooler and drier conditions.

Laelia Gouldiana
- **Intermediate conditions**
- **For everyone**
- **Easy to bloom**

A popular 30in (75cm) orchid, this bears large lilac pink flowers in autumn; the leaves are leathery. The plant can be depended on to bloom and is an ideal indoor subject.

Grow this orchid at your sunniest window—it must have direct sun rays to bloom. Pot in medium-grade fir bark, kept quite moist in warm months, but not so moist in autumn and winter. Provide ample ventilation and good humidity (40 percent). Do not feed. Repot only every fourth year. This plant is never bothered by insects. New plants from suppliers.

To encourage bloom:
Must have sun.

Photo left: **Laelia Gouldiana**
This fine orchid from Brazil has 5in (12.5cm) lilac pink flowers; it is an ideal windowsill plant and grows for years indoors without trouble.

Lantana camara
(Common lantana; shrub verbena; yellow sage)
- **Intermediate conditions**
- **For everyone**
- **Difficult to bloom**

This is a colorful pot plant up to 36in (90cm) with oval wrinkled leaves and many 2in (5cm) wide flat clusters of yellow and orange flowers in spring and summer. Many hybrids are available with white, pink, or red flowers. A good accent plant in the indoor garden.

Grow on a sunny windowsill—it needs direct light to bloom. Pot in standard packaged soil. Water evenly throughout the year but never allow the soil to become soggy. Feed every 2 weeks in warm months, not at all the rest of the year. Propagate from cuttings or seed in spring.

Above: **Lantana camara**
Lantanas make fine indoor plants, with their yellow and orange flowers and rather odd wrinkled leaves. Good for your brightest window.

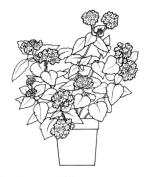

To encourage bloom:
Grow in sun. Observe a winter rest period at 50°F (10°C).

Lapageria rosea
(Copihue; Chilean bellflower)
● **Cool conditions**
● **For a challenge**
● **Difficult to bloom**

A vining plant to 10ft (3m) with leathery dark green leaves and handsome funnel shaped crimson flowers spotted white inside. A white-flowered variety is also available. Plants bloom on and off through summer and autumn, and make quite a sight at the window. Can tolerate abuse if necessary and still bloom. Excellent indoor plant.

Grow in a shady exposure – a north window is satisfactory, or a west exposure. Too much sun will burn the leaves. Use a rich lime-free potting mix of equal parts of humus and houseplant soil. Keep quite moist with lime-free water in spring, summer and autumn. In winter allow the plant to rest. Provide suitable support, such as a trellis. Feed moderately, about 4 times a year. These robust plants bloom best in the second year in new conditions.

Leptospermum scoparium
(Manuka; tea tree)
● **Cool conditions**
● **For everyone**
● **Easy to bloom**

An evergreen shrub growing to 40in (1m), *L. scoparium* has dark green oblong leaves, and white 5-petaled flowers in summer. Cultivars are available with pink and red flowers. Only mature plants bear flowers. Many varieties. Easily grown once established. Makes a good specimen plant.

This plant needs a sunny window – a south exposure is fine. Grow in equal parts of humus and soil, and water evenly. The soil should never be too soggy or too dry. Feed monthly with plant food. This plant can tolerate coolness(45°F, 7°C) if necessary. Generally it is easily grown indoors and rarely bothered by insects. Repot every third year. New plants from cuttings in spring.

Get new plants from seed or by layering shoots in spring.

To encourage bloom:
Grow plants in small pots.

Photo left: **Lapageria rosea**
The beautiful flowers of this vining plant – here the red with the white-flowered variety – make a stunning show in summer and autumn.

To encourage bloom:
For best results buy mature plants (several years old).

Right: **Leptospermum scoparium**
White five-petaled flowers are borne by this rather large bushy plant in summer, and the dark green leaves act as a perfect foil.

Lilium auratum
(Golden-rayed lily)
● **Cool conditions**
● **For a challenge**
● **Difficult to bloom**

These showy bulbous plants, up to 48in (120cm) tall, have trumpet-shaped fragrant white flowers striped with gold, and strap shaped leaves. Many hybrids have been developed and most are excellent in the home. Fine cut flowers.

Pot the bulbs in equal parts of humus and lime-free soil in autumn and keep cool (50–60°F, 10–16°C) until growth is 4in (10cm) high. Then move to bright light and slightly warmer conditions; keep the medium moist until flowering time and leaves start to yellow; then keep just moist with lime-free water in cool conditions (55°F, 13°C) until autumn. Do not feed. Provide ample air circulation. Repot bulbs each year in fresh potting soil.

To encourage bloom:
Start in shade and coolness. Be sure to plant the bulb at least 5in (12.5cm) deep; this lily develops secondary roots from the stem that feed and maintain the flowers.

Photo left: **Lilium auratum**
What could be nicer than these fine large white lilies in the home? In pots they add a colorful note to the window garden during the summer.

Lithops
(Living stone; pebble plant; stone face)
- **Warm conditions**
- **For a challenge**
- **Difficult to bloom**

Lithops is a genus of 50 succulent plants from South Africa that resemble small stones. Most grow no more than a few inches tall and have fleshy leaves. Daisy-like white or yellow flowers appear in autumn. Unusual. For a good display grow several plants together. There are many species and varieties.

These plants need the sunniest window you have. Grow in equal parts of sand, soil and gravel. Water just enough to keep the medium barely moist, but never soggy; plants die quickly if watered too much. Do not feed. Grow warm; use small pots. Plants appreciate an area with good air circulation Get new plants by sowing seed in spring.

To encourage bloom:
Give ample sun; do not overwater. Rest throughout the winter at 40°F (4°C) with no water at all.

Below: **Lithops**
Perhaps boasting the largest blooms of any tiny plant, lithops create a sensation at the window with their bright yellow or white flowers. Well worth the extra care needed.

Lobivia aurea
(Golden lily cactus)
- **Warm conditions**
- **For everyone**
- **Easy to bloom**

This globular cactus is about 4in (10cm) tall with closely ribbed dark green stems and light brown spines. Lovely golden-yellow flowers open to 2in (5cm) across in summer. A fine indoor plant.

Grow this cactus in your sunniest spot. Pot in equal parts of sand and soil. Water freely during the summer months. Be sure drainage is good. Do not feed. Do not get water on the plant, or rot may result. It can be depended upon to bloom if given sufficient sun and less water in winter. Grow new plants from offsets or seed in spring. Dry offsets for a few days if not already rooted.

To encourage bloom:
Observe winter rest time, and provide a temperature of 40°F (4°C).

Right: **Lobivia aurea**
This cactus is not difficult to bloom indoors, and bears colorful, though short-lived, yellow flowers.

Lycaste aromatica
(Cinnamon orchid)
- **Intermediate conditions**
- **For everyone**
- **Easy to bloom**

This charming 14in (35cm) orchid from Mexico is ideal for home growing, taking little space. The 2in (5cm) yellow scented flowers stay fresh for three weeks. Leaves are semideciduous and papery thin. A mature plant bears as many as 30 flowers in early spring. An excellent houseplant, sure to please.

Grow the cinnamon orchid at a bright window, but sun is not necessary. Use medium-grade fir bark as a potting mix, and a 5–6in (12.5–15cm) clay pot is fine for the container. Keep the mix evenly moist all year except in January, when little water should be given until flower buds show: then increase watering. Rest severely with only scant moisture after bloom, until you see new growth starting, and then resume watering. Do not feed. Repot only when absolutely necessary – this plant hates to be disturbed. Provide good humidity (about 40 percent) and maintain good air circulation. Rarely bothered by insects. New plants by division in spring (only a mature plant) or buy from specialist orchid suppliers.

To encourage bloom:
Observe resting times after the plant has finished flowering.

Photo left: **Lycaste aromatica**
This popular small orchid with perky yellow flowers is an excellent plant for those new to orchid growing.

149

Mammillaria zeilmanniana
(Rose pin cushion)
- **Warm conditions**
- **For beginners**
- **Easy to bloom**

A 4in (10cm) diameter globular cactus, this fine plant bears violet flowers in summer. Not difficult to coax into bloom if given a cold period in winter, after which even small plants will bloom. Nice indoor accent for limited space.

This cactus needs sun and plenty of it – place it in a south window. Pot in equal parts of soil and sand and dress the top with chipped gravel. Water moderately in summer and do not feed. Likes a buoyant atmosphere and requires artificial light in autumn to bear flowers. In winter rest it in cool conditions with little water. Grow new plants from offsets freely produced in spring.

Above: **Mammillaria zeilmanniana**
White and brick red spines decorate this cactus, and flowers are violet-red. Very showy. Ideal for beginners and easy to propagate.

To encourage bloom:
Give plenty of sun and keep cool (40°F,4°C) and almost dry throughout the winter.

Manettia bicolor
(Candy corn plant; firecracker plant; firecracker vine)
- **Intermediate conditions**
- **For beginners**
- **Easy to bloom**

This vining plant, which with pruning can be kept to 40in (1m) tall, has narrow shiny green leaves, and bright scarlet tubular flowers tipped with yellow from late spring to autumn. A nice plant if you have space for it.

Grow the firecracker plant in a fairly shady place – a west or north window is fine. Use standard packaged houseplant soil. Water freely all year but do not let the soil get soggy. Feed every 2 weeks during warm months. Use a small trellis support to train the plant. Mist occasionally with tepid water to maintain good humidity. Grow new plants from cuttings taken in spring.

Right: **Manettia bicolor**
A vining plant with scarlet and yellow flowers, Manettia graces many windows in late spring to autumn.

To encourage bloom:
Give plenty of water when growing.

Masdevallia coccinea
- **Cool conditions**
- **For everyone**
- **Easy to bloom**

One of the famous cool growing orchids, this is a showy plant in winter with its 2in (5cm) lilac to scarlet flowers. The leaves are straplike, and grow to about 12in (30cm). A true beauty of nature.

This plant likes a shady place in an airy situation. Plant in small-grade fir bark. Keep evenly moist all year – do not allow to dry out. Use clay pots. Provide ample humidity (about 40 percent) and mist plants with tepid water in warm weather. Do not feed. Repot every third year but use the same small pot: overpotting results in sparse flowering. Never bothered by insects but occasionally, if grown too damp, leaf rot may result. Must have ample ventilation to thrive. Get new plants by division in spring.

Above: **Masdevallia coccinea**
Beautiful flowers shaped like kites make this plant look very unlike the orchid it is. Handsome foliage; certainly worth space in cool situations.

To encourage bloom:
Grow in small pots, 3–4in (7.5-10cm) in diameter for best results.

Medinilla magnifica
(Love plant; rose grape)
- **Intermediate conditions**
- **For a challenge**
- **Difficult to bloom**

This lush green-blue leafy plant, up to 40in (1m) tall, has pendulous panicles of carmine flowers in pink bracts, generally in spring but blossoming can also occur in late summer. Only recently available from suppliers, the love plant is showy and worth its space at a window. A real display of color.

This plant likes a very bright spot at your wihdow, but sun is not necessary. Use a potting mix of equal parts of soil and humus that drains rapidly: stagnant soil can ruin the plant. Keep soil evenly moist except in winter, when it should be barely moist but never bone dry. Give a winter rest period at 60°F (16°C). Feed every 2 weeks when in growth. Provide ample humidity, as this plant likes moisture in the air. Rarely bothered by insects. Propagate by cuttings or buy young plants from suppliers.

To encourage bloom:
Keep in humid conditions. Only mature plants will bloom.

Right: **Medinilla magnifica**
And magnificent it is in bloom, with pendulous panicles of carmine flowers in pink bracts. A real find, which always causes comment.

Miltonia 'Peach Blossom'
(Pansy orchid)
- **Cool conditions**
- **For everyone**
- **Easy to bloom**

Growing to 12in (30cm), this fine small plant has grassy leaves and lovely flat-faced 2in (5cm) pink flowers, several to a stem. Bloom is generally in autumn, but the plant may bear flowers in summer some years. Many *Miltonia* hybrids are available. They make excellent pot plants for the indoor garden.

This plant likes a bright but not sunny location where there is excellent ventilation – it does not thrive in a stagnant place. Grow in medium-grade fir bark kept moist all year, and spray the growing area with tepid water to maintain humidity of not less than 40 percent. Do not feed. Dry out slightly after flowering but never allow the fir bark to

Above: **Miltonia 'Peach Blossom'**
A fine small orchid with flat-faced pink flowers, large for the size of the plant. A popular variety.

become bone dry. Rarely bothered by insects, this is generally a most amenable plant. Get new plants from suppliers or by division.

To encourage bloom:
Grow in a well-ventilated and bright place. Provide humid conditions.

Miltonia roezlii

(Pansy orchid)
- **Intermediate conditions**
- **For everyone**
- **Easy to bloom**

A 12in (30cm) orchid with blue-green leaves, this plant bears pansy shaped white flowers marked with purple in autumn. It is very pretty, and takes up little space, making it ideal for windows. A gem not to be missed for dependable bloom.

Grow this orchid at a west window – some sun is needed but no direct rays. Pot in medium-grade fir bark; be sure drainage is good. Water thoroughly and then allow to dry out before watering again. Do not feed. Keep cooler and drier in winter. Rarely bothered by insects. Get new plants from suppliers or division.

To encourage bloom:
Allow to dry out a little in winter in cool temperatures (50°F, 10°C).

Above: **Miltonia roezlii**
An easy orchid to grow in most situations, this miltonia has white flowers tinged with purple, which last many weeks on the plant.

153

Narcissus tazetta 'Paper White'
- ● Cool conditions
- ● For beginners
- ● Easy to bloom

Nothing is as pretty as these winter flowering beauties to liven a room. Plants grow to 20in (50cm) tall from bulbs, and the flowers are sweetly scented. In handsome trays, they make an ideal room decoration for Christmas. Very easy to grow.

Grow in gravel, bulb fiber or soil in autumn, in shallow bowls. Plant bulbs with tips showing. Water little at first and keep in a dark, cool place at 50°F (10°C). When leaves are 4in (10cm) high move to bright light and warmer conditions. Keep the medium uniformly moist at all times. After blooming, the plants are discarded. Other cultivars are available in different colors and all are handsome to grow.

To encourage bloom:
Start in a cool, shady place, then move to light and warmer conditions after 6 to 8 weeks. Do not allow to dry out while they are growing.

Below: **Narcissus tazetta 'Paper White'**
Even the novice gardener can bring this lovely white-flowering plant into bloom indoors. The sweet fragrance is an additional bonus.

Neomarica caerulea
(Apostle plant; walking iris)
- ● Intermediate conditions
- ● For a challenge
- ● Difficult to bloom

With fragrant blue flowers on tall stalks and straplike foliage, this lovely plant grows to 40in (1m). It is difficult, but not impossible, to bloom at home – it just requires a little care.

Place the walking iris at a sunny window; plant in a mix of equal parts of sand and soil that drains readily. Keep evenly moist all year and provide ample humidity – spray the plant with tepid water in warm months. Repot only every fourth year. Keep artificial light from the plant in late autumn, or bloom will be thwarted. Feed monthly during the summer only. Rarely bothered by insects. Get new plants by splitting rhizomes in early spring and starting them in a sterile medium.

To encourage bloom:
Be sure no artificial light reaches the plant during the late autumn.

Below: **Neomarica caerulea**
An unusual iris very suitable for house culture. It has straplike foliage and fragrant flowers.

Neoregelia carolinae
- ● Intermediate conditions
- ● For everyone
- ● Easy to bloom

A handsome 12in (30cm) rosette, this bromeliad is valued for its lovely straplike green leaves. The center of the plant turns fiery red at bloom time and tiny pinkish white flowers are borne from the heart of the plant in spring. Very pretty and unusual. Impossible to kill – grows with minimal care. A find.

Grow at a west or east window; pot in equal parts of soil and medium-grade fir bark. Keep potting mix moist – never soggy – and 'vase' of plant filled with water at all times. No resting period is necessary. Do not feed, as it can harm the plant. Provide ample humidity – mist occasionally in warm weather with tepid water. Rarely bothered by insects. New plants from offsets that appear at the base of the plant. Sever when 2in (5cm) high and rooted and pot separately in small clay pots. The parent plant dies after blooming.

To encourage bloom:
Allow the plant to receive some sun.

Right: **Neoregelia carolinae**
Very popular with people who 'cannot grow anything', this plant grows for everyone. Striking red bracts.

Neoregelia carolinae 'Tricolor'

(Blushing bromeliad)

● **Intermediate conditions**
● **For everyone**
● **Easy to bloom**

A fine 30in (75cm) rosette of exquisite foliage, this plant bears tiny pink flowers in the center of the rosette in summer. The leaves, striped yellow and green, are very impressive; they turn red in the center to accompany flowering. An amenable plant sure to please.

Grow this bromeliad in sun – an east or south window is fine. Pot in equal parts of soil and medium-grade fir bark. Keep evenly moist all year. Mist the plant with tepid water in summer. Do not feed. Remove offsets when they are 3in (7.5cm) tall and rooted and pot in separate containers to get new plants.

To encourage bloom:
Ensure plants get some sun.

Right: **Neoregelia carolinae 'Tricolor'**
Perhaps better known for its colorful leaves than for its flowers. The variegated leaves turn red at flowering time. This bromeliad grows in almost any situation. Colorful in one way or another all year.

Nerine bowdenii
- **Cool conditions**
- **For beginners**
- **Easy to bloom**

This beautiful South African bulbous plant reaches 20in (50cm), and has soft pink flowers in the autumn, blooming before foliage starts to grow. Flowers are exotic, several to a cluster, and last several days. Very pretty for that unusual touch indoors.

This plant needs a sunny location; start bulbs in late summer using equal parts of sand and soil. Grow one bulb to a 5in (12.5cm) pot. Water sparsely at first and increase watering as flowers appear and then as leaves mature. Do not feed. Provide good humidity (40 percent) and an airy place for the plant. Allow foliage to ripen naturally and then reduce water somewhat for several months. Repot in fresh soil mix.

To encourage bloom:
Observe summer resting time.

Below: **Nerine bowdenii**
This bulbous plant produces a welcome display of attractive pink flowers in autumn. Very easy to grow and ideal for beginners.

Nerium oleander
(Oleander; rose bay)
- **Intermediate conditions**
- **For everyone**
- **Difficult to bloom**

Growing to 40in (1m), this leafy plant bears fine pink flowers on and off throughout the summer. Forms with lovely white or red flowers are also available. Mature plants are best and generally require little care. Take care when handling the plant, it is extremely poisonous.

Grow oleanders at your sunniest window, because they like heat. Use a potting mix of equal parts of soil and humus. A thirsty plant, the oleander needs plenty of tepid water all year except in winter, when soil should be slightly damp. Feed every other watering. Repot yearly in fresh soil. In October or November cut back the plant to about 10in (25cm), and move to a cooler place at 50 °F (10 °C). Grow new plants from stem cuttings taken in spring or autumn.

To encourage bloom:
Give plenty of water; always tepid. Keep warm and sunny with maximum ventilation in summer.

Below: **Nerium oleander**
Bushy and big but colorful, with pink, white or red flowers at intervals throughout the summer. Mature plants flower best.

Nertera granadensis
(Bead plant; coral bead plant)
- **Cool conditions**
- **For everyone**
- **Easy to bloom**

This small low-growing plant has tiny oval leaves and inconspicuous flowers, followed by bright orange berries that last for many weeks from summer to autumn. The plant is unusual in appearance and a nice complement to more leafy plants. Best grown in hanging baskets. More bizarre than beautiful, but still warranting space indoors.

Grow coral beads in your brightest window – an eastern exposure is fine. Use standard houseplant packaged mix; keep uniformly moist all year. Do not feed. This plant likes humidity, so mist occasionally. Cool conditions are fine (60°, 16°C) and plants are generally easy to grow indoors. Get new plants by division or from seed in spring.

Above: **Nertera granadensis**
Insignificant flowers are followed by this striking display of tightly-packed orange berries, which may last for several weeks. Unusual.

To encourage bloom and fruit:
Do not mist during flowering, it will prevent berries forming. To ensure a good crop of berries, pollinate the flowers using a fine brush.

Nidularium innocentii
(Bird's nest bromeliad)
- **Intermediate conditions**
- **For everyone**
- **Easy to bloom**

A very handsome bromeliad that grows to 20in (50cm) across, *N. innocentii* has finely toothed, strap shaped leaves that become orange-red at the center of the rosette during flowering. The creamy white flowers are small and hidden in the cup of the plant; bloom starts in summer. Several varieties are available.

Grow this bromeliad at a north or west exposure – sun is not needed. Pot in equal parts of lime-free soil and medium-grade fir bark. Keep evenly moist all year. Occasionally mist the foliage with tepid water, and maintain good ventilation. Do not feed. It is rarely bothered by insects. Grow new plants from offsets: cut when 3in (7.5cm) tall and rooted and pot in separate containers.

Right: **Nidularium innocentii 'Striatum'**
One of the fine bromeliads, with rosette growth and attractive multicolored leaves; tiny pink or white flowers appear in the center.

To encourage bloom:
No special requirements.

Notocactus leninghausii

- **Warm conditions**
- **For everyone**
- **Difficult to bloom**

Growing to 5in (12.5cm) across and up to 36in (90cm) tall this fine desert cactus bears lovely yellow flowers in summer. It makes a very suitable indoor subject and lives for years with minimum care.

Grow this cactus at a sunny window – a south or east exposure is fine. Pot in equal parts of sand and soil, and dress the surface with chipped gravel. Water freely in midsummer, not so much the rest of the year. Do not feed. It is rarely attacked by insects. In winter rest the plant in a cool (50°F, 10°C) place with little water but where there is sun. Return it to the window in early spring, and resume watering. Grow new plants from offsets or from seed; start both in spring.

Above: **Notocactus leninghausii**
A very pretty cactus with soft yellowish spines and bright yellow flowers. Only mature plants bloom.

To encourage bloom:
Provide ample sun and winter resting period. Plants must be mature and quite tall before they will bloom.

Notocactus ottonis
(Ball cactus)
● **Intermediate conditions**
● **For everyone**
● **Easy to bloom**

A small 4in (10cm) globe cactus, *N. ottonis* has large 1½in (4cm) yellow flowers in spring, several to a plant. Charming and worthwhile.

Grow at a sunny window; use a potting mix of equal parts of soil, sand and gravel. Topdress the surface of the soil mix with gravel to avoid any possibility of rot at the base of the plant. Keep evenly moist with soft water except in winter, when it needs a 4 to 8 week rest at cooler temperatures – about 60°F (16°C) – and less water. Do not feed. Repot only every fourth year. This plant likes good ventilation, and is sure to bloom if given winter rest and sun. Grow new plants from offsets or from seed; start both in spring.

To encourage bloom:
Grow in small pots with winter rest.

Below: **Notocactus ottonis**
Very easy to grow and a splendid sight in bloom. It produces many offsets, making propagation simple.

Odontioda
● **Cool conditions**
● **For beginners**
● **Easy to bloom**

These hybrids of *Odontoglossum* and *Cochlioda*, up to 12in (30cm) tall, are robust plants with dark green leaves and colorful flowers, as many as 6 or 8 to a stem. There are many varieties, so colors vary greatly, but they are generally mauve-purple. Blooms are stunning and appear in summer and autumn. Flowers can be cut, and will stay fresh in a vase for a week or more.

Grow these orchids in a bright but never sunny place; the plants need good light but direct sun will harm them quickly. Use a potting mix of medium-grade fir bark kept moist all year. Do not feed. Spray plants with tepid water frequently during hot weather. These are cool-loving orchids and heat quickly desiccates them. They prefer temperatures of 50°F (10°C) at night. Get new plants by division in spring.

To encourage bloom:
Grow cool and well-ventilated.

Right: **Odontioda Jumbo 'Mont Millais'**
One of the brilliantly colored hybrids of Odontoglossum and Cochlioda. A stunning indoor plant.

Odontoglossum grande

(Clown orchid; tiger orchid)

● **Cool conditions**
● **For beginners**
● **Easy to bloom**

A popular 18in (45cm) orchid, *O. grande* has leathery dark green leaves, and bears lovely 6in (15cm) brown and yellow flowers in summer that last for several weeks. This is one of the finest orchids for home growing and requires little special care. Ideal for beginners.

Grow the tiger orchid in a bright window. Pot in clay containers, using medium-grade fir bark. Keep the bark moist with lime-free water all year except in winter, when moisture can be reduced somewhat. Provide adequate humidity but do not directly spray the plants, as the bulbs can rot with excessive moisture and gray days. Do not feed. Repot every fourth year.

After plants bloom, allow a definite resting time, keeping the bark barely moist. When new growth starts, increase watering. Rarely bothered by insects. Get new plants by division, or from orchid suppliers.

To encourage bloom:
Observe a 6–7 week resting period.

Below: **Odontoglossum grande**
A most dependable orchid, with large yellow and brown flowers that last for weeks. Sure to bloom.

Oncidium papilio
(Butterfly orchid)
- **Intermediate conditions**
- **For everyone**
- **Easy to bloom**

A fine 18in (45cm) orchid with thick succulent leaves, *O. papilio* bears one handsome 5in (12.5cm) chestnut brown-and-yellow flower per stalk in summer. Mature plants may have several flowers, opening one at a time in succession. A good accent plant at the window.

Grow the butterfly orchid at a bright window – sun is not necessary. Use a potting soil of medium fir bark; small pots are best. Keep the bark evenly moist all year. Do not feed. Provide adequate humidity (40 percent) and be sure the plant is in a well ventilated area. Flowers last a long time cut and placed in a vase of water. A care-free plant sure to please. New plants from orchid suppliers or by division.

To encourage bloom:
Provide good air circulation.

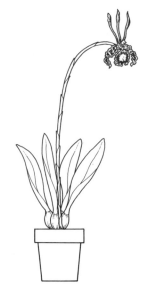

Below: **Oncidium papilio**
Appearing one at a time, each bloom of this orchid sways like a beautiful hovering butterfly. Stunning.

Oncidium ornithorhynchum
- **Cool conditions**
- **For beginners**
- **Easy to bloom**

A charming small orchid about 24in (60cm) tall, with blue-green leaves, *O. ornithorhynchum* bears sprays of tiny lilac-pink fragrant flowers in autumn and winter, hundreds to a plant. Nice spot of color for the indoor garden. Very attractive and desirable and easy to grow.

Grow this orchid at a bright exposure – a west or east window is fine. Pot in medium-grade fir bark. Be sure drainage is good. Water freely in summer months, but not so much the rest of the year. Do not feed. Provide ample humidity (40

Above:
Oncidium ornithorhynchum
Dainty sprays of lilac-pink flowers make this autumn to winter blooming orchid welcome indoors.

percent) and good ventilation. Let the plant rest after flowering. New plants from suppliers or division.

To encourage bloom:
Give winter rest of 4–8 weeks.

Oxalis rubra
(Wood sorrel)
- Cool conditions
- For a challenge
- Difficult to bloom

This small bulbous plant grows to 10in (25cm), with cloverlike leaves, and lovely pink flowers in summer. Flowers close at night and on dull days. It is a pretty little pot plant. Grow several plants to a pot for a special effect.

Grow in sun – a west or south window is fine. Pot in packaged houseplant soil; be sure the drainage is good. Feed every 2 weeks during growth only; in winter allow the plant to rest, with scant waterings. Repot in fresh soil during early spring. Propagate by separating side tubers from the main plant when repotting or from seed planted in autumn.

To encourage bloom:
Give plenty of sun when in growth.

Right: **Oxalis rubra**
Perhaps a weed outdoors, but indoors this is a pretty pot plant, with fine pink flowers in summer.

Pachystachys lutea
(Golden hops; golden shrimp plant; lollipop plant)
● **Intermediate conditions**
● **For everyone**
● **Easy to bloom**

Sometimes known as Jacobinia or Beloperone, this 20in (50cm) plant has lance shaped dark green leaves, and yellow bracts contrasting with white flowers in late summer. It is an easy plant to grow and fine indoors.

Grow at a bright window – an east or west exposure is fine. Use a potting mix of equal parts of soil and humus that drains readily. Water plant freely in warm weather, but allow to dry out between waterings the rest of the year. Feed monthly during warm weather. Prune back occasionally: cut off tip growth 4–6in (10–15cm) to encourage bushiness. After 2 years, start new plants from cuttings in spring. This plant has a tendency to legginess after a time.

To encourage bloom:
No special requirements.

Below: **Pachystachys lutea**
A shrubby plant with lance shaped leaves and clearly marked veins; overlapping yellow bracts protect the white tubular flowers.

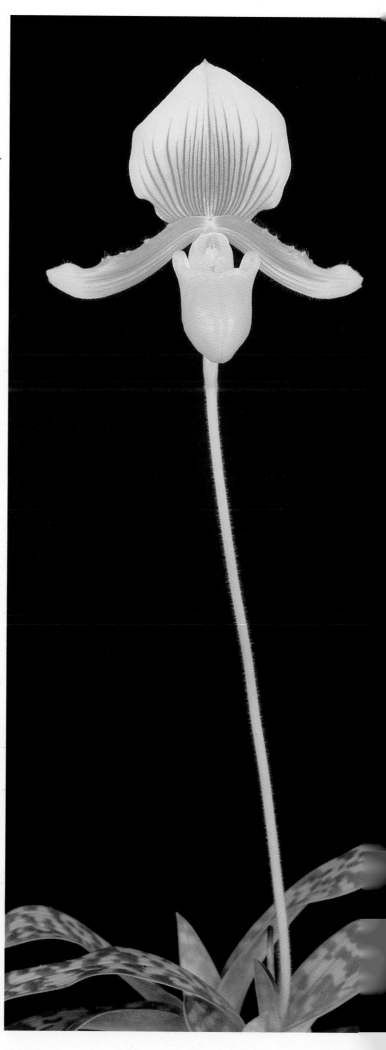

Paphiopedilum maudiae

(Lady's slipper orchid; slipper orchid; Venus' slipper)
- **Cool conditions**
- **For everyone**
- **Easy to bloom**

This 16in (40cm) orchid is a hybrid between *P. callosum* and *P. lawrenceanum*. Leaves are light green and marbled; flowers appear in summer, and are white with delicate green shadings. A very pretty pot plant, and dependable to bloom every year – a real find for the indoor garden.

Grow this orchid at a west or east window – avoid direct sun on the plant. Use a potting mix of equal parts of medium-grade fir bark and soil that drains readily. Water evenly all year. Provide adequate humidity (30 per cent) and mist the plant with water occasionally. Do not feed. It is rarely bothered by insects.

Propagate by careful division once the flowers have died.

To encourage bloom:
Provide good ventilation and adequate humidity.

Photo left:
Paphiopedilum maudiae
Beautiful to behold, a mature plant bears 6 or 7 stunning green and white flowers in summer.

Parodia sanguiniflora

(Prairie fire cactus; Tom Thumb cactus)
- **Warm conditions**
- **For beginners**
- **Easy to bloom**

This pretty little cactus grows to 3in (7.5cm) across, pale green with a white wooly top and white spines. Brilliant red flowers in summer make this a spectacular plant.

Grow in a sunny window. Use a potting mix of equal parts of soil and humus – it likes a rich soil. Be sure drainage is good. Water sparingly, even during growth; too much water can cause rot. In winter, rest in a cool place (50°F, 10°C) and keep the soil just barely moist. Do not feed. Excellent for growing under artificial light. Grow new plants from offsets, seed or buy from suppliers.

To encourage bloom:
Give plenty of sun.

Below: **Parodia sanguiniflora**
Tom Thumb is its name and tiny it is; this pale green globe with wooly top and white spines has fine red flowers, though for a few days only.

Pelargonium
(Geranium)
- ● **Cool conditions**
- ● **For beginners**
- ● **Easy to bloom**

These are popular indoor plants with three main types: zonals (*P. zonale*), regals (*P. grandiflorum*), and the trailing, or ivy-leaved, geraniums (*P. peltatum*). Most are medium-sized plants up to 24in (60cm) tall, and flowers come in many colors, but mainly from the red end of the spectrum. A large versatile group of plants that thrive in cool conditions.

Plants like a sunny place; grow in a rich, slightly alkaline potting mixture of equal parts of humus and soil with some sand added. Be sure the medium drains readily. Water freely, then allow to dry out between waterings. Geraniums bloom best when potbound, so grow in small pots. All types rest in winter; water sparingly then, and do not feed. Keep them at 50°F (10°C). Feed

Below:
Pelargonium peltatum 'Rouletti'
A new bicolored hybrid. Trailing geraniums, ideal for hanging baskets, prefer a little shade.

Passiflora caerulea
(Blue passion flower; common passion flower; passion vine)
- ● **Cool conditions**
- ● **For everyone**
- ● **Difficult to bloom**

Known for its spectacular 3in (7.5cm) flower of beautiful white, blue and purple, this vine grows very rapidly and can become very large. Flowers appear in late summer, followed by attractive orange-yellow fruits. Excellent for and best suited to greenhouse growing.

It needs a fairly bright but not sunny place at the window. Grow in a large tub of packaged soil that drains readily. Water heavily during growth but less in winter, when the plant rests. Feed every 2 weeks when in growth. Supply a suitable trellis support. Grow new plants from cuttings or seed in spring.

To encourage bloom:
Give plenty of water. Rest in winter at 50°F (10°C). If leaves are produced at the expense of flowers, stop feeding and allow the plant to become potbound. It is quite natural for some of the leaves to turn yellow and drop off the plant.

Above: **Passiflora caerulea**
Known for its spectacular 3in (7.5cm) flowers of white, blue, and purple, here is nature at her best. A large vine that needs space.

every other week when in active growth. Avoid overwatering and high humidity; do not mist leaves and provide good ventilation. Grow new plants from seed or cuttings taken in spring for winter bloom; in autumn for spring or summer bloom. Discard old plants, which will decline in flowering vigor.

To encourage bloom:
Provide the cool period in winter. Keep in full sun and do not overwater or overfeed. Keep potbound.

Below: **Pelargonium grandiflorum 'Fanny Eden'**
Large, multicolored flowers make these hybrids a particular favorite.

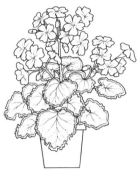

Right: **Pelargonium zonale**
Compact clusters of single or double blooms above ring-marked leaves signify these classic geraniums.

Pentas lanceolata
(Egyptian star cluster; Egyptian star flower)
- **Intermediate conditions**
- **For beginners**
- **Easy to bloom**

An overlooked plant but one with great beauty. Its showy umbels of pink flowers appear on and off throughout the warm months. Hybrids are available with purple and white flowers. Kept to 24in (60cm) with careful pruning, these plants make excellent indoor subjects and add great color to a window. Flowers last a long time when cut and put in a vase of water. Even small plants bloom so these are indeed worthy additions to the indoor garden. An ideal plant for beginners

Grow in plenty of sun – a south window is fine. Use a standard houseplant soil kept evenly moist all year. Feed every 2 weeks when the plants are in active growth. Old plants have a tendency to get leggy so start new ones from stem cuttings taken every spring.

Above: **Pentas lanceolata**
Showy umbels of pink flowers make Pentas a great beauty. A compact and amenable houseplant.

To encourage bloom;
Grow in small clay pots; likes to be potbound. Provide at least 4 hours of sunshine each day.

Petrea volubilis
(Purple wreath; queen's wreath)
- **Intermediate conditions**
- **For a challenge**
- **Difficult to bloom**

This twining 6–8ft (1.8–2.4m) vine has brittle, dark green leaves, and blue flowers in spring and summer – a refreshing sight. The large plant does best in a garden room or greenhouse, where it makes a handsome accent.

Grow at your sunniest window; use a potting mix of equal parts of soil and humus that drains readily. Water heavily in warm weather, not so much the rest of the year. Feed every 2 weeks during the warm months. Have a suitable support for the plant, such as a trellis or pole, and train it to the support. Plants must be 3 to 4 years old to produce a harvest of flowers, so have some patience. Propagate by stem cuttings taken in spring or summer.

To encourage bloom:
Get mature plants.

Right: **Petrea volubilis**
A twining vine, with blue flowers in spring and summer. Needs space and suitable support.

Phalaenopsis hybrids
(Moth orchid)
● **Intermediate conditions**
● **For everyone**
● **Easy to bloom**

A popular and beautiful orchid with straplike broad dark green leaves growing to 14in (35cm) and long stems of flat handsome white, pink or yellow flowers, usually in summer or autumn. It is a favorite of orchid enthusiasts. Flowers last for weeks and a mature plant may bear as many as 100 flowers. Impressive and sure to please.

Grow the moth orchid at a bright window – a west exposure is fine. Sun will desiccate this plant. Pot in medium-grade fir bark and provide excellent humidity (50 percent). Good ventilation is necessary as well. Water evenly throughout the year with a slight drying out in winter. Do not feed. The plant is rarely bothered by insects. New plants from suppliers or by division.

To encourage bloom:
Do not overwater. Allow plant a period of rest in winter.

Left: **Phalaenopsis hybrids**
Now available in yellow, pink, white or 'peppermint' stripes like this P. Hennessy, these are the beauties of the orchid group.

Pittosporum tobira
(Japanese pittosporum)
● **Cool conditions**
● **For everyone**
● **Easy to bloom**

A decorative evergreen plant that will
easily grown to 40in (1m) in a tub, *P.
tobira* has glossy green leaves, and
tiny white flowers in spring that smell
of orange blossom. Where there is
space this makes a fine indoor
accent and is easy to grow. There is
also a variegated one available –
quite handsome.

This evergreen will grow in any
exposure – even succeeding in a
shady window. Use an acid soil. Add
some peat moss to standard
houseplant soil – about 2 cups to a
10in (25cm) container. Water, and
allow to dry out before watering
again. Feed twice monthly all year.
Rarely bothered by insects.
Propagate by heeled stem cuttings
taken in midsummer.

To encourage bloom:
Keep cool in winter (40–50°F,
4–10°C). Provide good ventilation in
summer or place plant outside.

Right: **Pittosporum tobira
'Variegata'**
*The tiny white flowers may not be
spectacular but the superb,
orangelike fragrance makes this a
fine indoor plant.*

Pleione formosana
'Snow White'
● **Cool conditions**
● **For everyone**
● **Easy to bloom**

This is a small terrestrial 10in (25cm)
orchid with ribbed green leaves; it
has lovely flowers in spring or
sometimes in autumn. Plants make
exceptionally good house subjects
and grow easily in 4in (10cm) pots. A
real find for houseplant enthusiasts,
and sure to bloom even when grown
in shaded corners.

Grow in a shady location – a north
window is fine, or a west window with
a little sun. Pot in equal parts of
medium-grade fir bark and soil, and
keep uniformly moist except in
winter, when a resting period of
about 6 weeks with little water is
advisable. It will tolerate and need
coolness (50°F, 10°C). Do not feed.
It is rarely bothered by insects. Grow
new plants from bulbils in spring.

To encourage bloom:
Observe resting time.

Right: **Pleione formosana
'Snow White'**
*Can't grow anything? Try this
exquisite white flowering orchid from
China. Sure to please – with lovely
4in (10cm) blooms in spring.*

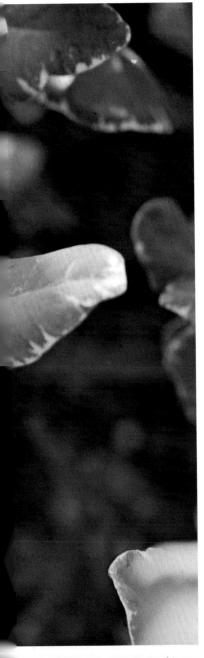

Plumbago auriculata/ capensis

(Blue Cape plumbago; Cape leadwort; leadwort)

● **Cool conditions**
● **For everyone**
● **Easy to bloom**

This large bushy shrub is not spectacular, but it can be depended upon to bear pretty blue flowers in summer. Plants grow to 6ft (1.8m) unless pruned and so do best in large tubs.

Grow at a bright window – direct sun is not necessary. Use standard houseplant soil but be sure drainage is perfect. Give plent of water when in active growth, not so much the rest of the year. In winter cut back to 6–10in (15–25cm). Keep somewhat dry. Feed every 2 weeks in spring and summer; this is a greedy plant. Sometimes attacked by red spider; use suitable precautions. Propagate by heeled stem cuttings.

To encourage bloom:
Get mature plants. Provide winter rest at 45°F (7°C).

Above and right:
Plumbago auriculata/capensis
A dependable but large bushy plant, with plentiful blue or white flowers (depending on variety) in summer. In tubs, it makes a handsome show.

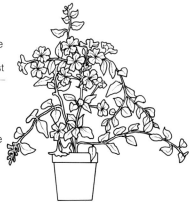

Primula malacoides
(Baby primrose; fairy primrose)
- Cool conditions
- For beginners
- Easy to bloom

With wavy edged circular leaves, this 14in (35cm) plant bears lovely pink, red, purple or white flowers in winter and spring, making it a valuable addition to the indoor garden. Generally an outdoor plant, it also does well in the home if kept really cool. Nice seasonal color.

Select a somewhat shady place for this primula – a west or north window is fine. Grow in standard houseplant soil that drains well. Keep soil moist to the touch; a dry soil will harm the plants. Feed every 2 weeks during the growing season. Grow cool (50°F, 10°C) if possible; warm weather can harm these plants. Occasionally attacked by red spider, so use appropriate remedies. Get new plants by sowing seed in spring.

To encourage bloom:
Keep soil quite moist during growing

period. Good ventilation helps; preferably grow in a cold frame until buds appear, then bring the plants into a cool room in the house.

Right: **Primula malacoides**
Whorls of rose-purple flowers make this outdoor plant an indoor favorite. Handsome wavy edged leaves.

Primula obconica
(Primula)
- Cool conditions
- For beginners
- Easy to bloom

This fine pot plant from China, growing to 12in (30cm) in height, has round hairy leaves and 2in (5cm) purple, red, white or pink flowers in winter and spring. It is a very pretty indoor subject for cool conditions.

Grow in a bright window, or an exposure with a little sun. Keep temperatures as cool as possible (50–60°F, 10–16°C). Provide a soil of equal parts of sand, soil and humus – be sure drainage is perfect. Plants require a great deal of water when growing, not so much the rest of the year. This particular species has leaves that can cause a rash with some people, so handle with gloves. New plants should be started from seed every spring.

Above: **Primula obconica**
An excellent pot plant from China with 2in (5cm) flowers in many colors. Leaves can cause a rash.

To encourage bloom:
Do not allow to dry out. Keep in a very cool and airy place. Feed weekly when about to flower.

Primula vulgaris/ acaulis
(Primrose)
- Cool conditions
- For everyone
- Easy to bloom

Clusters of yellow flowers make this pretty 8in (20cm) plant a desirable one for the window. Blooms appear in spring. Hybrids are available with flowers of various colors including white, pink, red and blue. Primroses make nice accent plants.

Grow in a bright but not sunny window – a west exposure is fine. Pot in packaged houseplant soil. Keep evenly moist all year except in winter, when a drying out is necessary. Feed every 2 weeks during growth. Provide good ventilation. Easily grown in coolness (55°F, 13°C). Grow new plants from seed in spring; they do well when raised under artificial light.

Right: **Primula vulgaris/acaulis**
Flower color of cultivated varieties may be yellow, white, pink, purple or blue. Makes a fine indoor subject.

To encourage bloom:
Keep cool with good ventilation. Grow outside in cool shade after flowering if you want flowers again the following spring.

Rebutia krainziana
(Crown cactus)
- **Warm conditions**
- **For beginners**
- **Easy to bloom**

This miniature cactus is a gem, growing to 2in (5cm) in diameter, with bright red flowers in a circular pattern in summer. It is one of the dependable cacti, sure to please, and it grows under adverse conditions. There are many fine species of *Rebutia*, most of which have red flowers.

This plant needs ample sun in summer to bear flowers, so grow it at a sunny window. Use equal parts of sand and soil for potting and allow 1in (2.5cm) at the top of the pot for a layer of gravel. Water copiously in spring and summer but the rest of the year keep somewhat dry. Feed once a month in warm weather, but not at all the rest of the year. Plants seem immune to any insect attack. Propagate by seeds or offsets.

To encourage bloom:
Give plenty of sun.

Right: **Rebutia krainziana**
Tiny and charming, this ball cactus bears very large red flowers in the summer. Ideal for beginners.

Punica granatum 'Nana'
(Dwarf pomegranate)
- **Intermediate conditions**
- **For beginners**
- **Easy to bloom**

A fine miniature indoor tree, growing to about 14in (35cm) in a pot, the dwarf pomegranate has tiny green leaves, and large bell shaped scarlet flowers in summer followed by small yellow inedible fruits. It is a charming plant for indoors and does well with little care. Plants make handsome bonsai subjects and can be trained with little problem. In summer the pomegranate appreciates an outdoor vacation on a sunny patio or terrace, where it can add beauty to the scene. If this is not possible, ensure that plants kept indoors have good ventilation.

Grow the dwarf pomegranate in sun at a west or south window. Use equal parts of soil and humus for a potting medium. Keep evenly moist throughout the summer and feed

Above: **Punica granatum 'Nana'**
Scarlet red flowers always create a sensation when you grow this miniature pomegranate. Desirable.

every 2 weeks. Rarely bothered by insects. Propagate by heeled stem cuttings or seed in spring.

To encourage bloom:
Keep cool in winter (45°F, 7°C) and reduce amount of water.

Rechsteineria cardinalis
(Cardinal flower)
- **Intermediate conditions**
- **For everyone**
- **Easy to bloom**

An overlooked gesneriad, growing to 24in (60cm), with handsome dark green heart shaped leaves, and brilliant red flowers in summer. The tubular flowers are unusual and highly decorative. An easy indoor plant, sure to please. This is a good plant for the windowsill, neither too large nor too small.

Grow at a bright window, as they like light, but sun can be harmful; a west window is usually ideal. Pot in a loose mix of equal parts of soil and humus, and water heavily in warm weather, not so much the rest of the year. Feed every 2 weeks during growth; provide 50 percent humidity. After plants bloom, leave the tubers in the pot and store them dry in a shady place at 55°F (13°C). Let them rest for about 4 months. When new

Above: **Rechsteineria cardinalis**
An overlooked gesneriad, this fine plant has brilliant red 2in (5cm) flowers for many weeks in summer.

growth starts, repot for next season. Use small pots. Start new plants from seed or division of tubers in spring.

To encourage bloom:
Keep in a cool place in winter.

Reinwardtia trigyna
(Yellow flax)
- Cool conditions
- For a challenge
- Difficult to bloom

Above: **Reinwardtia trigyna**
Sometimes called the yellow petunia, this plant has yellow flowers in spring. Not often seen but worth the search.

Rivina humilis
(Baby pepper; bloodberry; rouge plant)
- Intermediate conditions
- For everyone
- Easy to bloom

Right: **Rivina humilis**
This small plant from tropical America is delicate in appearance and almost everblooming, with white flowers followed by bright red berries. An overlooked plant.

.A splendid spring flowering shrub, up to 30in (75cm) in height, with bright yellow flowers. It has shrubby twining growth; a good offbeat plant.

Grow in shade in spring and summer and then place in sun for the rest of the year. Pot in packaged houseplant soil that drains readily. Mist in summer to provide humidity. Pinch plants back to make them compact. Water freely during growth; also feed moderately during growth. It is sometimes attacked by red spider; use the appropriate remedies. Grow new plants from cuttings taken in spring.

To encourage bloom:
Provide ample humidity. Give winter rest at 55°F (13°C). Place in sun in late summer and during the autumn to ripen the flowering wood.

A fine bushy plant growing to 24in (60cm), with thin textured leaves, and erect spikes of tiny pinkish white flowers blooming from summer to autumn. Red berries follow the flowers to give an extra bonus of color for the indoor garden.

Grow in a bright location — a west window is fine. Pot in packaged soil that drains readily. Water freely in summer, but less during the rest of the year. Feed every 2 weeks when in growth. Provide good ventilation. It is sometimes attacked by red spider; use an appropriate remedy. Grow new plants from seed or cuttings started in spring — artificial light is fine during this early period.

To encourage bloom:
No special requirements.

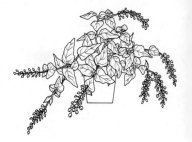

Rosa chinensis minima
(Miniature rose)
● **Cool conditions**
● **For a challenge**
● **Difficult to bloom**

Tiny replicas of the familiar roses, these fine 6–10in (15–25cm) plants have dark green leaves, and 1in (2.5cm) pink flowers in summer and autumn. Many other miniatures have been raised from *Rosa chinensis* in every conceivable color. They are temperamental but worth the time.

Grow miniature roses in a bright sunny window. Pot in equal parts of humus and soil that drains readily. Water freely during growth, but not so much the rest of the year. Feed every 2 weeks when in growth. Cool temperatures are fine (50°F, 10°C). Mist with tepid water to maintain humidity. Watch for red spider mites; if present, use the appropriate remedy. New plants from stem tip cuttings taken in late summer.

Above: **Rosa chinensis minima**
Fine miniature replicas of their outdoor cousins, these tiny roses are charming and full of flowers. Many varieties are now available.

To encourage bloom:
Give plenty of sun. Plunge them outdoors in winter and bring inside when buds show, or allow to rest inside the house at 45°F (7°C).

Ruellia makoyana

- **Intermediate conditions**
- **For everyone**
- **Easy to bloom**

A graceful but overlooked plant with dark green leaves, and pale pink or red flowers from autumn into spring. Desirable for its winter color, it grows to about 24in (60cm). A good accent plant for indoor gardens. Plants are excellent for hanging baskets, and need little care.

Grow in sun; a west or east window is fine. Use a potting mix of standard houseplant soil, and provide good air circulation. Mist the leaves occasionally. Water moderately – allow to dry out between waterings; moisture is needed all year. Feeding is optional. Grow new plants from stem cuttings, which should be taken in spring.

To encourage bloom:
No special requirements.

Below: **Ruellia makoyana**
Don't overlook this beauty; it has dark green leaves and rich pink flowers in autumn. Easy to grow. It should be in every collection.

Russelia equisetiformis

(Coral plant; fountain plant)
- **Intermediate conditions**
- **For everyone**
- **Easy to bloom**

A shrubby plant to 36in (90cm) with grassy leaves, it bears pretty tubular two-lipped flowers with a fiery red corolla at intervals throughout the year. A pretty addition to the indoor garden. Though not a spectacular plant, it is desirable where there is space for it. It is a nice accessory plant, easily grown indoors and good for hanging containers.

Grow the coral plant in a bright window, but sun is not necessary. Use standard houseplant soil and clay pots. Keep the soil evenly moist all year except in winter, when the plant should be cut back to 10in (25cm) and moisture withheld somewhat, though the soil should never be allowed to become bone dry. Do not feed, as this encourages the grassy foliage and thwarts bud formation. Rarely bothered by insects. Propagate by division in spring or stem cuttings in summer.

To encourage bloom:
No special requirements.

Below: **Russelia equisetiformis**
Not often seen but very amenable to indoor culture. It has pretty tubular red flowers. Good for hanging baskets.

Saintpaulia

(African violet)
- **Intermediate conditions**
- **For everyone**
- **Easy to bloom**

These immensely popular gesneriads are free-flowering and dependable indoor plants. Leaves may be somewhat velvety or smooth, scalloped or wavy, lance or heart shaped, variegated or solid green. Flowers are single or double in shades of pink, blue, lavender, purple or white. There are countless hybrids. Plants grow up to 8in (20cm) across the rosette.

Grow African violets at a bright but not sunny window in an area of good air circulation. A little winter sun is fine. Use standard houseplant soil that drains readily, and small pots. Water the soil moderately to keep it slightly moist but never wet. Use tepid water; allow it to stand overnight in a watering can. Feed once a month in spring, summer and autumn; plant food rich in superphosphate will be particularly beneficial. Do not get water on the foliage, it will leave ugly marks. Dry air causes leaf curl and bud drop so maintain good humidity (but do not spray the plants). Turn the plants a quarter round monthly so that all the leaves get light. Easily propagated from leaf cuttings in spring.

To encourage bloom:
Do not pamper – allow to grow naturally. If few flowers are produced, pick them off and keep the plant on a dry regime for 6 weeks. This should induce heavier bloom.

Photo left: **Saintpaulia**
A huge group of favorite plants with varieties in many colors. Also available as miniatures. Perhaps the most popular of houseplants.

Schizanthus pinnatus
(Butterfly flower; poor man's orchid)
● **Cool conditions**
● **For everyone**
● **Easy to bloom**

This outdoor annual, up to 24in (60cm) tall, can be grown indoors in small pots. Leaves are ferny, flowers colorful. Many varieties with blooms in pink, mauve or yellow are available. Fine one-season plant for accent color in the indoor garden. Unusual houseplant and worth a try.

Grow in sunlight – without it, there will be no flowers. Select a south window or grow in a greenhouse. Water freely: soil must be damp to the touch at all times. Feed moderately. Good ventilation will help plants stay healthy. Usual garden insects, such as aphids and thrips, may attack, so use appropriate remedies. Plants are generally not available from suppliers; you should start seed in late summer for a spring display.

To encourage bloom:
Give plenty of sun.

Below: **Schizanthus pinnatus**
Easy to raise from seed, this dazzling outdoor annual can be grown indoors for marvellous spring color.

Schizocentron elegans
(Spanish shawl)
● **Intermediate conditions**
● **For beginners**
● **Easy to bloom**

This is a thoroughly delightful 12in (30cm) plant with dark green hairy leaves and pretty pink-purple flowers, 1in (2.5cm) across, starting in late winter and continuing colorful until early summer. Makes a fine hanging basket plant.

Grow the Spanish shawl in a bright location – a west window is fine. Use a standard houseplant soil and clay pots are best so that water evaporates slowly from the soil. Keep soil reasonably moist all year, never too dry nor too wet. Feed every 2 weeks in warm weather, once a month at other times. Occasionally, trim back the plant to encourage new growth – cut off 3 to 4in (7.5–10cm) of tip growth. Rarely bothered by insects. All in all a very amenable indoor plant. New plants from division of rooted shoots.

To encourage bloom:
Grow potbound.

Right: **Schizocentron elegans**
Blooming at intervals through winter into early summer, this is an easy and colorful pot plant. Not to be missed.

...e different species provide a continuous display of colour throughout the year needs quite a large area.

However, it is possible to have a very attractive display on a much more limited scale in the average garden.

Heaths and heathers belong to the genus Erica. Heaths have small needle-like leaves growing in whorls along the stems whereas heathers have a tiny coniferous type of foliage. Both types are usually called heathers.

There are an enormous [nu]mber of heather species [and] varieties. Their flowers [ran]ge in colour from white [throu]gh yellow and orange to [re]ds and reds and purples. [The]re are also foliage spe[cies] with an equally attractive [range of] colours and variega-

Continuous colour in heaths and heathers

tions. They vary from a few inches high to a couple of feet with an equal spread.

Because you can grow spring, summer, autumn and winter flowering varieties they provide an invaluable source of colour in the garden.

Heaths are hardy and evergreen and stand up well to wind. Bought in containers they can be planted at any time from October to the beginning of April if conditions are good but the earlier the better since the plants then have a good chance to become established by spring.

Avoid planting heathers under trees or in shade and make sure your soil is not limey. Heathers will not grow well in lime although the winter and spring-flowering species will tolerate it in small quantities.

Prepare the ground well, removing all weeds and working in plenty of peat. Do the same for heavy clay soil, breaking it up thoroughly and working in a good quantity of sharp sand as well.

Plants in drifts made up of not less than three plants of each contrasting species.

Space them at least two feet apart for the larger species and not less than 15in. apart for the smaller ones.

They will take four of five years to grow together and completely cover the ground. Into each planting hole place a large fistful of peat and work it well into the soil.

Place the plant with its foliage resting on the soil to encourage rooting on the stems. Firm in well, water thoroughly and give a top dressing of peat.

The young plant must never be allowed to dry out. This is particularly important

Cut off flowers of winter and spring-flowering heathers when they fade. Summer flowering plants can be dead-headed in spring.

from March throughout the first summer. Spraying the foliage is helpful as moisture is taken in through the leaves.

Schlumbergera ×
buckleyi
(Zygocactus truncatus)
(Crab cactus; Christmas cactus; lobster cactus; Thanksgiving cactus)
● **Intermediate conditions**
● **For beginners**
● **Easy to bloom**

The Thanksgiving cactus grows to 30in (75cm), and has toothed branches that distinguish it from *Schlumbergera gaertneri.* Dozens of flowers appear in autumn, and a mature plant is a fine sight. Excellent for hanging baskets. Many varieties are available, in different colors — red, pink, orange, white.

Grow this jungle type cactus at a bright but not sunny window; it does not like direct sun. Use a potting mix of equal parts of medium-grade fir bark and soil. Keep plants moderately moist except in autumn, when roots should be fairly dry and plants grown quite cool (55 °F, 13 °C) with 12 hours of uninterrupted darkness each day for a month to encourage flower buds. Do not feed. Pieces of stem root easily in sand for new plants. Allow cuttings to dry first.

To encourage bloom:
Observe period of darkness. Do not move plants about — it causes the buds to fall.

Below: **Schlumbergera x buckleyi**
An excellent plant for superb autumn color and so easy to propagate from simple stem cuttings. A must.

Schlumbergera gaertneri
(Rhipsalidopsis gaertneri)
(Easter cactus; leaf cactus; link-leaf cactus)
- ● **Intermediate conditions**
- ● **For beginners**
- ● **Easy to bloom**

The Easter cactus is a fine epiphytic plant growing to 24in (60cm) and has scalloped branches that distinguish it from the toothed *Zygocactus* varieties. With red flowers in spring, this is an example of nature at her best. Very beautiful. Mature plants excellent for hanging baskets.

Grow this cactus at a sunny window in autumn and winter – in bright light the rest of the year. For a potting mix use equal parts of lime-free soil and medium-grade fir bark for the best results. In spring and summer water plants freely with lime-free water, but in autumn and winter reduce watering. Feed monthly. In mid-October or November give plants 12 hours of uninterrupted darkness per day, and cool nights (55 °F, 13 °C), and they will set buds. When buds form, return the plant to the window. Provide good humidity (40 percent); spray with water in warm months. Propagate by cuttings in spring.

To encourage bloom:
Must have a period of darkness with cool, dry conditions. Do not move plants about or the buds will drop.

Below: **Schlumbergera gaertneri**
Lovely scarlet flowers make this forest dwelling cactus a must for all indoor gardeners. Easy to grow

Smithiantha cinnabarina
(Temple bells)
- ● **Warm conditions**
- ● **For everyone**
- ● **Easy to bloom**

A fine 24in (60cm) gesneriad with large lush green leaves, and handsome bell shaped flowers from November through March, when color is so needed at windows. The orange-red flowers are exquisite. Plants adjust well to indoor conditions. Dependable. Many hybrids in vivid colors.

Grow temple bells at a bright window, but no sun is necessary. Be sure the air circulation is good. Use a potting mix of equal parts of soil and humus that drains readily. In March or April start each rhizome in a 4–5in (10–12.5cm) pot, planting 1in (2.5cm) deep. Keep the soil evenly moist. After the flowers fade, store the rhizome dry in the pot in a cool shaded place at 55 °F (13 °C) for about 3 months. Then repot and return to the bright window. Propagate from seed, division of rhizomes or from leaf cuttings.

To encourage bloom:
Observe resting time. Feed weekly when flower buds appear.

Below: **Smithiantha cinnabarina**
Lush green leaves and handsome bell shaped orange-red flowers make this plant welcome indoors.

Sinningia
(Gloxinia)
- ● **Cool conditions**
- ● **For a challenge**
- ● **Difficult to bloom**

These glamorous Brazilian plants up to 12in (30cm) tall have single or double tubular flowers in vivid colors – red, purple, pink, white, blue and bicolors. Although species are dormant in winter, today's hybrids can bloom at different seasons of the year, depending on when the tubers are started into growth. Enjoy plants in bloom as spot decoration on desk or table.

Gloxinias like a location where there is subdued light, and sun is not necessary: a west or north window is fine. Grow plants in equal parts of soil and humus. Start the tubers in spring or autumn, using one to a 5in (12.5cm) clay pot. Set the tuber hollow side up and cover with soil (but only just). Keep evenly moist at a temperature of about 60 °F (16 °C). When growth starts, increase the watering somewhat and move the plant to a slightly warmer location.

When the flowers fade, gradually decrease watering, remove tops, and store tubers in a dry place at 55 °F (13 °C). Keep soil barely moist and rest from 6 to 8 weeks (no more) or tubers lose their vitality. Repot in fresh soil. Propagate by taking basal shoot cuttings, leaf cuttings or raise plants from seed.

To encourage bloom:
Observe resting time. Feed weekly when flower buds form.

Photo left: **Sinningia**
Many fine hybrids are now available, all with brilliantly colored flowers that are stunning in bloom.

Solanum
capsicastrum

(Jerusalem cherry; Christmas cherry; winter cherry)
- ● **Intermediate conditions**
- ● **For beginners**
- ● **Easy to bloom**

A small dark-leaved shrub from Brazil, the Jerusalem cherry grows up to 15in (38cm) tall and has white starry flowers in summer followed by non-edible fruits that stay on the plant well into winter. They ripen through green to yellow and then orange-red. Very pretty.

Grow the Jerusalem cherry in a bright window – a west or east exposure is fine. Use standard houseplant soil that drains readily. Keep the soil evenly moist except in winter, when plants can be grown somewhat dry and cool (55 °F, 13 °C), without letting them dry out completely. Plants like an airy place. Mist leaves daily with water. Rarely bothered by insects. Generally good for the season only and then must be discarded or placed in the garden and pruned back to 8in (20cm); it can then be brought inside before the first frost. New plants from seed.

To encourage bloom:
Pollinate the flowers by hand using a brush. Keep plants cool during fruiting. Replace plants after 2 years; they decline in flower/fruit vigor. Take care; the fruits are poisonous.

Below: **Solanum capsicastrum**
Prized mainly for its orange fruits rather than its small white flowers, this compact plant brings color to the windowsill in winter.

Spathiphyllum 'Mauna Loa'

(Peace lily; spathe flower; white flag; white sails)

● **Intermediate conditions**
● **For everyone**
● **Easy to bloom**

This plant from South America has shiny green leaves and white spathe flowers that resemble anthuriums. Plants grow up to 18in (45cm) tall. In good growing conditions this hybrid will produce fragrant flowers intermittently throughout the year. Although spathiphyllums are not spectacular plants, they seem to adjust to almost any indoor location and do well.

Grow these at any exposure – they can tolerate sun or shade. Use standard houseplant soil. Allow the soil to dry out between waterings. Use a plant food about 4 times a year. Plants are rarely bothered by insects and seem trouble free. For a good

show grow in 12in (30cm) pots. Excellent room plants even in shady corners. Propagate by seed or division of the rhizomes in spring.

To encourage bloom:
Keep warm and humid.

Photo left:
Spathiphyllum 'Mauna Loa'
Striking flowers, compact growth and ability to endure neglect make this a recommended houseplant.

Sprekelia formosissima

(Aztec lily; Jacobean lily)

● **Cool conditions**
● **For beginners**
● **Easy to bloom**

This bulbous plant has narrow strap shaped leaves usually appearing after the flowers. The flowers are bright scarlet, exotic in appearance, and borne on 18–24in (45–60cm) stems in late spring or early summer. A very dependable plant and a real beauty for the indoor garden.

Grow this lily in a sunny place – a west or south window is fine. Pot the bulbs, two thirds buried, in equal parts of soil and humus that drains readily. Water freely while in growth. Do not feed. When leaves yellow, let the soil go almost dry and rest for several weeks. Repot in fresh soil in autumn. Grow new plants from the small bulbs that form next to the main one. Remove these in the autumn.

To encourage bloom:
No special requirements.

Below: **Sprekelia formosissima**
A lily in the home? Yes, here is a magnificent example. The plant has exotic red flowers, and bloom comes year after year with little care.

Stanhopea wardii
- **Warm conditions**
- **For beginners**
- **Easy to bloom**

This unusual orchid from Mexico, Central and South America grows to 24in (60cm) in height; it has large dark green leaves, and bears pendent flower spikes in late summer. Flowers are up to 5in (12.5cm) across, white or yellow with brown markings, and heavily scented. The plant blooms from the bottom of the pot so open orchid baskets or clay pots with several large drainage holes are necessary; get these from specialist suppliers.

Grow at a bright but not sunny window – good light is needed to encourage flowers. Pot in medium-grade fir bark – basket culture is recommended and drainage must be perfect. Flood with water in the warm months but in winter allow plants to be fairly dry. Do not feed. Provide adequate humidity (40 percent) and good ventilation. Rarely bothered by

insects. Flowers are short lived but the plant is still worth the space – they are spectacular. Buy new plants from suppliers or divide the pseudobulbs during the summer.

To encourage bloom:
Give plenty of water while in growth.

Right: **Stanhopea wardii**
An unusual orchid with large leaves and waxy flowers borne from the bottom of the plant. Heavily scented with a pleasing menthol fragrance.

186

Stephanotis floribunda

(Madagascar jasmine)
- **Intermediate conditions**
- **For a challenge**
- **Difficult to bloom**

Here is a fine plant for the indoor garden, with handsome dark green leaves, and scented white flowers in midsummer. Plants climb, so supply a suitable support. Very pretty. One plant can perfume an entire room. Somewhat difficult to grow but not impossible and worth a try. Plants will grow to 10ft (3m).

Plants thrive in an east or west window – they must have bright light but sun is not necessary. Pot in equal parts of soil and humus. Keep soil evenly moist with lime-free water all year except in winter, when it can be slightly drier. Provide adequate moisture by misting with water. Feed every 2 weeks in summer. Watch for mealy bugs, which sometimes attack plants (use appropriate remedies). Propagate by cuttings in spring.

Photo left: **Stephanotis floribunda**
It is hard to beat the fragrance of Madagascar jasmine. White star shaped 1in (2.5cm) flowers appear in clusters in summer. A valuable plant.

To encourage bloom:
Must have coolness (55°F, 13°C) in winter resting period. Do not move the plant or the buds will drop.

Strelitzia reginae

(Bird of paradise flower)
- **Warm conditions**
- **For a challenge**
- **Difficult to bloom**

Called 'bird of paradise' because its flowers resemble exotic birds, this 40in (1m) plant has gray-green spatulate leaves, and bright orange and purple flowers in summer. Only mature plants with 7 or more leaves bloom and then reluctantly indoors. Even so, it is worth a try because of the spectacular flowers.

Grow this plant at your sunniest window – it must have at least 3 hours of sun daily to prosper. Use a standard houseplant soil and feed every 2 weeks in summer, but not at all the rest of the year. In winter keep cool at 50°F (10°C) and allow the soil to dry out somewhat, but in summer flood the plants with water. Use large tubs. Rarely bothered by insects. Propagate by division of tubers or from seed; either way new plants will take several years to flower.

Above: **Strelitzia reginae**
A stunning plant with 6in (15cm) blooms. Needs warmth and space.

To encourage bloom:
Buy mature plants. Leave undisturbed – dividing plants stops flowering for several years.

Streptocarpus hybrids
(Cape primrose; Cape cowslip)
- **Intermediate conditions**
- **For everyone**
- **Easy to bloom**

There is a fine new group of hybrids available that bloom almost all year, but mainly in the summer. Flower colors are white, pink or violet, and the tubular flowers are indeed handsome. Plants grow to about 8–12in (20–30cm) in height. Highly recommended.

Grow the Cape Primrose in a bright window, protected from direct sun. Use standard houseplant soil that drains readily; feed every 2 weeks when in growth. After a bloom cycle reduce watering, let the plant rest for about 4–6 weeks, and then resume watering. Always use lime-free water. Do not mist the leaves; water on the foliage can cause rot. Repot annually for best results. Grow new plants from seed or leaf cuttings taken in midsummer.

To encourage bloom:
Allow to rest slightly after blooming. Replace plants after 2 or 3 years as they decline in flowering vigor.

Right: **Streptocarpus hybrid**
If you want dazzling flowers look to the fine streptocarpus hybrids Blooms come in wonderful shades of violet, pink or white.

Streptocarpus saxorum

(False African violet; spiral fruit)
● **Cool conditions**
● **For everyone**
● **Easy to bloom**

This 14in (35cm) gesneriad has large rich green leaves, and 1½in (4cm) lavender flowers in spring or sometimes in autumn. This species is good for hanging baskets.

Grow at a bright window, as they like light but no sun. Use a potting mix of equal parts of soil and humus that drains readily. Water and then allow to dry out between waterings. Avoid getting water on the leaves. Feeding is optional. After blooming reduce watering and let the plant rest. Watch for signs of dormancy and do not try to force plants into growth. When new growth starts, resume watering. It is best to repot every year. Propagate by seed or stem cuttings taken in spring.

To encourage bloom:
Dry out between waterings.

Photo left:
Streptocarpus saxorum
Less spectacular than the hybrids but no less delightful, this species produces a springtime display of delicate pale lavender blooms.

Thunbergia alata

(Black-eyed Susan vine; clock vine)
● **Warm conditions**
● **For a challenge**
● **Difficult to bloom**

This uncommonly beautiful plant, with funnel shaped yellow-orange flowers and attractive green foliage, climbs up to 10ft (3m). It makes a happy note of color in midsummer at the window, but is a difficult plant to keep from year to year. In some climates it may be easier to treat it as an annual and raise new plants from seed each year. Good for spot color only. Excellent hanging basket plant.

Grow this at your sunniest window – it will not bear flowers in shade. Use a standard houseplant soil that drains readily. Plants are greedy and need copious watering and feeding every 2 weeks during the warm months. Provide a suitable support and check the plant occasionally for insects – red spider mites are fond of the foliage. Use appropriate

Above: **Thunbergia alata**
A colorful tropical vining plant that grows lavishly in warm airy conditions. Difficult, but worthwhile.

remedies. Maintain good humidity. Grow new plants from seed.

To encourage bloom:
Must have at least 3 hours of sun daily to bloom successfully.

Tibouchina semidecandra
(Glory bush)
- Intermediate conditions
- For everyone
- Easy to bloom

This shrub, usually considered an outdoor plant, does well indoors in 8in (20cm) pots. Plants have hairy leaves, pale green maturing to red, and the flowers are a lovely purple. Blooms last only a day but are quickly replaced by new ones throughout the warm months. A nice addition to indoor gardens, needing little care.

Grow the glory bush at a sunny window – a west exposure is fine. Use standard houseplant soil that drains readily. Repot yearly. Feed 4 times a year. Pinch off tips of branches occasionally to encourage bushiness. Keep the soil evenly moist all year. Look for the plant in the outdoor section of a nursery. New plants from stem cuttings.

To encourage bloom:
Give plenty of water during growth. Pinch back occasionally.

Below: **Tibouchina semidecandra**
You can't go wrong with this bushy shrub at the window – it bears purple flowers day after day in summer.

Tillandsia cyanea
(Pink quill)
- Intermediate conditions
- For a challenge
- Difficult to bloom

This fine 10in (25cm) bromeliad has grassy dark green foliage and lovely purple flowers – dozens to a bract in early summer. Flowers last only a few days but are followed by others. A truly fine indoor plant.

Grow the pink quill in a bright location – a west window is excellent. Use equal parts of lime-free soil and small-grade fir bark for potting. Keep the medium evenly moist; do not feed. Plants need excellent ventilation – they will not thrive in a stagnant atmosphere. Provide ample humidity; spray leaves with tepid water during warm weather. Rarely bothered by insects. Get new plants from suppliers or from rooted offsets detached from the parent plant.

To encourage bloom:
Keep humid.

Right: **Tillandsia cyanea**
An unusual bromeliad with purple flowers, this grassy leaved plant is well worth space indoors.

Trichopilia tortilis
(Corkscrew orchid)
● **Intermediate conditions**
● **For everyone**
● **Easy to bloom**

Don't let the name fool you – this is an exquisite 14in (35cm) orchid that does better in the home than in a greenhouse. Plants have narrow dark green leaves and 5in (12.5cm) tubular white flowers spotted in orange with corkscrew petals – very handsome. Blooms last several weeks in spring or autumn, and are undemanding. A very fine plant that should be in every indoor garden.

Grow this orchid in a bright place – a west or north window is fine. Use small-grade fir bark and pot somewhat tightly. Keep the bark evenly moist at all times of the year. Mist with water to provide adequate humidity and be sure the plant is in a place where there is good air circulation. Do not feed. Repot only every third year – this plant does not like to be disturbed. Rarely bothered by insects. Get new plants from suppliers or divide pseudobulbs.

To encourage bloom:
Do not overwater.

Photo left: **Trichopilia tortilis**
A fine indoor orchid that really does grow and bloom indoors. Very unusual flowers with corkscrew petals.

Tulipa
(Tulip)
- **Cool conditions**
- **For everyone**
- **Easy to bloom**

These plants need little introduction, and their handsome flowers are available in dozens of colors. The best tulips for indoor cultivation are the early dwarf varieties, which grow to about 12in (30cm) tall; choose single or double flowered varieties.

Grow tulips in your sunniest place. Use a potting mix of equal parts of sand and soil that drains readily. Pot bulbs in autumn (covering completely) and keep cool (50 °F, 10 °C) and shaded until the flower buds begin to show color; then move them into warmer, bright conditions. High temperatures while plants are in bud will cause the buds to die off. Water sparingly, keeping mix just moist. Start new bulbs each year.

To encourage bloom:
Grow in cool conditions.

Below: **Tulipa (Triumph type)**
These fine flowers can be forced during the winter to provide post-Christmas color in the home.

Vallota speciosa
(Scarborough lily)
- **Cool conditions**
- **For everyone**
- **Easy to bloom**

A bulbous plant with strap leaves, *V. speciosa* has bright scarlet funnel shaped flowers 3in (7.5cm) across on 24in (60cm) stems in summer. A spectacular plant.

Grow in sun – a west or south window is fine. Pot in equal parts of soil and humus that drains readily. Use a 4 or 5in (10–12.5cm) clay pot and leave the top of the bulb uncovered. Water evenly throughout the year, never too much or too little. Do not feed. Maintain good ventilation and humidity of 30 percent. Plants can be grown in the same container for several years. Grow new plants from seeds or from the offset bulbs that develop beside the parent bulb. Remove in autumn.

To encourage bloom:
Do not overwater.

Right: **Vallota speciosa**
A bulbous plant from South Africa, this beauty is easy to grow and quite spectacular in bloom.

Vanda suavis var. tricolor

● **Intermediate conditions**
● **For everyone**
● **Easy to bloom**

This popular vanda grows to 48in (120cm) or more with long straplike leaves: flowers are 4in (10cm) across, usually white and spotted with red and purple. As many as 10 flowers to a scape are borne on mature plants in summer or autumn. Excellent plant if you have the space.

Like most vandas, this one needs sunshine at its best so place it at a south exposure. Use a potting mix of large-grade fir bark kept moist most of the year. Do not feed. A slight drying out is permissible in winter. Maintain excellent ventilation and mist plant with tepid water occasionally to maintain humidity. This plant is relatively free of insects. Propagate from side shoots.

To encourage bloom:
Must have sun.

Below: **Vanda suavis** var. **tricolor**
This beautiful orchid from Java and Bali produces fragrant waxy flowers freely during summer and autumn.

Veltheimia viridifolia
(Forest lily)
● **Cool conditions**
● **For everyone**
● **Easy to bloom**

This 20in (50cm) bulbous plant from the lily family is hard to beat for winter color. It has large dark green glossy leaves and a yellow-green to rosy pink cone of small flowers borne at the tip of a tall stem. Not to be missed and a dependable houseplant.

Grow in bright light – almost any exposure is fine. Pot in standard houseplant soil in 8in (20cm) pots. Place one bulb to a pot with the top ¼in (6mm) extended above the soil line. Be sure drainage is good. Keep soil moist except after flowering, when the plant can be kept somewhat dry and moved to a cooler location, 50 °F (10 °C). Feed monthly when in growth. Increase watering as growth starts, and after flowering allow to die back and rest through the summer months. Repot in fresh soil in early September for new flowers. Grow new plants from offset bulbs that develop next to the main bulb.

To encourage bloom:
Observe summer rest period.

Photo left: **Veltheimia viridifolia**
This member of the lily family can be relied on to provide a wonderful show of color in winter.

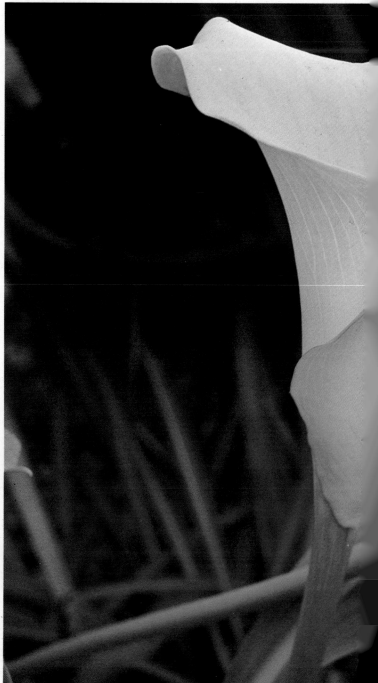

Vriesea splendens
(Flaming sword)
● **Intermediate conditions**
● **For everyone**
● **Easy to bloom**

A rosette shaped bromeliad, *V. splendens* has glossy green leaves banded with brown, and a sword shaped spike up to 18in (45cm) tall, bearing bright red bracts and yellow flowers, that appears in summer and lasts for weeks. The plant is more unusual in appearance than pretty, but its vibrant color makes it a popular indoor subject. Easy to grow.

Grow the flaming sword at a sunny window – it likes light. Use a potting mix of equal parts of medium-grade fir bark and soil. Keep the center of the plant filled with water, and the soil moist to the touch. Provide an airy place. Mist the leaves to furnish adequate humidity. Never bothered by insects. Grow new plants from offsets at the base of the parent plant: remove these when they are

3in (7.5cm) tall and have developed roots, and pot in separate containers.

To encourage bloom:
No special requirements.

Right: **Vriesea splendens**
This favorite bromeliad offers not only striking foliage but also a long-lasting 'sword' of red bracts.

Zantedeschia rehmannii
(Calla lily; pink arum; pink calla; trumpet lily)
● **Cool conditions**
● **For beginners**
● **Easy to bloom**

This tuberous plant growing to 20in (50cm) in height has handsome spear shaped leaves, and pink to cream flower spathes in summer. Generally grown outdoors, it also makes a fine pot plant indoors.

Grow this calla lily in bright light until foliage develops, and then move it to a sunny window for bloom. Use a potting mix of equal parts of soil and humus that drains readily. Water moderately at first, and when growth appears keep the soil fairly moist. Plant one tuber to a 4–5in (10–12.5cm) pot. Give liquid plant food once a month. After flowering, allow tubers to ripen off naturally by reducing water. Then rest in pots in a cool shady place at 50 °F (10 °C) and withhold water entirely. In August, repot the bulbs in fresh soil. Grow new plants from tiny offshoots or by dividing the tubers when repotting.

To encourage bloom:
Observe the strict resting time. Do not omit feeding.

Left: **Zantedeschia rehmanni**
The pink calla graces many windows with elegant flowers and spearlike leaves. Small, attractive plants.

Zephyranthes candida

(Fairy lily; flowers of the western wind; rain lily; swamp lily; zephyr lily; zephyr flower)

● **Cool conditions**
● **For a challenge**
● **Difficult to bloom**

Growing only to 12in (30cm), the zephyr lily has grassy foliage, and pretty white flowers in summer. There are also pink and orange species. These overlooked plants do very well indoors.

The zephyr lily needs a sunny window; in spring pot 4 or 5 bulbs to a 6in (15cm) pot. Cover completely with a mix of equal parts of soil and humus that drains readily. Let the soil dry out between waterings. Do not feed. In winter, store the bulbs dry in a cool shaded place. Repot in fresh soil in spring. Bulbs are good for about three seasons. Grow new plants from offset bulbs that develop beside the main bulb.

To encourage bloom:
Observe resting time.

Right: **Zephyranthes candida**
Zephyr lilies are pretty and bear graceful little white flowers in late summer and autumn. Pink flowering species of Zephyranthes (shown below) are also available.

Zygopetalum crinitum

● **Intermediate conditions**
● **For beginners**
● **Easy to bloom**

A handsome orchid growing to 20in (50cm), this plant has papery green leaves, and exquisite flowers of green, purple and brown in winter. Flowers last several weeks on the plant. This is an overlooked but beautiful orchid.

Grow at a bright window; sun will harm this plant. Pot in medium-grade fir bark kept reasonably moist but never wet, and provide good ventilation. Keep humidity at about 40 percent. Do not feed. When growth stops in autumn (when the leaves are fully expanded), rest the plant without water and only an occasional misting. Sometimes the leaves develop black streaks and are unsightly, but the plants are not unhealthy. Get new plants from suppliers or divide pseudobulbs.

To encourage bloom:
Do not overwater. Do not disturb plants – they resent repotting.

Right: **Zygopetalum crinitum**
Another popular orchid, this one bears lovely fragrant green and purple flowers in midwinter. A welcome addition to any indoor garden.

Common and Latin Names

Common/Latin Names

African violet
Saintpaulia
Alpine violet
Cyclamen
Amaryllis
Hippeastrum
Amazon lily
Eucharis grandiflora
Amazonian zebra plant
Aechmea chantinii
Angelwing begonia
'Begonia 'Orange Rubra'
Apostle plant
Neomarica caerulea
Aztec lily
Sprekelia formosissima
Baby pepper
Rivina humilis
Baby primrose
Primula malacoides
Ball cactus
Notocactus ottonis
Barberton daisy
Gerbera jamesonii
Basket vine
Aeschynanthus lobbianus,
Aeschynanthus speciosus
Bead plant
Nertera granadensis
Bear's breeches
Acanthus mollis
Bellflower
Abutilon hybrid,
Campanula isophylla
Bird of paradise flower
Strelitzia reginae
Bird's nest bromeliad
Nidularium innocentii
Black-eyed Susan vine
Thunbergia alata
Bleeding heart vine
Clerodendrum thomsoniae
Bloodberry
Rivina humilis
Blood flower, lily
Haemanthus katharinae
Blue African lily
Agapanthus africanus
Blue Cape plumbago
Plumbago auriculata/capensis
Blue glory flower
Clerodendrum ugandense
Blue passion flower
Passiflora caerulea
Blushing bromeliad
Neoregelia carolinae tricolor
Bottlebrush plant
Callistemon citrinus/lanceolatus
Brazilian plume
Jacobinia carnea
Busy Lizzie
Impatiens walleriana
Butterfly flower
Schizanthus species
Butterfly orchid
Oncidium papilio
Calamondin orange
Citrus mitis
Calla lily
Zantedeschia rehmannii
Candy corn plant
Manettia bicolor
Cape cowslip
Streptocarpus hybrids
Cape jasmine
Gardenia jasminoides
Cape Leadwort
Plumbago auriculata/capensis
Cape primrose
Streptocarpus hybrids
Cardinal flower
Rechsteineria cardinalis
Cathedral bells
Cobaea scandens
Chameleon plant
Brunfelsia calycina
Chenille plant
Acalypha hispida
Cherry pie
Heliotropium hybridum

Chilean bellflower
Lapageria rosea
Chinese hibiscus, rose
Hibiscus rosa-sinensis
Christmas cactus
Schlumbergera x buckleyi
(Zygocactus truncatus)
Christmas cherry
Solanum capsicastrum
Christmas pepper
Capsicum annuum
Cigar flower
Cuphea ignea
Cinnamon orchid
Lycaste aromatica
Clamshell
Epidendrum cochleatum
Clock vine
Thunbergia alata
Clown orchid
Odontoglossum grande
Cineraria
Senecio cruentus
Cockleshell orchid
Epidendrum cochleatum
Cockscomb
Celosia argentea 'Cristata'
Comet orchid
Angraecum eburneum
Common allamanda
Allamanda cathartica
Common camellia
Camellia japonica
Common hydrangea
Hydrangea macrophylla
Common lantana
Lantana camara
Common passion flower
Passiflora caerulea
Copihue
Lapageria rosea
Coral berry
Ardisia crispa/crenata
Coral bead plant
Nertera granadensis
Coral plant
Russelia equisetiformis
Corkscrew orchid
Trichopilia tortilis
Corn lily
Ixia speciosa
Corsage flower
Cattleya hybrids
Crab cactus
Schlumbergera x buckleyi
(Zygocactus truncatus)
Crimson bottlebrush
Callistemon citrinus/lanceolatus
Crown of thorns
Euphorbi milii (splendens)
Cup and saucer vine
Cobaea scandens
Cupid's bower
Achimenes hybrids
Desert rose
Adenium obesum 'Multiflorum'
Dwarf pomegranate
Punica granatum 'Nana'
Easter cactus
Schlumbergera gaertneri
(Rhipsalidopsis gaertneri)
Egyptian star cluster, flower
Pentas lanceolata
Elephant's ears
Haemanthus albiflos
Elfin herb
Cuphea hyssopifolia
Epicactus
Epiphyllum
Exotic brush
Aechmea fasciata
Eyelash begonia
Begonia boweri
Fairy lily
Zephyranthes candida
Fairy primrose
Primula malacoides
False African violet
Streptocarpus saxorum
False heather
Cuphea hyssopifolia
Fiery costus
Costus igneus

Firecracker flower
Crossandra infundibuliformis
(C. undulifolia), Cuphea ignea
Firecracker plant, vine
Manettia bicolor
Flame of the woods
Ixora coccinea
Flame plant
Anthurium andreanum,
Anthurium scherzerianum
Flame violet
Episcia cupreata
Flaming Katy
Kalanchoe blossfeldiana
Flaming sword
Vriesea splendens
Flamingo flower
Anthurium andreanum,
Anthurium scherzerianum
Florist's mum
Chrysanthemum
Flowers of the western wind
Zephyranthes candida
Flowering maple
Abutilon hybrid
Flowering onion
Allium neopolitanum
Forest lily
Veltheimia viridifolia
Fountain plant
Russelia equisetiformis
Foxtails
Acalypha hispida
Geranium
Pelargonium
Gherkin cactus
Chamaecereus silvestrii
Glory bower
Clerodendrum thomsoniae
Glory bush
Clerodendrum speciosissimum,
Tibouchina semidecandra
Glory lily
Gloriosa rothschildiana
Gloxinia
Sinningia
Golden hops
Pachystachys lutea
Golden lily cactus
Lobivia aurea
Golden-rayed lily
Lilium auratum
Golden shrimp plant
Pachystachys lutea
Golden trumpet
Allamanda cathartica
Goldfish plant
Hypocyrta nummularia
Goldfish vine
Columnea microphylla
Grass lily
Ixia speciosa
Grecian urn plant
Acanthus mollis
Guatemala rhubarb
Jatropha podagrica
Heath
Erica
Heliotrope
Heliotropium hybridum
Hot water plant
Achimenes hybrids
House hydrangea
Hydrangea macrophylla
Hyacinth
Hyacinthus orientalis
Impala lily
Adenium obesum 'Multiflorum'
Indian azalea
Azalea indica
(Rhododendron simsii)
Indian jasmine
Ixora coccinea
Indian shot
Canna hybrids
Italian bellflower
Campanula isophylla
Jacobean lily
Sprekelia formosissima
Japanese pittosporum
Pittosporum tobira
Jasmine plant
Bouvardia x domestica

Java glorybean
Clerodendrum speciosissimum
Jerusalem cherry
Solanum capsicastrum
Kaffir lily
Clivia miniata
Kahili ginger
Hedychium gardnerianum
Kangaroo thorn
Acacia armata
King's crown
Jacobinia carnea
Kiss me plant
Hypocyrta nummularia
Hypocyrta strigillosa
Lace flower
Episcia dianthiflora
Lady of the night
Brassavola nodosa
Lady's eardrops
Fuchsia
Lady's pocketbook
Calceolaria hybrids
Lady's slipper orchid
Paphiopedilum maudiae
Lady's slippers
Calceolaria hybrids
Leadwort
Plumbago auriculata/capensis
Leaf cactus
Epiphyllum,
Schlumbergera gaertneri
(Rhipsalidopsis gaertneri)
Lily of the Nile
Agapanthus africanus
Lily of the Valley
Convallaria majalis
Link-leaf cactus
Schlumbergera gaertneri
(Rhipsalidopsis gaertneri)
Lipstick vine
Aeschynanthus lobbianus
Living stones
Lithops
Lobster cactus
Schlumbergera x buckleyi
(Zygocactus truncatus)
Lollipop plant
Pachystachys lutea
Love plant
Medinilla magnifica
Madagascar jasmine
Stephanotis floribunda
Madagascar periwinkle
Catharanthus roseus
(Vinca rosea)
Manuka
Leptospermum scoparium
Mexican cigar plant
Cuphea ignea
Mexican love vine
Dipladenia 'Amoena'
Miniature eyelash begonia
Begonia boweri
Miniature rose
Rosa chinensis minima
Miniature wax plant
Hoya bella
Morning glory
Ipomoea
Moth orchid
Phalaenopsis hybrids
Oleander
Nerium oleander
Orange star
Guzmania lingulata
Orchid cactus
Epiphyllum
Ornamental chilli
Capsicum annuum
Painter's palette
Anthurium andreanum
Pansy orchid
Miltonia 'Peach Blossom',
Miltonia roezlii
Paper flower
Bougainvillea
Passion vine
Passiflora caerulea
Patient Lucy, plant
Impatiens walleriana
Peace lily
Spathiphyllum 'Mauna Loa'

Peanut cactus
Chamaecereus silvestrii
Pebble plant
Lithops
Persian violet
Exacum affine
Pigtail plant
Anthurium andreanum,
Anthurium scherzerianum
Pineapple lily
Eucomis bicolor
Pink allamande
Dipladenia splendens 'Rosea'
Pink arum, calla
Zantedeschia rehmannii
Pink jasmine
Jasminum polyanthum
Pink quill
Tillandsia cyanea
Plume celosia
Celosia argentea 'Pyramidalis'
Pocketbook plant
Calceolaria hybrids
Poinsettia
Euphorbia pulcherrima
Poor man's orchid
Cyclamen, Schizanthus species
Porcelain flower
Hoya australis
Pouch flower
Calceolaria hybrids
Prairie fire cactus
Parodia sanguiniflora
Primula, primrose
Primula obconica,
Primula vulgaris/acaulis
Prince of Wales feathers
Celosia argentea 'Pyramidalis'
Purple wreath
Petrea volubilis
Queen of the bromeliads
Aechmea chantinii
Queen's tears
Billbergia pyramidalis
Queen's wreath
Petrea volubilis
Rainbow cactus
Echinocereus baileyi
Rain lily
Zephyranthes candida
Red ginger
Alpinia purpurata
Red hot cat's tail
Acalypha hispida
Red pepper plant
Capsicum annuum
Rose bay
Nerium oleander
Rose grape
Medinilla magnifica
Rose mallow
Hibiscus rosa-sinensis
Rose pin cushion
Mammillaria zeilmanniana
Rouge plant
Rivina humilis
Saffron spike
A. squarrosa 'Louisae'
Sand dollar cactus
Astrophytum asterias
Saucer plant
Aeonium tabulaeforme
Scarborough lily
Vallota speciosa
Scarlet plume
Euphorbia fulgens
Scarlet star
Guzmania lingulata
Sea urchin cactus
Astrophytum asterias
Shell flower
Epidendrum cochleatum
Shooting star
Cyclamen
Shrimp plant
Beloperone guttata
Shrub verbena
Lantana camara
Silver vase
Aechmea fasciata
Slipper flower
Calceolaria hybrids

Slipper orchid
Paphiopedilum maudiae
Slipperwort
Calceolaria hybrids
Small-leaved goldfish vine
Columnea microphylla
Snapweed
Impatiens walleriana
Snowball flower
Hydrangea macrophylla
Spathe flower
Spathiphyllum 'Mauna Loa'
Spear flower
Ardisia crispa/crenata
Spiral fruit
Streptocarpus saxorum
Star cactus
Astrophytum asterias
Star of Bethlehem
Campanula isophylla
Stone face
Lithops
Sultana
Impatiens walleriana
Summer torch
Billbergia pyramidalis
Swamp lily
Zephyranthes candida
Tail flower
Anthurium andreanum,
Anthurium scherzerianum
Tea plant
Camellia japonica
Tea tree
Leptospermum scoparum
Temple bells
Smithiantha cinnabarina
Thanksgiving cactus
Schlumbergera x buckleyi
(Zygocactus truncatus)
Tiger orchid
Odontoglossum grande
Tom thumb
Kalanchoe blossfeldiana
Tom Thumb cactus
Parodia sanguiniflora
Touch-me-not
Impatiens walleriana
Trailing campanula
Campanula isophylla
Transvaal daisy
Gerbera jamesonii
Tree gloxinia
Kohleria amabilis
Treasure flower
Gazania hybrids
Trompetilla
Bouvardia x domestica
Trumpet lily
Zantedeschia rehmanii
Tulip
Tulipa
Tulip orchid
Anguloa ruckeri
Urn plant
Aechmea fasciata
Vase plant
Aechmea fasciata
Venus' slipper
Paphiopedilum maudiae
Walking iris
Neomarica caerulea
Wattle
Acacia armata
Wax begonia
Begonia semperflorens
Wax plant
Hoya australis, Hoya carnosa
Wax vine
Hoya australis
White flag
Spathiphyllum 'Mauna Loa'
White paintbrush
Haemanthus albiflos
White sails
Spathiphyllum 'Mauna Loa'
Winter cherry
Solanum capsicastrum
Wood sorrel
Oxalis rubra
Yellow flax
Reinwardtia trigyna

Yellow sage
Lantana camara
Yellow tulip orchid
Anguloa clowesii
Yesterday, today, and tomorrow
Brunfelsia calycina
Zebra plant
A. squarrosa 'Louisae'
Zephyr flower, lily
Zephyranthes candida

Latin/Common Names

Abutilon hybrid
Bellflower, Flowering maple
Acacia armata
Kangaroo thorn, Wattle
Acalypha hispida
Chenille plant, Foxtails,
Red hot cat's tail
Acanthus mollis
Bear's breeches,
Grecian urn plant
Achimenes hybrids
Cupid's bower, Hot water plant
Adenium obesum 'Multiflorum'
Desert rose, Impala lily
Aechmea chantinii
Amazonian zebra plant,
Queen of the bromeliads
Aechmea fasciata
Exotic brush, Silver vase,
Urn plant, Vase plant
Aeonium tabulaeforme
Saucer plant
Aeschynanthus lobbianus
Basket vine, Lipstick vine
Aeschynanthus speciosus
Basket vine
Agapanthus africanus
Blue Africa lily, Lily of the Nile
Allamanda cathartica
Common allamanda,
Golden trumpet
Allium neopolitanum
Flowering onion
Alpinia purpurata
Red ginger
Angraecum eburneum
Comet orchid
Anguloa clowesii
Yellow tulip orchid
Anguloa ruckeri
Tulip orchid
Anthurium andreanum
Flame plant, Flamingo flower,
Painter's palette, Pigtail plant,
Tail flower
Anthurium scherzerianum
Flame plant, Flamingo flower,
Pigtail plant, Tail flower
A. squarrosa 'Louisae'
Saffron spike, Zebra plant
Ardisia crispa/crenata
Coral berry, Spear flower
Astrophytum asterias
Sand dollar cactus, Sea urchin
cactus, Star cactus
**Azalea indica
(Rhododendron simsii)**
Indian azalea
Begonia semperflorens
Wax begonia
Begonia boweri
Eyelash begonia,
Miniature eyelash begonia
Begonia 'Orange Rubra'
Angelwing begonia
Beloperone guttata
Shrimp plant
Billbergia pyramidalis
Queen's tears, Summer torch
Bougainvillea
Paper flower
Bouvardia x domestica
Jasmine plant, Trompetilla
Brassavola nodosa
Lady of the night
Brunfelsia calycina
Chameleon plant,
Yesterday, today, and tomorrow

Calceolaria hybrids
Lady's pocketbook, Lady's
slippers, Pocketbook plant,
Pouch flower, Slipper flower,
Slipperwort
Callistemon citrinus/lanceolatus
Bottlebrush plant,
Crimson bottlebrush
Camellia japonica
Common camellia, Tea plant
Campanula isophylla
Bellflower, Italian bellflower,
Star of Bethlehem,
Trailing campanula
Canna hybrids
Indian shot
Capsicum annum
Christmas pepper, Ornamental
chilli, Red pepper plant
**Catharanthus roseus
(Vinca rosea)**
Madagascar periwinkle
Cattleya hybrids
Corsage flower
Celosia argentea 'Pyramidalis'
Plume celosia,
Prince of Wales feathers
Celosia argentea 'Cristata'
Cockscomb
Chamaecereus silvestrii
Gherkin cactus, Peanut cactus
Citrus mitis
Calamondin orange
Chrysanthemum
Florist's mum
Clerodendrum speciossimum
Glory bush, Java glorybean
Clerodendrum thomsoniae
Bleeding heart vine, Glory bower
Clerodendrum ugandense
Blue glory flower
Clivia miniata
Kaffir lily
Cobaea scandens
Cathedral bells,
Cup and saucer vine
Columnea microphylla
Goldfish vine,
Small-leaved goldfish vine
Convallaria majalis
Lily of the valley
Costus igneus
Fiery costus
**Crossandra infundibuliformis
(C. undulifolia)**
Firecracker flower
Cuphea hyssopifolia
Elfin herb, False heather
Cuphea ignea
Cigar flower, firecracker flower,
Mexican cigar plant
Cyclamen
Alpine violet, Poor man's
orchid, Shooting star
Dipladenia 'Amoena'
Mexican love vine
Dipladenia splendens 'Rosea'
Pink allamande
Echinocereus baileyi
Rainbow cactus
Epidendrum cochleatum
Clamshell, Cockleshell orchid,
Shell flower
Epiphyllum
Epicactus, Leaf cactus,
Orchid cactus
Episcia cupreata
Flame violet
Episcia dianthiflora
Lace flower
Erica
Heath
Eucharis grandiflora
Amazon lily
Eucomis bicolor
Pineapple lily
Euphorbia fulgens
Scarlet plume
Euphorbia milii/(splendens)
Crown of thorns
Euphorbia pulcherrima
Poinsettia

Common and Latin Names

Exacum affine
 Persian violet
Fuchsia
 Lady's eardrops
Gardenia jasminoides
 Cape jasmine
Gazania hybrids
 Treasure flower
Gerbera jamesonii
 Barberton daisy, Transvaal daisy
Gloriosa rothschildiana
 Glory lily
Guzmania lingulata
 Orange star, Scarlet star
Haemanthus albiflos
 Elephant's ears,
 White paintbrush
Haemanthus katharinae
 Blood flower, Blood lily
Hedychium gardnerianum
 Kahili ginger
Heliotropium hybridum
 Cherry pie, Heliotrope
Hibiscus rosa-sinensis
 Chinese hibiscus,
 Chinese rose, Rose mallow
Hippeastrum
 Amaryllis
Hoya australis
 Porcelain flower, Wax plant,
 Wax vine
Hoya bella
 Miniature wax plant
Hoya carnosa
 Wax plant
Hyacinthus orientalis
 Hyacinth
Hydrangea macrophylla
 Common hydrangea, House
 hydrangea, Snowball flower
Hypocyrta nummularia
 Goldfish plant, Kiss me plant
Hypocyrta strigillosa
 Kiss me plant
Impatiens walleriana
 Busy Lizzie, Patience plant,
 Patient Lucy, Snap weed,
 Sultana, Touch-me-not
Ipomoea
 Morning glory
Ixia speciosa
 Corn lily, Grass lily

Ixora coccinea
 Flame of the woods,
 Indian jasmine
Jacobinia carnea
 Brazilian plume, King's crown
Jasminum polyanthum
 Pink jasmine
Jatropha podagrica
 Guatemala rhubarb
Kalanchoe blossfeldiana
 Flaming Katy, Tom Thumb
Kohleria amabilis
 Tree gloxinia
Lantana camara
 Common lantana, Shrub verbena,
 Yellow sage
Lapageria rosea
 Copihue, Chilean bellflower
Leptospermum scoparum
 Manuka, Tea tree
Lilium auratum
 Golden-rayed lily
Lithops
 Living stones, Pebble plant,
 Stone face
Lobivia aurea
 Golden lily cactus
Lycaste aromatica
 Cinnamon orchid
Mammillaria zeilmanniana
 Rose pin cushion
Manettia bicolor
 Candy corn plant, Firecracker
 plant, Firecracker vine
Medinilla magnifica
 Love plant, Rose grape
Miltonia 'Peach Blossom', roezlii
 Pansy orchid
Neomarica caerulea
 Apostle plant, Walking iris
Neoregelia carolinae tricolor
 Brushing bromeliad
Nerium oleander
 Oleander, Rose bay
Nertera granadensis
 Bead plant, Coral bead plant
Nidularium innocentii
 Bird's nest bromeliad
Notocactus ottonis
 Ball cactus
Odontoglossum grande
 Clown orchid, Tiger orchid

Oncidium papilio
 Butterfly orchid
Oxalis rubra
 Wood sorrel
Pachystachys lutea
 Golden hops, Golden shrimp plant,
 Lollipop plant
Paphiopedilum maudiae
 Lady's slipper orchid,
 Slipper orchid, Venus' slipper
Parodia sanguiniflora
 Prairie fire cactus,
 Tom Thumb cactus
Passiflora caerulea
 Blue passion flower, Common
 Passion flower, Passion vine
Pelargonium
 Geranium
Pentas lanceolata
 Egyptian star cluster, Egyptian
 star flower, Purple wreath
Petrea volubilis
 Queen's wreath
Phalaenopsis hybrid
 Moth orchid
Pittosporum tobira
 Japanese pittosporum
Plumbago auriculata/capensis
 Blue Cape plumbago,
 Cape leadwort, Leadwort
Primula malacoides
 Baby primrose, Fairy primrose
**Primula obconica, vulgaris/
 acaulis**
 Primula, primrose
Punica granatum 'Nana'
 Dwarf pomegranate
Rechsteineria cardinalis
 Cardinal flower
Reinwardtia trigyna
 Yellow flax
Rivina humilis
 Baby pepper, Bloodberry,
 Rouge plant
Rosa chinensis minima
 Miniature rose
Russelia equisetiformis
 Coral plant, Fountain plant
Saintpaulia
 African violet
Schizanthus species
 Butterfly flower, Poor man's orchid

**Schlumbergera x buckleyi
(Zygocactus truncatus)**
 Crab cactus, Christmas cactus,
 Lobster cactus,
 Thanksgiving cactus
**Schlumbergera gaertneri
(Rhipsalidopsis gaertneri)**
 Easter cactus, Leaf cactus,
 Link-leaf cactus
Senecio cruentus
 Cineraria
Sinningia
 Gloxinia
Smithiantha cinnabarina
 Temple bells
Solanum capsicastrum
 Jerusalem cherry,
 Christmas cherry, Winter cherry
Spathiphyllum 'Mauna Loa'
 Peace lily, Spathe flower,
 White flag, White sails
Sprekelia formosissima
 Aztec lily, Jacobean lily
Stephanotis floribunda
 Madagascar jasmine
Strelitzia reginae
 Bird of paradise flower
Streptocarpus saxorum
 False African violet, Spiral fruit
Streptocarpus hybrids
 Cape cowslip, Cape primrose
Thunbergia alata
 Black-eyed Susan vine, Clock vine
Tibouchina semidecandra
 Glory bush
Tillandsia cyanea
 Pink quill
Trichopilia tortilis
 Corkscrew orchid
Vallota speciosa
 Scarborough lily
Veltheimia viridifolia
 Forest lily
Vriesea splendens
 Flaming sword
Zantedeschia rehmannii
 Calla lily, Pink arum, Pink calla,
 Trumpet lily
Zephyranthes candida
 Fairy lily, Flowers of the
 Western wind, Rain lily, Swamp
 flower, Zephyr lily, Zephyr flower

Further Reading

Arnold, J., **The Illustrated Encyclopedia of House Plants,**
 Ward Lock, London 1979
Bracken, J., **Your Window Greenhouse,** T.Y. Crowell Publishers,
 New York 1977
Crockett, J. U., **Flowering House Plants,** Time-Life Books Inc.
 1972, 1977
Davidson, W., Rochford, T. C., **The Collinridge All Colour Guide to
 Houseplants, Cacti and Succulents,** Hamlyn, London 1976
Elbert, G. & V. **Plants That Really Bloom Indoors,**
 Simon & Schuster, New York, 1974
Fitch, C. M., **The Complete Book of Growing Houseplants Under
 Lights,** Hawthorn Publishers, New York 1975
Free, M., **Houseplants,** Doubleday & Company, New York,
 Revised edition, 1979
Grayson, E. & R., **The Complete Book of Bulbs,**
 Lippincott Publishers, New York 1977
Haring, E., **The Complete book of Growing Plants From Seeds,**
 Hawthorn Publishers, New York 1967
Hay, R., McQuown, F. R., and Beckett, G. & K., **The RHS Dictionary of
 Indoor Plants in Colour,** Ebury/Michael Joseph, London 1974
Herwig, R., **House Plants in Colour,** David and Charles,
 Newton Abbot 1977
Hellyer, A., **The All-Colour Book of Indoor and Greenhouse Plants,**
 Hamlyn, London 1973
Huxley, A. & A., **Huxley's House of Plants,** Paddington Press,
 London 1978
Johns, L., **Collins Book of Houseplants,** Collins, London 1977
Kramer, J., **Bromeliads, The Colorful Houseplants,** Van Nostrand,
 New York 1977
 Cacti, Harry N. Abrams, Inc., New York 1978
 1000 Beautiful Houseplants and How to Grow Them,
 William Morrow & Company, 1969
 Growing Orchids at Your Windows, Hawthorn Publishers,
 New York 1973
Longman, D. **The Care of Houseplants,** Peter Lowe, London 1979

Mills, B., **The Complete Guide To Bulbs,** Octopus Books Ltd.,
 London 1977
Neal, C. **Build Your Own Greenhouse,** Chilton Publishers,
 Radnor, PA, 1978
Northen, R. T., **Home Orchid Growing,** Van Nostrand Reinhold
 Company, New York 1970
Perry, F., Hay, R., et al., **The Complete Book of Houseplants and
 Indoor Gardening,** Octopus Books Ltd., London 1978
The Readers Digest Encyclopedia of Garden Plants and Flowers,
 The Reader's Digest Association Ltd., London 1978
Rochford T. & Gorer R., **The Rochford Book of Houseplants,**
 Faber and Faber, London 1973 **The Rochford Book of Flowering
 Pot Plants,** Faber and Faber, London 1974
In Association with the House of Rochford, **The Complete Book of
 Houseplants and Indoor Gardening,** Octopus Books, London 1978
Rowley, G. **The Illustrated Encyclopedia of Succulents,**
 Salamander Books Ltd., London 1978
Schwarg, D., **World Encyclopedia of Indoor Plants and Flowers,**
 Octopus Books Ltd., London 1978
Seddon G., **Your Indoor Garden,** Mitchell Beazley Publishers Ltd.,
 London 1976
Squire, D., and McHoy, P., **The Book of Houseplants,** Octopus Books
 Ltd., London 1978
Taloumis, G. **House Plants for Five Exposures,** Abelard Schuman,
 New York 1973
Unwin, C. W. J. (Advisor), **Flowering Bulbs in Colour,** Hamlyn,
 London 1973
Westcott, C., **The Gardener's Bug Book,** Doubleday & Company,
 Garden City, NY 1964
Wickham, C., **The Houseplant Book,** Marshall Cavendish Editions,
 London 1977
Williams, B. et al., **Orchids for Everyone,** Salamander Books Ltd,
 London 1980
Wright, M. (Ed.), **The Complete Indoor Gardener,** Pan Books Ltd.,
 London 1974

Glossary

Words in *italics* refer to separate entries within the glossary.

Adj. = Adjective; cf. = compare; Pl. = Plural.

Androecium The male organs of the flower; collectively the *stamens*.

Annual A plant which grows from seed, flowers and dies in one year.

Anther The top part of a *stamen* that contains the *pollen*.

Apex The tip of a shoot or root.

Areole The spine cushion of a cactus from which arise wool, spines, leaves (when present), lateral branches and flowers.

Axil The upper angle between a stem and a leaf arising from the stem. Adj. axillary.

Bedding plant A plant used for seasonal display in beds or tubs.

Berry A fleshy fruit with one or several *seeds* enclosed.

Bicolor A flower which has more than one distinct color.

Bisexual Two sexed, the flowers possessing both *stamens* and *pistils*.

Bloom 1. A collective term for *flowers*. 2. A waxy, powdery substance on the leaves of some *succulents*.

Bottom heat In propagation, heat applied from below, usually via electric cables, to assist rooting.

Bract A leaf or leaf-like structure, often *scale*-like, which usually has a *flower* in its *axil*.

Bud A small lateral or terminal growth containing the developing parts of a branch or *flower*.

Bulb A swollen underground *bud*-like structure with a shortened stem enclosed by fleshy inner and *scale*-like outer leaves. An organ of food storage and *vegetative propagation*.

Bulbil A small *bulb* formed among the *flowers*, in the *axil* of a leaf or beside another bulb.

Bulbous With the nature of a *bulb*.

Buoyancy Of atmosphere, the upward movement of air. (cf. *Stagnant*).

Cactus A member of the Cactaceae, the cactus *family*. Pl. cacti.

Calyx The outer part of the *flower*, the *sepals*, which can be separate or fused.

Canes Of some orchids, the jointed, erect stems.

Carpel One female reproductive unit of a *flower*, consisting of an *ovary*, *style* and *stigma*. The carpels may be separate or fused.

Chlorophyll A green pigment found in the cells of algae and higher plants which is fundamental in the use of light energy in *photosynthesis*.

Column The central body of a flower formed by the union of the *stamens* and *pistil*.

Corm A swollen underground stem surrounded by *scales* and replaced every year as a food store and an organ of *vegetative propagation*.

Corolla The part of a *flower* within the *calyx* consisting of a group of *petals*, which may be separate or fused and are usually colored.

Corymb A flat-topped *inflorescence*.

Cotyledon The first leaves that emerge from the *seed*.

Crocks Broken pieces of clay pot used in pots or trays to aid drainage.

Crown The base of a plant from which the roots and shoots emerge.

Cultivars Cultivated varieties that are propagated, not by seeds, but by cuttings or grafting.

Cutting A piece of stem, leaf, or root cut and used to grow a new plant.

Cyme A type of *inflorescence*. The oldest flower is at the center and younger growth branches beneath it.

Dead-heading A gardening term for the removal of fading flower heads.

Desiccation The drying out of a plant through exposure to heat, usually scorching sunlight.

Dibber A small stick used for lifting seedlings when *pricking out*.

Division The means by which a single plant is divided into two or more plants.

Dormancy Resting period. Adj. Dormant.

Double A flower with more than the usual number of *petals*.

Epiphyte A plant growing above ground level, usually upon another plant for support only. Epiphytic plants, such as bromeliads, gain nourishment from rain and debris. Adj. Epiphytic. (cf. *Terrestrial*).

Eye The bud of a growth.

Family A taxonomic grouping made up of related *genera*.

Fertilization Fusion of the male and female *gamete* (contained in the *pollen* and *ovule*) to form an embryo.

Fibrous Of roots, thin and wiry.

Floret A single *flower* of a dense *inflorescence*, as in the Compositae.

Flower A specialized reproductive shoot, usually consisting of *sepals*, *petals*, *stamens* and *ovary*.

Forcing The encouragement of *bulbous* plants into bloom earlier than their normal flowering season.

Gamete The sex cell of a plant. Male gametes are contained within *pollen* grains; female within the *ovule*.

Genus A subdivision of a *family*, consisting of one or more *species* which show similar characteristics and appear to have a common ancestry. Adj. generic. Pl. genera.

Germination The first stirrings of life in a seed as it grows into a plant.

Grafting The joining of a *bud* or stem of one plant to the root of another, so forming a separate plant.

Gynoecium The female portion of a *flower* formed by the *carpels*.

Heel A piece of the main stem or *old wood* left on a side shoot when taken as a *cutting*. It may assist rooting.

Hormones Chemical messengers that control physiological processes such as growth. In rooting powder they assist the rooting of *cuttings*.

Hybrid A plant produced from the crossbreeding of two different *species* and possessing characteristics from both parents.

Inflorescence A general term for the flowering part of a plant, whether of one *flower* or many, typically consisting of *bracts*, flower stalks and *flowers*.

Inorganic A chemical compound which does not contain carbon.

Internode The part of a stem between two *nodes*.

Lateral shoot A side shoot.

Layering The establishment of a new plant when a shoot makes contact with the ground and roots into it.

Legginess Of growth, thin and elongated. Adj. leggy.

Long-day plant A plant that flowers only in response to increasing day length. (cf. *Short-day plant*).

Midrib The central *vein* of a leaf.

Misting The spraying of a plant with a very fine spray or 'mist'.

Monopodial Growing only from the *apex* of the plant.

Nectary A gland, usually located in the *flower*, that secretes a sugary fluid, nectar, to attract pollinators.

Node The position on a stem where one or more leaves arise.

Offset (Offshoot) A young plant growing at the base of its parent.

Old wood Any growth made previous to the current season and hence more mature.

Organic Containing carbon. Substances formed from the decay of living material.

Ovary The basal part of the *carpel* containing the *ovules* and later the *seeds*.

Ovule The 'egg' of a plant which, on *fertilization*, develops into a *seed*.

Panicle A *raceme* of racemes.

Pedicel The stalk of an individual *flower*.

Peduncle The secondary axis of an *inflorescence* that bears the *pedicels*. Adj. pedunculate.

Perennial A plant living for more than two years and usually flowering each year.

Perianth A collective term for the *sepals* and *petals* that together form the asexual part of the *flower*.

Petiole A leaf stalk.

Pendulous (Pendent) Hanging downwards or inclined.

Petal A segment of the *corolla* surrounding the sexual parts of the *flower*. Petals are usually colored or brightly marked.

pH Mathematical notation for the degree of acidity or alkalinity of a soil or fertilizer. pH 7 is neutral, pH 8 is alkaline, pH 4 very acid.

Photoperiodism The response of plants, especially flowering and fruiting plants, to relative lengths of light and darkness.

Photosynthesis A series of chemical reactions in the tissues of green plants that synthesize *organic* compounds from water and carbon dioxide using energy absorbed by *chlorophyll* from light.

Pinching out (back) The removal or 'stopping' of growing points to produce *lateral shoots*.

Pistil The female organ of a *flower*; the *ovary*, *stigma* and *style*.

Plume A feathery *inflorescence*.

Plunge A bed of soil or ashes used to embed potted plants to prevent then drying out in the summer.

Pollen Dustlike grains produced by the *anthers* of flowering plants carrying the male gamete in *fertilization*. (cf. *Pollination*).

Pollination The process by which *pollen* is transferred from the *anther* to the *stigma*.

Potbound (rootbound) The crowding of roots in a pot, easily seen when the pot is removed.

Pricking out (off) The first transplantation of seedlings into trays.

Pseudobulb A structure formed from thickened stem *internodes*, typically a storage organ of orchids.

Raceme A type of *pendulous inflorescence* which bears its youngest flowers at the tip.

Receptacle The *apex* of a flower-stalk bearing the flower-parts.

Respiration The reverse of *photosynthesis*, wherein *organic* matter is broken down into carbon dioxide and water, and energy released.

Rhizome A root-bearing horizontal stem, which often lies on or just beneath the ground surface.

Rootstock The lower half of a graft, supplying the root system.

Runner A prostrate stem that produces a daughter plant at its tip.

Scale A small leaf or *bract*. The term is loosely applied to many structures, such as bud sale and bulb scale.

Scape A flower stalk without leaves, arising directly from the ground, as seen in *Cyclamen*.

Seed A structure within the *ovary*, produced by *fertilization* of the *ovule* and consisting of a seed coat, food reserves and an embryo capable of *germination*.

Seedling Very young plant arising from a germinating *seed*.

Sepal One of the segments of the *calyx*. Sepals are usually green and serve to protect the flower bud.

Sessile Of *flower* or leaf, stalkless.

Short-day plant A plant that flowers only in response to shortening day length. (cf. *Long-day plant*).

Single A *flower* with the normal number of *petals*.

Spadix A flower *spike*, usually fleshy, and surrounded by a *spathe*.

Spathe A large *bract*, sometimes colored, surrounding a *spadix*.

Species A group of plants sharing one or more common characteristics which make it distinct from any other group. Adj. specific.

Spike A single elongated *inflorescence* with *sessile* flowers occurring up the stem, the youngest at the top.

Stagnant Of atmosphere, unmoving. (cf. *Buoyancy*).

Stamen One of the male sexual parts of the *flower* consisting of a filament (usually) and an *anther* that contains *pollen*.

Stigma The part of the *style* that receives the *pollen*.

Stolon A creeping stem which roots at the *nodes* and produces plantlets.

Strain A selection of a *species* raised from *seed*.

Style The middle, often elongated, part of a female sexual organ of a *flower* between *stigma* and *ovary*.

Succulent Storing water in specially enlarged spongy tissue of the roots, stems or leaves; a plant of this type.

Sympodial A form of growth in which each new shoot, arising from the *rhizome* of the previous growth, is a complete plant in itself.

Systemic A pesticide that is absorbed by the plant and poisons the cells against pests.

Tender Half-hardy. Plants which will not survive frost outdoors.

Terrestrial Growing at ground level. Gaining nourishment from the soil. (cf. *Epiphyte*).

Topdressing The replacement of the surface layer of soil in a pot by fresh compost.

Transpiration The loss of water from a plant by evaporation, mainly through the leaves.

Tuber A swollen part of a stem or root, often formed beneath the ground each year and serving as a food store and an organ of *vegetative propagation*.

Umbel An *inflorescence* in which three or more *pedicels* arise from the same level.

Variety A subdivision of a *species*. The term is used mainly for natural variation within a *species* rather than for new plants produced by cultivation. (cf. *Cultivar*).

Variegation The markings on leaves or petals resulting from localized failure of development of pigment. Adj. variegated.

Vegetative propagation Asexual reproduction in which part of a plant becomes detached and subsequently becomes a new plant.

Vein A strand of strengthening and conducting tissue running through a leaf or modified leaf.

Virus An infectious agent which invades living cells causing disease.

Whorl A type of *inflorescence* where the flowers all arise from one point.

General Index

A beautiful red species of Strelitzia.

Figures in *Italics* refer to illustrations.

A

Achimenes see gesneriads:
   Achimenes
adaptation 24
aechmeas *see* bromeliads:
   aechmeas
aeoniums 69
Aeschynanthus see gesneriads:
   Aeschynanthus
air circulation 24
Allium 10
Angraecum see orchids:
   Angraecum
anthuriums *45,* 46, 76, 77
ants *see* insects: ants
aphelandras 46, 77
aphids *see* insects: aphids
   'apple-in-the-bag' bloom
   stimulator 68, 69, 82
Ascocentrum x *Vanda* hybrids 78

B

baskets *see* containers: baskets
begonias *17, 30, 43,* 56
   coloration 56
   revised classification 56
benomyl *see* fungicides: benomyl
billbergias *see* bromeliads:
   billbergias
bloom stimulation 27, 68, 69, 82
bonsai 174
Bougainvillea 23, 83
bromeliads 10, 23, 24, 46, 56, 68, 69,
   82, 126, 154, 156, 158, 195
   aechmeas 56
   billbergias 56
   coloration 56
   Cryptanthus 56
   Hohenbergia 56
   neoregelias 56
   nidulariums 56
   potting medium 30
   Tillandsia cyanea 47, *190*
   Tillandsia lindenii 56
bulbous plants 10, 18, 29, 60, 157,
   163
   Eucharis 10, 61
   Eucomis 10, 12, 61
   potting mixture 30, *61*
   repotting 33, 61
   Vallota 10, 47, 61
   Veltheimia 61, *194*

C

cacti 12, 22, 26, 114, 127, 148, 150,
   159, 160, 165, 174
   Cereus 22
   echeverias 58
   euphorbias 58
   lobivias 59
   parodias 59
   potting *32*
   potting mixture 30
   Rhipsalis 58
caladiums *20*
Calanthe vestita see orchids:
   Calanthe vestita
captan *see* fungicides: captan
carbaryl *see* insecticides: carbaryl
Caryota 22
Cattleya hybrids *see* orchids:
   Cattleya hybrids
central heating 29
Cereus see cacti: *Cereus*
choice of plants 10
chrysanthemums *17,* 46

Index to Plants

The elegant and fragrant blooms of *Gardenia jasminoides*.

Index to Plants

Credits

Picture credits
The publishers wish to thank the following photographers and organizations who have supplied photographs for this book. Photographs have been credited by page number and position on the page: (B) Bottom, (T) Top, (C) Center, (BL) Bottom left, etc.

Photographs
A–Z Collection: Endpapers, 66–7(C), 73(TL), 73(BR), 80–1(TC), 82(BL), 100(L), 104(TL), 133(TR), 136–7(C), 141(L), 177(BL), 178–9(C), 186(B), 187, 189

Bernard Alfieri: 43

Pat Brindley: 61, 89(R), 95, 105(BL), 107(R), 116–17(B), 140(R), 166, 167(B), 177(T).

Peter Chapman: 112, 113(T), 127(BR), 148, 149(T), 150, 159(T), 160, 165.

Eric Crichton: Title page, Contents page, 11, 13(R), 14(TL), 14–15(C), 15(TR), 16–17(C), 17(TR, BR), 20, 20–1, 25, 28(BL), 31, 32(TL, C), 34(T, B), 36, 37, 48(TL), 49, 50(TL), 52–3, 59(B), 60, 62, 64, 65, 66(L), 68–9(B), 69(TR), 72–3(B), 74–5, 76–7, 78–9(B), 79(TL), 80(L), 80–1(BC), 81(TR, BR), 82(T), 84–5(BC), 85(TR), 86–7, 91(B), 92–3, 99(R), 100–1(C), 101(R), 104–5(T), 106(L), 106–7(C), 109(TR, BR), 110(BL), 114, 117(TL), 120–1(B), 121(BR), 122(L), 125(T), 128, 128–9(BC), 130(TR), 131(TR), 132(L), 134(TL), 134–5(B), 137(R), 140(TL), 142, 143(R), 144–5, 147(TR), 149(BL), 151, 152(L), 153(R), 156(TR), 156–7, 160–1(C), 161(R), 162(BL), 162–3(T), 164(R), 168(TL), 168–9(TC), 170–1(BC), 171(TR, BR), 172(C), 178(L), 179(R), 183(R), 184, 186(TR), 191(BL), 193, 197, 208

Jan van Dommelen: 33(T), 94(R)

Derek Fell: 96(R), 155, 163(BR), 188(TR), 202

Kees Hageman: 16(TL), 28–9(T), 35, 124(TL), 205

Jack Kramer: 22–3(C), 39(TR)

B. J. van der Lans: 56(TL), 70(L), 84(L), 139(T), 196(BL)

Dean Lockhart: 113(BL)

Gordon Rowley: 67, 79(R)

Daan Smit: 10(TL), 12–13(C), 38, 91(T), 110(TR), 117(BR), 120–1(TC), 141(TR), 154(L), 183(L), 192, 196(TR)

Harry Smith Photographic Collection: 18(TL), 42, 44, 50–1(C), 56(TR), 68(TR), 70(BR), 97, 98–9(TC), 102–3, 111, 119, 130(L), 132–3(C), 139(BR), 143(L), 147(BL), 154(R), 159(BL), 164(L), 172(TR), 176, 190, 191(T), 194–5(B), 195(T)

David Stone: 169(B)

Michael Warren: 22(TL), 52(TL), 96(L), 125(BR), 136(L), 146, 152–3(C), 170(T), 180–1(B), 188(B)

Artists
Copyright of the drawings on the pages following the artists' names is the property of Salamander Books Ltd.

Alan Hollingbery: 27 (in part), 29 (in part), 35, 36, 39

Lydia Malim: 54

Gordon Riley: 51

Tyler/Camoccio Design Consultants: 12, 14, 27, 29, 32, 33, 42, 43, 44, 45, 64–197. (The illustrations on pages 32, 33, 42, 43, 44, and 45 were redrawn from originals by Carol Carlson).

Acknowledgements
The publishers would like to thank the following individuals for their help in preparing this book.

Eric Crichton (for taking many of the photographs specially for the book); Fran Fisher (for styling the interior photographs); Maureen Cartwright (for copy-editing and proof-reading); Stuart Craick (for preparing the index); David Papworth (for help with choosing interior locations); Valerie Noel-Finch, Steve Thompson and Jeff Grimes (for editorial help); Wilma Rittershausen, W. Davidson and Gordon Rowley (for botanical advice).

Thanks are due also to the following companies and stores for their help in providing material for photographs.

Thomas Rochford and Sons Ltd.; Magnet Joinery Ltd.; The Brass Monkey, 11 Sicilian Avenue, London WC1; Dickins and Jones, 224 Regent Street, London W1; Liberty and Company Ltd., Regent Street, London W1; The Conran Shop, 77–79 Fulham Road, London SW3.

The delicate flowers of Begonia 'Orange Rubra.'

PRINTED IN BELGIUM BY
proost
INTERNATIONAL BOOK PRODUCTION

Epiphyllum hybrids 'London Gaiety' (left) 'Ackermannii' (right)